Ena Chamberlain was ⟨...⟩
south-west London; she w⟨...⟩
matriculating she became ⟨...⟩
She has a son, two daughters and six grandchildren. She
now lives in Devon.

In this autobiography, her first book, Ena Chamberlain
reveals herself to be an accomplished writer with the rare
ability to recapture, and bring to life, a time and place
which now live only in the thoughts and feelings of the
intelligent, observant child who inhabited them.

29 *Inman Road*

ENA CHAMBERLAIN

Published by VIRAGO PRESS Limited 1990
20–23 Mandela Street, Camden Town, London NW1 0HQ

Copyright © 1990 Ena Chamberlain

*A CIP Catalogue record for this book
is available from the British Library*

Printed in Great Britain by
Cox & Wyman Ltd, Reading, Berkshire

For my family

Chapter One

My mother sat by the kitchen window; she had opened it to let the sunlight in. Two small girls attended her – one was my friend, Rene Collins, the other was me.

'There you go again,' said my mother, 'making me all behind with my jobs.'

We were combing the hair which she had unpinned; it fell like water, it whistled down the back of the chair when she pulled the pins away. 'Once upon a time I could sit on it but there, it had to be chopped off, for it was such a weight to carry around. One day,' she threatened, 'I'll go and get it shingled.'

Rene and I ignored the defiance, mourned the chopped hair which we might have boasted about, and wielded the combs to make it long once more. Soon there was no other sound but the hush of combing and the girls' breathing. Waving strands were stroked into parallels, locks were picked out to be held against the light of the window so that sunbeams danced between the threads and glittered copper and ruby-brown. We combed the hair as sleek as cats' fur and as brown as leaves.

'Your hair, Em, is your crowning glory,' the aunts had told my mother.

'Everyone has some good feature,' she had replied, so that they agreed and looked one another up and down with suspicion.

Rene had more than one good feature, she was beautiful. I had nice teeth and nicely shaped fingernails and neither were much satisfaction, but here, in the middle of this afternoon, we devoted ourselves to my mother's hair. It smelt warm and of my mother. Her eyes closed; see how wound about in her tiredness she was becoming. All we asked of her was compliance, and that she was giving willingly at last. We stood over her, at once concentrated and pensive while lazy Mother drooped into the sunshine, eyelids concealing eyes, hands open on lap, holding a cup for emptiness.

All at once the eyelids jerk open, eyes shine bright with the recollection of who and where she is. Hands fly to throw the hair back, hairpins fang her lips as she coils and twists and jabs her head of hair into order. Quick! Into a knot at the back, scragged tight and painful to the very top – and – another time perhaps . . . funny girls . . . yes, another time.

And another time must wait until she allows herself to be tired, or until she has washed her hair with the block of Sunlight soap. Then we shall brush and comb and soothe the hair again until it is silk and satin. It will smell of soap and not of Emma; it will, as it dries, be free of her, it will fan out from her head, showing it to be small and shapely. It will fly about her cheeks, clinging to the combs wonderfully.

'I must be a sight for sore eyes,' she will say, as she wipes away the webs of her hair. 'It's all up to the electric,' she will explain. 'I've got a lot of the electric.'

The girls will nod agreement and will continue to comb her down until something outside the circle, anything, the hustle of the kitchen clock or the collapse of coals in the range, or the cry of a street trader, rallies her to the facts of the next meal, or to the socks which wait to be mended, or, if all else fails, to the eternal supply of untidinesses.

Her reputation as a good housekeeper had to be maintained, for without it she had no name or place or

2

small glory. With that reputation she knew what she was and that was enough to know.

'Let's do your hair soon,' the girls begged.

'We'll see. When it's got more grease, when it behaves itself.'

Rene made a face; she liked the soap smells better.

'Run along then, Rene.'

My mother dismissed Rene and I would follow my friend. There was no appeal. Mum was proud to be harassed by duties, grumbled and worked hard to produce more. She might have been a queen, my mother, cherished by Rene and me; instead she chose to be a housewife.

'You don't have to keep on at the house,' I told her. 'Rene's mother doesn't. She says life's too short.'

'You don't understand. You're only a child. Any case, I enjoy it, it's all I ever wanted. That – and to keep myself to myself. Not much to ask, eh, ducks?'

Those are the words I think she said, though perhaps I put them into her mouth – out of pity? Certainly I felt no pity for her when I was her child.

Inman Road joins together the long thoroughfares of Earlsfield and Wilna Roads. In the 1920s it was called 'The Street' by its inhabitants. It might just as well have been called 'The Village', for it carried every mark of a village except a church. It was even feudal in character; at the apex of its society were my dad and my uncle, who ran the laundry where many women and one young man worked. At the top of the street were the shops, the few which supplied everyday food, and the Off-Licence which supplied everyday beer; though not for Number 29 where I lived. There was one shop in the street; really it was only a front room which was filled to the brim with the vast, sugary-smelling body, arms and legs of the

3

lady who sold sweets: yellow bags of sherbet dabs, black liquorice braids, and newspaper cones of fruit drops and toffee pieces, in accurate exchange for our halfpennies. Gully's, the greengrocer's, was at the turn of the street. It was dim and earthy, the door was never closed, and on rare occasions it was visited by Mrs Gully, who wore green cabbage dresses and a velvet band around her long and twitching throat.

'Like Queen Alexandra,' said my mum.

'To hide her scar,' whispered Auntie Annie.

They couldn't tell me anything about scars and an errand to Gully's was performed with all speed in case Mrs Gully should appear.

The street itself furnished our social needs – friends, enemies, we possessed our own witch. We had a leader, a lord. He was my father.

Although the slums of Earlsfield weren't far away Inman was not a slum, neither was it entirely respectable. Irrefutable respectability breathed thinner air at the top of the hill where quiet roads led to Wandsworth Common through avenues of acacias. Sometimes, instead of taking the direct and busy route up Earlsfield Road, Mum and I walked along the avenues. In summertime we went sedately under lace parasols of leaves and leaf-shadows; in wintertime we marched between stubs of tree trunks that fisted up from paving stones. The trunks bristled into warts, hunched against the cold they made a picture of winter for me.

'We had trees in Inman Road once,' Mum said, 'but the boys pulled them down.'

I was curious about this exploit of the boys and asked why? And when? And how? Especially – how?

'Oh well – the boys always do things like that. Don't you keep on and on about it now. Please.'

But she kept on and on, this time about the trees and hedges which bordered Garratt Lane from Tooting

4

Broadway to Wandsworth High Street when she had come as a bride to Earlsfield. 'Just like the country it was. Buttercups and all.'

For a while we would walk in silence, out of respect I suppose.

Mum wasn't a country girl, she only seemed to long for the pictures in her head, neither was she aware that when she spoke in such wistful tones of banks of buttercups and of 'little white starry flowers – no – not daisies' she was painting them in my head too. Probably she was telling me that she detested Inman. For all the work she put into the house she had other ideas, like my sister Elsie. Mum saw herself in one of the new houses in Morden; Elsie saw herself in Canada; for me and for my dad the only possible place to live was Inman Road.

My mother kept within the walls of Number 29, inside them she knew what was what; inside them she fought out her wars against dirt and poverty, a hobby beyond understanding, enemies which were invisible. Because of the laundry weren't we, the Chamberlains, the most spotless people in Earlsfield? Again, because of the laundry and because of Number 29, both of which we owned, neither of which did we share with other families, weren't we rich? It wasn't much fun being rich, to judge by the glad old times which the poorer folk seemed to enjoy. From the pavement I caught the tuning-up of bellyfuls of laughter, the gusts of swearing. Nothing like that went on inside Number 29. When I complained of being rich Mum muttered about me being like the rest, just because we had a business, kept our heads above water, didn't throw money about like wildfire – which picture opened wide my eyes. In time I learnt to avoid references to affluence as this provoked her to action of a disagreeable kind, and to a scatter of aphorisms like – 'We'll have to draw our horns in'. Like – 'Looks as though we'll have to pinch a bit or else . . .'

5

'Or else' was left open, but the prospect was a grim one, no doubt of that. From habit she practised small economies, the sort of thing I found later in other homes: the scraping of the butter papers, the unfolding of sugar packets to chase out the fugitive sugar grains. Rene's mother was lavish with the marg, careless with its papers, piled her treacle high on bread. When she had treacle. Sometimes her extravagance took my breath away. But when my mother was upset about poverty it was me who bore the brunt of her remedies. At worst I had to eat – well, to try then – the cheap fat meat; at best I was the one who had to run up to the butcher's to ask for twopenn'orth of marrow bones, and to Gully's for a penn'orth of pot herbs. She wouldn't light the fire in winter, although she had to cook on it, until the last possible moment. There were also the automatic maxims.

'Don't scuff your shoes.'

'Don't pull the chain unless you – you know – have to.' She saved water also.

Economies shaped my mother's life. They were her pride, they were her torment. They obliged her to make rather than buy, whether the end product was a cake or a dress. Ready-made was a nasty word and suspect, so from it came a kind of snobbery. It was a real struggle which involved her, a tug of war which was never resolved, for against parsimony she set her instinct for generosity which would not let go.

Above everything she delighted in clothes and it was when she and I were alone in the kitchen that she let slip her hopes and confidences, forgetting that I was her child. She had more time for me, although less energetic interest, than she had had for my sisters and brother.

'They came all in a rush,' she said, 'while you . . .'

I, the afterthought, had arrived ten years later. So – we were allies in the quiet kitchen, and we entered her

6

fairy tale of sumptuous dressing until, when we had done with her, she was clothed like a princess. Then the tug of war would pull the other way and it would all come down to buying by the yard, or, if things were more drastic, to the business of unpicking an old garment. Usually the remnants (and in some extraordinary way it made no difference how large the original garment was) were too skimpy to be made into a dress for anyone but me.

My dresses were either sparse or exuberant, the latter made from a piece of stuff bought in a sale which was a real bargain – of course there was too much material, but it could be made up to last. Auntie Annie was in on these shopping expeditions; she was a trained dress-maker and made all my clothes: coats, underwear, everything. She made my dresses long and wide, gave the skirts deep hems which, as – everyone hoped – I grew taller, could be let down. No one hoped for the letting down as earnestly as I did. And up above, the exquisite tucks in the bodices waited their turn for the letting out to accommodate my expansion when every prick of the needle would give evidence of my growth.

'She's bound to develop.' Mum and Auntie nodded to one another as I stood on the table to be fitted. It was a triumph of confidence, though I, in gloom, crossed my fingers and shrank back from the battery of pins which attacked each sway of the dress.

'It will happen overnight,' people said. 'One day she'll be down here, the next day – upsadaisy!'

Until that startled moment I had to make an entrance either as a leggy insect, short in skirt and sleeve, or swing into sight as a pleated balloon. On such appearances even Auntie Annie called me 'Lizzie Tin Ribs' or 'Polly Long Frock', and laughed when I turned up my nose. All I wanted from clothes was to be dressed like the others, to

7

be as threadbare as them, to be as dirty as they were, and I knew this was too much to ask.

Auntie Annie could sew but she was no baker. All she could make were bread puddings. To atone for her clumsy sponges and thickset rice puddings she hoarded raisins and sultanas, suet and cinnamon and nutmeg, and bread of course, and when all these alluring smells and names and flavours were gathered she flung them into a huge earthenware bowl in which, she told me, she had bathed her children when they were babies. She let me stir the sticky mess, three times and wish, and then I helped her fill trays and trays which she lifted into the range. One thing at a time was Auntie Annie's way. Where Mum would have set to and found a dozen jobs while she was waiting for the food in the oven to cook, Auntie was happy to sit with me on her coping outside in Wilna Road. Others joined us to chat and sniff the spicy air and wait. My friends came. There was quite a cluster of friends waiting on Auntie's bread pudding days, and when the time was up she fed us every one. When the pudding was cold and moist she exported a slab to old Mr Bothwell who lived at the top of Wilna and who had, they said, the ooperspudicks in his pondi-corium. She distributed the stuff among the laundry women. She wrapped a piece up in a tea towel for me to take home and not to mention it but to leave it on the table to be discovered. She was on tiptoe with the euphoria of her bread pudding expertise. I didn't doubt that if it had been feasible she would have sent some to the starving Indians who, so faddy eaters were advised, were willing to take anything from runny boiled eggs to nice glasses of milk.

Mum was an excellent cook, her pastry was as light as a feather, her loaves of bread crusty but soft within, her sponge cakes were swansdown; everyone said so. But I brought her down with a reference to Auntie's bread

8

pudding which, though she tried, Mum could not equal. They were very fond of one another, Mum and Auntie Annie, and the bread puddings were a real test of that affection.

One other person challenged Mum's fame as a cook but wasn't considered as a serious rival because she was Mrs Collins next door, who was after all a bit of a topsy-turvy person, who cooked only when food happened to find its way into her kitchen, who did her washing when it occurred to her to do it, not on Mondays when even the rowdiest members of the street obeyed the Monday washing rule. Certainly Rene dined well on the odd occasion when her mother was given leftovers to take home. Mrs Collins did a little charring, an activity which no one explained but which seemed mysterious and rewarding and was done in the big houses near the Common. Mrs Collins also brought home fancy clothes made of silk with tassels. They were usually torn and sometimes rather clammy but were fine for dressing up. Once she brought us a fan, an enormous fan with feathers which cried out for grand theatre but collapsed us into giggles. The feathers tickled. Mrs Collins was a widow with two grown-up sons, one of whom worked in the laundry, as well as Rene. They all lived downstairs quietly and a noisy family lived up above.

'I take life as it comes,' said Mrs Collins, and she sank back into the squeaky cane chair to take it. Like my mother she was always tired, but Mrs Collins's tiredness stopped her dead while Mum's whipped her into a frenzy to fly around even faster. Adults had infinite variety.

Mrs Collins liked me as a friend for Rene. This liking had to do with the laundry rather than with me although she did admire my nose, she said, and this approval I found quite endearing as my family called the nose a lump of putty and squashed it with a thumb to emphasize the fact. Mrs Collins, though, appreciated its roundness,

9

perhaps because her own nose was as sharp as a pencil; moreover the skin of it was pink and shiny as though it was starched. Whether my nose or my status as the daughter of my dad gave me the freedom of the Collins kitchen I never asked. It was peaceful to be there on washdays, for those were the days when she made and we ate the swimmers.

'There they go!' she cried with something of Auntie's bread pudding abandon. The clothes had finished boiling in the copper, the scullery was filled with steam, the cobbled floor was a skating rink, and she tossed fistfuls of flour and fat in the copper while Rene and I slid about waiting for the bobbing globules to rise up as swimmers. We were the fishers and none escaped us. If there was treacle in the cupboard, she poured it over the glistening lumps. If none, we ate them just the same. 'Don't tell me she boils them in soapy water,' Mum said. 'Not in dirty soapy water!'

Mum's justified pride in her cooking provoked me into teasing comparisons using swimmers and bread puddings and shop cakes. Shop cakes were forbidden on the grounds of extravagance and taste; therefore I brooded ostentatiously when we passed the window of the baker's shop in Earlsfield road, and was ecstatic about the shop cakes paraded in my friends' homes. Didn't tell of the dusty crumbs of them.

'We had pink and green cake – '

'Battenburg.'

'And one with tapes of coconut on top.'

Her lips curved tighter.

'And – guess what! – Devil cake!'

'You'll be sick tonight. I'll put the pot beside your bed.'

'And they buy shop cakes and they're poor. Poorer than us.'

Instead of shop cakes she gave me watercress and

home-baked bread. She gave me cod-liver oil and malt which I tried to claw from the roof of my mouth. She made me sit up straight for a soldier and not take sweets from anyone unless I knew the person and unless I was asked twice. She didn't praise my good marks for English composition but was stern with my muddled arithmetic. The hat with the red cherries was denied me and she placed me, scowling, under a broad-brimmed panama like the hats the royal children wore. That hat was indestructible. The most I could do was sling it on the back of my head with the elastic in my teeth.

My sister Edie said, 'Crikey. She lets you get away with anything. She wasn't half strict with us.'

But my mother, during one of our unguarded moments together, when we were friends and could tell the secret things, had confessed that she had not wanted another child. Not wanted me. And since I had insisted on coming alive, I might have come alive as a boy – think of the clothes Bill had grown out of; she could have kept them for me. And since she was over forty when I came along – well. Suddenly she stopped, realized that we were not, after all, friends, but mother and daughter.

'Of course once you had arrived it was all forgotten. I wanted you, ducks; we all did.'

Arrived? Like an unwelcome guest? Another girl! And now, she was sorry she had been so slow to greet me. Without hesitation I used her guilt against her when she annoyed me by one restriction or another, and this is what Edie was indignant about.

'She never smacks you. We used to get a wallop and no mistake.'

It was only when I was ill or when I fell over that she found the words. They were – 'That's my brave girl.' They were – 'Come on, ducks. Where's my little ray of sunshine?'

She bound my ears in warm rags when I sat up in bed with the terrible earache; she held my forehead when I hung over the bowl, vomiting, dying, beyond hope. And there were the times which caught us unawares, when we were alone and quiet together, when I glanced up to intercept the soft brown gaze from behind her glasses and looked away, quickly, too shy to stand up to such a love.

Chapter Two

THE first years of my life belonged to my mother and to my sister Edie, and both of them selected what I should know of those years, although the occasional recollections, the mind-drifters, I kept to myself. There was no coherence in them, they lifted out of the darkened times like shoals of fish, curved and shone and sank again, leaving me entranced and bewildered. No. Mum and Edie could not be told such things. But out of the earliest years one event stood up as sturdy as a break-water; it was theirs to tell but it was mine to possess.

The place was St Thomas' Hospital. I was four years old, and was laid on a trolley and wheeled along corridors to the clang of Big Ben across the river. Corridors rattled, ceilings swayed overhead as dizzy as railway lines and – 'Watch the nurses dress up,' ordered a man in white with bare, hairy arms. 'Comic, aren't they?' Was the reverse of everyday comic? Ceilings instead of floors? Upside-down faces, where lips opened instead of eyes?

'Take a deep breath – that's a good girl . . . girl . . . girl . . .' I fought against the cage which was held to my face and the wicked gas sucked into me. Became me. When I opened my eyes it was all to put together again; throat hurt, legs were a fish tail. I had washed up on a foreign shore where ice birds stalked about and came now and then to peer and demand my wrist to hold. Then they became nurses who were alert to ask all kinds of private things. It was plain that the questions were private, for the nurses spoke so softly, waiting to mark their little books.

'How are we today?'

'Have your bowels moved, dear?' (A solemn and incomprehensible enquiry.)

One afternoon a nurse whispered, leaning behind the screen at the doors to the ward; she hurried across to my bed with a bunch of sweet peas and I knew that my mother was behind the screen, hiding. They took her away, poor Mother; the screen doors swung back and I heard her voice and wept with pity for her, and soon after with envy of the boy next to me, who was the focus for the nurses' attention. He was brought in, having been squashed by a steamroller. Horror and glory! When they took the screens away I tried to see whether he was absolutely flat; at any rate his head was as round as a football and his hair stuck up in bristles and he stuck his tongue out at me. I was sent home before I could find out how flat he was, but carried with me material for nightmares sufficient to last a lifetime. The odour of chloroform and reeling ceilings and eyes with teeth . . . and . . . a scar in my neck.

Saint Thomas had removed my TB gland and left me with a neat piece of needlework. So neat was the stitching that I was to be remarkable because of it and for little else. I was warned to be grateful, for similar operations had resulted in permanent disfigurement, in necks as twisted and bulged as the acacia stumps in the roads to the Common.

'It hardly notices unless she bends her neck. Fancy!' So I had to bend my neck to each newcomer; before long this became an automatic response to 'And how is she today?'

Saint Thomas also took away my curly hair and sunny disposition. Mum said, 'Lovely hair you had before you went in. Fair and curly. See?' There was a photograph to prove it.

'Everyone said what a dear little girl you were.'

Looking at the photograph, there was no doubting the

truth of that either. Mum was sad, the way she was sad when she spoke of my eldest sister, Winnie, who had died when she was two years old. Around the house were grey and flowery pictures of guardian angels and in my imagination they had some kind of connection with my dead sister; there was something about the way they perched on the edge of cliffs or lakes which at best was careless of the children they were supposed to be guarding and at worst . . . Still, Mum thought of Winnie as an angel child. Now she was wistful for the dear little girl that had been me. Hard luck for her, left with only a scarred child to comfort her, that and the fact that I had been saved from TB. TB – too fearful to be spoken, except by the initials.

However, she said that I was quick on the uptake – that is when I wasn't a Dreamy Daniel, and – my teeth were good, thanks to Uncle Ernie the dentist, and – my fingernails were a nice shape. 'Filberts,' she said, 'quite classy.'

Loss of charm turned out to be a blessing as it set me free to play in the street and permitted a neglect which would not have been extended to a dear little girl. The term was 'Kept-In' and it was applied to nicely brought up children. For example, there was a 'Kept-In' child who lived in Dingwall Road; when we ran round the block we saw her, peeping out of her lace curtains. I was to play with her, it was to be an honour bestowed; instead it became a disgrace.

Meanwhile I was a scavenger, roaming the streets, gathering the bits and pieces together to make up the world I was to live in. For one thing, I had to assemble the jigsaw of my mother's past – in a way it was my past too, for I had grown up listening to her stories; her childhood and mine were inextricably linked.

Eleven children. A scramble of children and all in one tenement? 'Squashed up like peas in a pod we were.

15

Four to a bed. Heads to toes. And the washing! Your grandmother had to do the washing on the roof. And some of the women there with her! Proper old scally-wags. The language! My mum wasn't like that . . . refined she was . . . kept herself to herself.'

'On the roof?'

Surely – quite slippery – interesting though – and I thought of my heavy grandma, who was a martyr to her feet.

'Don't be daft – it was a flat roof, of course.'

And then the picture changed, became fine as I saw the spires and domes of London.

Mum told me, bit by bit, of the WC shared in the courtyard with other families. 'Agony it was, if you had to wait.' And back to the washing and the water which had to be lugged up from the ground floor because the tap on the landing was broken. And the noise from all the children playing in the courtyard, and the women shouting.

'Poor old Mum, she was a bit afraid of the women, but she was more afraid of the – ' her voice hushed ' – of the – insects. Well, the lice. They were in the walls, you see. Nothing to do with her goings-on. She was as white as snow, poor Mum. Oh dear, she had a hard time trying to make ends meet. Nowhere to turn round in either, beds to be taken down every morning, put up again at night, until the boys began to leave home.'

Mum's brothers had jet-propelled themselves from the rooms in Peabody Buildings, Blackfriars, with such a spurt of energy that they had landed on the other side of the world: two in New Zealand; one in Australia; one in South Africa. The rest had stayed behind. The pattern had been explained in fairy stories, but in Mum's family it was the eldest, not the youngest, who was rewarded. All the adventurers prospered, but only Uncle Walter felt himself rich enough to keep a hold on his relations back in England. To prove he was in New Zealand he sent home copies of the *Auckland Weekly News*, where he was an engineer. Within the pages were pressed leaves from some of the New Zealand forests. These were passed between the relations and after all the fingers had experienced the thick grey hairiness the leaves splintered into New Zealand dust.

Uncle Walter did more than send magazines and leaves and photographs of his timbered house with his new black motorcar outside; he brought himself back to London, to check on his family and to reserve seats in the Victoria Theatre, in London – real London, not Earlsfield, not Clapham Junction. He bought seats for a complete spread of relations. 'Bluebell in Fairyland' was written in lights above the theatre but that proclamation, and indeed the whole performance, was outshone by the astonishing display of the line of aunts and uncles and cousins and grandparents who preened in the front row of the stalls.

'What a turn-up,' Mum said, 'for your first trip to a show – to go in the stalls. Not the pit, mind you, but the stalls. Bit of all right, eh?'

My eldest sister Elsie enjoyed the theatre, she came home singing; and Edie, she shone bright when she went to the Sunday League concerts in Clapham. Mum told me about pantomimes, but couldn't take me; 'The gods are too high up for me, I'd come over all anyhow, I'd chuck a dummy. Elsie will take you when you're older.'

Dad was too busy for theatres and considered that because of Elsie we were getting a bit above ourselves. In any case, he would rather be in the Conservative Club with his friends. But when Uncle Walter came to London my dad was in the theatre with all the rest and as splendid to look at as the rest, set out as they were in the crimson seats like decorated chocolates. Uncle Walter was proud of them. I heard him say to my dad, 'They've certainly turned up trumps, Joe.'

Best Christmas and wedding clothes were on display, and necklaces and bangles. Auntie Florrie had bought a dress specially, ready-made from Arding and Hobbs. Shoes twinkled, so did smiles; the men's hair was flat and solid with oil; the women's was crimped into precise and parallel waves; powder settled in drifts around nostrils and noses shone; a confusion of scents, Eau de Cologne, Ashes of Roses, Californian Poppy and violet cachous, hung over men and women alike.

'This is the life,' Uncle Will grinned. 'Good old Wollie! One of the nobs now, eh, Wol?'

We had arrived early and there was plenty of time to look about, to buy programmes, to buy sweets, to find the lavatories, to change seats. Uncles sweated cautiously from out of stiff collars; reckoned the price of the seats we sat in; raised eyebrows; but recovering from the shock they took heart and passed the bags and boxes of sweets with a display of generosity which took my breath away.

I was slotted in between adults and was told by my mother not to fidget or to be sick. I was too astonished to do either. I had not dreamt that the theatre would be so . . . would be so . . . I was desperate for adequate vocabulary. It was my first visit to a theatre and all night and all the next a hundred candles lit the dark around my bed.

Mum leaned over to reassure me. 'You won't have to wait much longer. Look. The orchestra is arriving. The show will start soon.'

Start? But it had begun. It was enough for me to be there. I was more and more excited by the atmosphere, I hugged myself with the thrill of the place. I could hear wild noises from the orchestra, they were all part of the wonder. People, grand people in velvet, were appearing in gilded shelves at the sides of the stage. My aunt saw me gazing and said, 'They are the boxes. Very swish. And close your mouth up.' When I twisted to look up and back I saw the hundreds of people high up near the roof; they hardly seemed to be real, more like painted blobs, and were overwhelmed by the golden cherubs curved above them.

From the orchestra came a proper tune, the instruments had had their fun; the lights went down; the lights went up along the hems of the tasselled stage curtains, and the family turned lines of faces towards the stage. As one face they were lit, as one they were brought face to face (when the curtains swung back) with enchantment. As my eyes too were dazzled I heard their unison of '*A-ah!*'

Then there were people shouting and swaggering from one side of the stage to the other, taking no notice of the darkened rows of faces waiting on them. Until they sang. All their songs were aimed straight at us, especially us, the family who were strung across the theatre. One song, quite sad and shivery, was sung to an accompaniment of paper windmills which were twirled by dancers as frail as the pink sails they were holding. 'Windmills, windmills, pretty little windmills, won't you buy my windmills, turning for you now?'

Uncle Will whispered loudly to Uncle George, 'Take a dekko of that one on the end, boy. What thighs, eh?'

On either side of me the walls of bodies grew steamy and I was dizzy with the colours and the music.

'What did you like best?' Edie asked on the cold way home in the bus.

'Don't know.'

It was the moment, the shock, when all the faces, the day-by-day faces of the family, were lit up like the faces of saints in church windows. That sudden lift to paradise. But I wouldn't tell. Like? No, I didn't exactly *like* it. 'P'raps – it was Fairyland.' She nodded, satisfied.

If Uncle Walter had expected a wave of admiration on his return to London, he must have been disappointed. Face-to-face comparison proved too much for his brother and sisters, and for his parents too. 'Wol's got too big for his boots,' Grandma Peggs muttered when he had insisted on taking her out to tea in Fullers' tea shop. 'Joe Lyons was good enough for me.'

As she gave few opinions, the words were taken seriously. It was, they said, the way Wollie had shot back to them, like a comet – didn't seem like the old Wol. True, they had to admit it was true, the fact of his posh house in Auckland, and . . . he did own a motorcar. He swore that the leaves he had sent them, to show, were leaves from genuine forest trees and ferns. Well, there was the photo. You couldn't deny the photo. Like rabbits' ears, those leaves. But – your London, that was where the real world was and they were glad to be stay-at-homes. So they gave him high tea wherever he visited and asked his opinion as a man of the world and were relieved when he sailed back over the edge of it again.

Auntie Lizzie settled them all down when she said, 'Well, your brother Walter has made his bed, now he must lie on it.'

Peabody Buildings remained the reference for Mum's attitudes and practices.

'I'll take you there one day, if you're good,' she said to me. The contingency of my goodness to any treat was inevitable but could be worked upon. All the same I wasn't sure I wanted to see the place, for pictures which people painted in my head were often misleading. Peabody Buildings – had Mum exaggerated the savage place, the allure of its shadows, the raw women, the bellowing court?

While she ironed my sisters' blouses (they were too precious to pass through the laundry women's hands) she told me the stories. 'Like lost souls,' she said, 'the

20

river noises at night. Sometimes we used to go down to the bridge and get on the mud and find things . . .'

'What things?'

'Oh . . . I d'know . . . shoes . . . I found a half-crown once! Guess what I did?'

'I know, you gave it to your mother.'

She glanced up suspiciously.

'And your poor mother was led such a dance by her sons.'

'It's the truth, so don't smile like that. She had to go to the lav in the yard – that was when they wouldn't leave her be – just to get a bit of peace and to count her money. And then, guess what? The blighters stuck the spout of the teapot into the window and watered her where she sat. Blighters! She let fly when she come out.'

But – London, was it really bad? Really wicked? I hoped so. 'Isn't London where the King and Queen live? Dirty? Isn't it where Jack the Ripper lived? Dull? You said it was dull in London.'

'Jack the Ripper! Who's been telling you about him?'

If I said Rene she wouldn't be allowed to come to tea, so I said that Big Ethel had been talking about him in the laundry.

Mum spat on the iron so that it hissed at the lawn sleeves, punishing each wrinkle, tormenting each fold.

'But did you see him? Jack?'

'When I was eleven years old I used to run across Blackfriars Bridge early in the morning to Ludgate Circus. It was dark then in the winter, and dark again when I ran back at night, and I was too cold or too tired at eight o'clock to worry about silly old Jack the Ripper. And if you think that the King – only it wasn't a King then it was the Queen, Queen Victoria – if you think that the Queen had nothing better to do than traipse over Blackfriars Bridge . . .'

21

The tale of the bridge now was postponed for the more immediate satisfaction of the tale of the boots.

'D'you realize how lucky you are? D'you realize that I wore my brother Will's boots until the day when I'd saved, scrimped and saved, enough to buy my own shoes? I hated' – *bang* on the dress she was ironing – 'hated having to wear my brother's boots. I used to nip along as quick as you like in those old boots . . . and – I can tell you for nothing – they slopped up and down something chronic. Tore at my chilblains they did.'

'Mean old Grandma Peggs,' I sympathized.

'Mean old! – You'd better wash out your mouth, young lady! Mean! My mother was a dear! Wore herself out for us she did. Wore herself to the bone.'

A perfect mother then, my silent Grandma Peggs, my squat and fleshy grandma. Irons were changed, Mum sighed as she turned to her girlhood once more. 'One day a week we had a short day, finished at four if we were lucky – and we had Sundays too.'

'The rest of the week you stood in the basement, washing dishes all of the day. And you were only a few years older than I am now,' I prompted. 'Poor old Mum.'

'Oh well. Don't look so mournful. We had a bit of a lark now and then, and when I went upstairs to be a waitress, then it was nice. City gentlemen, real toffs, ate at Stewarts'. They knew the way to go on, lovely manners. They called me their Emma, I had my own tables, see? My regulars gave me tips, but I didn't feel . . . didn't feel . . .'

'Didn't have to kiss them?' I suggested, thinking of my uncles' handouts to me and the obligatory scratching of moustache or beard.

'You're a one and no mistake, young Een. Wait till I tell Annie what you come up with. Kiss them – oh dear.'

She wiped her eyes. 'Tell the truth, I wouldn't have minded – but . . . well . . . there you are. We didn't

22

poach, us girls upstairs. Kept to our own tables, knew all our gentlemen, almost like friends we were with them, though never stepped out of line, not them or us. Mrs Stewart was most particular. My gentlemen were – oh yes – they really were . . .'

Smoothly, smoothly the iron slid across the lacy tablecloth and my mother had forgotten me. It was young Emma Peggs she contemplated, who moved deft hands among the knives and forks at the tables of her gentlemen. Supple and trim she was in her black-and-white uniform, light-footed in her slender shoes. The gentlemen had to tease her, she had to blush. Not one of them kissed her, but . . . perhaps . . . on a day of celebration . . . one of them would. Whatever happened, her own daughter whom she had forgotten would be a witness. She should remember that.

I listened to her talk of that improbable youth as I listened to fairy stories, and with the same kind of belief. She told of a time before I was born, before she was my mother – an unlikely time, but lively, so I concentrated with her on making up a past.

'At Stewarts' – Blow it!' she forgot to change the irons; one was cool, the other was red-hot, and she straightened her back while they were amended. 'At Stewarts' the roast meat was always on the bone. We waitresses learnt to carve it so straight and fine that you couldn't see the lines of the knife blade. I tell you as much – I could do it. Mind – they weren't 'arf hard taskmasters, Mr and Mrs Stewart.'

As a reward for Emma's services at the steaming sinks among the cockroaches, and above ground in the dazzle of white table linen, the Stewarts gave her, when she left to be married, a workbox lined with satin. All that remained of her youth Emma gave to me over the ironing table except certain items which she guarded jealously; they were – her skill at carving the roast; her workbox

23

lined with satin; and the spectre of poverty, poverty and dirt which followed her, beseeching her not to turn aside, until she was driven half mad and ran from it to scrub and scour and polish and save into exhaustion.

I listened to her, yes; understood these things, yes; but – without the language of understanding – what could I do? So I gave no sign, and suppose the words had come she would have taken no account of them, for I was a child, and her child what's more – except when she forgot that it was so, over the ironing.

Chapter Three

Mum's intention was that I should be different and this might have suited me well, but for the fact that difference began and finished with the ideal of my unadulterated cleanliness. I struggled against this, but cotton knickers were razor-edged, so were petticoats; my somersaults over railings were pyrotechnic displays; even my bouncings over hopscotched pavements were fluorescent. It was useless to kick off shoes and to grub in the gutter, for my socks would be changed as soon as the dirt was noticed. The laundry was on Mum's side, and – clean as a nut – I drove off the ghost of Peabody Buildings. I was starched sore, as white as snow, and bad-tempered. She didn't care what I was or what I did as long as I was spotless while I was being or doing it.

'I bet you married my dad because he had a laundry,' I said. And to my surprise both Mum and Auntie Annie giggled.

'What about Charlie, sparrer?' Auntie nudged my mother. 'Gave Charlie the glad eye, didn't you?'

There was more, but though I hung about they kept it to themselves with winks and knowing looks.

Uncle Charlie – there was only one Charlie in our lives – was my dad's youngest brother. He was a half-crown uncle – but had my mother considered him suited to be my father? I thought of my dad as I skipped behind his long strides up Inman. The smiles of people as they called out to him.

'Morning, Joe!'

''tcher, Guvnor!'

'All Sir Garnett, Mr Joe?'

His clogs struck sparks from the pavement and I followed in the wake of my dad, who was a fine figure of a man, they all said so. And – she had – what was it Auntie Annie had whispered?

'You set your cap at Charlie, eh, sparrer?'

It was time to watch my parents. I was old enough, about eight years old; moreover I knew about things from books, for I had read all the books in our house. Most of them were concerned with characters in crinolines or in uniforms, but I read everything, from *The Wide, Wide World*, to Louisa May Alcott's books, to *The Cat and the Canary*. This last book I found in the kitchen drawer one Saturday morning and stood there reading it while Mum was blessedly out of the house, shopping and talking. Eyes raced against time, toes curled in fright – and as a hand stretched from the panelling, as the girl opened her mouth to scream . . . and . . . there were feet on the stairs. The next time I opened the drawer the book was gone. Well, it had afforded nothing but the tingle of fear, unlike Louisa May Alcott, who showed families who were fond of one another – better than that, who seemed to share one communal family life, together painted one large picture. Not lots of small and separate ones. Louisa May Alcott wrote of affection between mother and father.

But – 'None of that lovey-dovey stuff,' Mum had said, pushing my dad from her lips when he returned from the Club on Sunday morning. It was her custom to do so and I had supposed it was the smell of Conservative beer which wrinkled her nose. But – suppose it was that she didn't like my dad? Suppose she still kept the glad eye for Uncle Charlie?

At midday I was often alone with my parents. After the meal Dad stretched himself out on the floor in front of the range, because his overalls would make the chair dirty. I tried lying down beside him to keep him

26

company, before going back to school. Both of us were covered by the *Daily Telegraph*, which didn't send me to sleep as it did my father. When his steady breathing lifted the pages it was time for me to go.

'Ssh. Get up now. Just look at your dad. He could sleep on a clothesline, the poor old chap.'

I tiptoed to the door of the kitchen, turned to whisper goodbye, and saw how gravely she bent her head above him. She didn't touch him, but just stood there. Lonely.

The others had got there first – even my sisters, Elsie and Edie, and my brother, Bill. All the aunts and uncles and all but two of the cousins had arrived before me; they were permanent fixtures; it was their world and their landscape and none of it would change and its regulations must stand. However, I could grumble.

'Ena will go. Just one more errand, ducks. Your legs are younger than ours.'

Bill was older; besides, he was a boy. My sisters were young ladies, they told me. It was pointless to glare at those older legs, those longer legs. I slouched off on one of their errands, which would no doubt involve me in an argument which I did not deserve, with a butcher or greengrocer who lowered his huge face to my level. It would be about quality. Quality was a substance of such unstable nature that on some occasions only my mother could lay her hands on it.

'Tell the butcher that the beef he sold us last weekend was stringy. This time we want something we can put our jaws around. And a nice lean chump chop for your dad. Tell him.'

It was for me to put my jaws around the tonguetwister of 'lean chump chop' while the butcher, taped into his bloody apron, clashed his knife up and down the steel and beamed down at me.

'Your mum's knowing what's what. Tell her as I'm sorry. It won't happen again, tell her. Now,' displaying the quivering chop on his broad palm, 'how's that for your dad?'

Meat smelt. It was buzzed by bluebottles; even when it was divided and chopped it was alarming; when it was hung and was a pig or half a sheep I looked down at the sawdust floor. Then I hated the butcher, hated the pigs and the sheep for letting it happen. They hung so meek and willing – as well as doleful. Errands brought you up against life.

'My giddy aunt!' Edie shouted. 'When I was your age I had to . . . clean the range . . . peel the spuds . . . scrub the passage . . . er . . . hearthstone the step . . . erm . . .' The catalogue of her slavery was interminable until Mum came into the room. 'Bill got away with it,' Edie muttered.

I saw her point and sometimes regretted, like my mother, that I had not been born a boy. Even at school boys were proposed for a separate and most probably a more exciting destiny than girls. Suddenly, after being cosy Infants, boys became Boys and girls became Girls. Titles to these effects were carved over the separate stone doorways; and to make certain of the distinction the doors faced into separate playgrounds each behind high walls, although the building itself was one establishment. At playtime the girls heard savage yells from behind the walls; we heard the thump of footballs or of fists; the idea of boys was growing; they were a tribe, they answered to surnames or to crude epithets; they wore belts which clasped by means of metal snake heads. Some girls were terrified of boys even outside school, but I was saved from this as in our street we had boys who were friends – who kept their ends up in school, were as wild as the rest, but in Inman those same boys were allowed to play our games, to follow our rules, were domesticated creatures.

In spite of being told frequently, first of the surprise of my birth ('Just when I thought I was safe') and then, as a syrup, the 'Never mind, you were a dear little baby' piece, it did appear that I wasn't. Not a dear little baby. Edie told me I wasn't. She returned to the services rendered, the songs she had sung to press me into sleep. Thanks were now overdue, but I resented giving them.

'Just as I'd got you off and was creeping out of the room, then you'd start up.'

I asked what songs she had sung.

'Oh, I don't know . . . something nice . . . "Oh! No John!" or "She was a sweet little dicky bird. Tweet, tweet, tweet, she went. Sweetly she" – '

'That's not a lullaby!'

'Well! I like that!'

And at this point we would both walk out on the screaming baby until the next time Edie felt the need to rehearse her story. One day it might keep her company as Mum's stories of her own youth did.

More than one aspect of Edie's tales was disturbing. Unlike my mother's stories of Peabody Buildings, Edie's described a place and a time in which I had played a part, and without knowing that I was playing it. Helpless and horrid I had been. So I drew back from Edie's portrait to the idea which came in a flash, that I was of noble birth. The more I considered, the more convinced I became. Brushing aside for the time being all whys and wherefores, I accepted with thanks the excitement of understanding why I was so different from the rest of the family. I worked on this assumption until Mum looked up and said, 'What are you bossing at?'

At first my noble birth poured torrents of purest blood through my veins and bred immunity to teasing and criticism, but its complications were numberless and, tiring of the whole thing, I took to myself the responsibility for my own difference.

If Edie had stayed by the baby's bed, Elsie had gone roving, which was what was expected of her. Elsie had no need to be anything but beautiful and clever and captivating. With these attributes she was the one who polished up the day. Edie told me more stories, of a time I could enjoy hearing about, before I was born. When she spoke of the fun they had had she forgot to mention those chores of hers. Elsie was the leader, she organized everyone, including the cousins who lived round the corner in Wilna Road, including those who came at weekends. What adventures they all had, under Elsie's banner. And how, while I listened, I wished to have been there, not to have been an afterthought and different, not to be, as I was now, merely listening, marooned in a separate childhood, dull and deprived.

With friends I converted wistfulness into pride, for not one of them had a sister like Elsie, so charming and lovely in her ways. She talked to me, when she had time to talk, as though I mattered more than anyone else in the world. It wasn't only telling that she did, for she asked me about – well – anything. Her friends were also nice to me because that would please Elsie. Young men came to see Bill and fell at Elsie's feet, which was stupid as they were too young for her. I read about the falling business in one of the magazines left about the house and when I told Elsie what they did she laughed. At the young men, not at me.

All these things I saw and heard from a sort of underworld which I inhabited, and down there I understood that Elsie was poised to leave home. Whatever the grown-ups said I knew the truth of it, but the prospect of her leaving brought a lump to my throat. There was no argument, however; she must go, I could see that she must, before something happened to her, before she married someone. While she was still singing and laughing.

Only once was she too angry to laugh. Bertie lived on the corner of Inman and Wilna with a set of relations who came and went in such numbers that the bricks of the house must have bulged. Bertie was the fixture. He went nowhere except on his donkey rounds. The donkey lived in the back yard and its braying gave a piquant and bucolic note to the normal shouts of the street. It was one of Inman's ornaments. From the cart Bertie sold oil and saucepans and dolly bags and candles and strings of onions which bounced about from the cart like the knobbly plaits which some girls at school possessed, and which I was not allowed to grow for fear of fleas. Bertie wore thick pebble glasses and his mouth stayed ajar and he wasn't all there. It was his enormous feet that you looked up at first when he galloped his donkey cart home down Earlsfield Road. He sat on top of the cart, high up on a half roof, and sometimes when he was excited he stood up on the seat and curled his whip like billyo and shouted at the donkey, at passers-by, at himself too.

'Bloody Bertie! Bloody Old Four Eyes!' All through fat sticky lips which grinned from side to side of his face as he turned his head, to bring goodwill to all men. A happy Old Four Eyes until he fell in love with my sister.

It was Edie who brought the news. 'That Bertie was yelling at the top of his voice all the way down Earlsfield Road: "Elsie Chamberlain! Elsie Chamberlain!" He didn't half look a guy.'

'Was that all he shouted?'

'Isn't that enough?'

Of course it was. Edie was smug. Elsie was humiliated. She was furious with the creature, she said, and what did you expect when you had to live here in Inman Road? It was nothing better than a slum, she said, and when my dad heard of this he was angry too. He was rarely angry with anyone; especially was he careful of Elsie.

'You'd best guard that tongue of yours, my girl. You've upset your mother, good and proper. Calling Inman a slum!'

Mum was pale, and very hurt. 'I'm feeling what I call drained,' she said. 'I wouldn't live here if I thought Inman was a slum. It's bad enough anyway with all the dust and dirt.'

Beside this argument Bertie's passion dwindled in importance. His flowers were left on the doorstep and I was sorry to see them fade, but too scared of Elsie to rescue them. Bertie persisted, though, with ropes of onions which I had to return as neither Elsie nor Mum would go near the house on the corner. When a pile of carrots and several oily bundles of kindling wood blocked the path to the front door, my dad was asked to have a word with Bertie.

'Elsie will come with me,' he said, 'and the nipper must stay indoors.' They came back with very straight faces; Elsie was white-lipped.

There were no more presents laid at our door. Bertie had set his sights too high; he was a fool and that was all there was to it. Also, he had upset my sister. If he was seen at all after his rejection it was as a bundle of a man limp on his donkey cart; he was older, and somehow less of a clown; seemed almost sensible when he raised his eyes. His donkey, too, had lost his dash; the whip which had been flourished about his head, but had never cut him, was now kept furled beside Bertie as correctly as Uncle Charlie's office umbrella.

One sunny afternoon Bertie was killed. Auntie Annie saw it all from the bus going to Clapham Junction.

'You should've been with me, Em,' she said to Mum. 'D'you know, he toppled off his cart like a sack of potatoes – slow – d'you follow? Fell – *plop* – in front of the bus coming the other way; not my bus, thank the Lord.' Her eyes shone. 'Oh Em! You should've been with me!'

Bertie's family gave him a good funeral. They got hold of a harmonium and played their favourite hymn all night: 'Fight the good fight'.

Soon afterwards the donkey was taken away as no one could manage him, and we missed his braying.

'A bit of the country,' Mum said. 'It's a pity the donkey had to go.'

What was left was a thickening of disapproval towards Elsie. Sides were taken. I was her champion, though it was difficult to understand how it was to be her; as I tried she became more remote, more of a mystery. Her days were spent in an office which, I gathered, was a splendid place to be working inside, but we had an office in Number 29 Inman and it was a muddle of papers, and although it had a desk no one used it except me. I was allowed to write on the long brown envelopes which had gummed together, and so I wrote stories which were wonderful, though I never read them back to myself, and hid them, again in the office, which was the only place in the house safe from Mum's duster.

'Thank goodness my office is nothing like this one,' said Elsie. 'This doesn't deserve the name of office.'

At the end of the day Elsie came home to change her clothes so that she might eat her dinner in night-time restaurants in town, or sit in a theatre while famous actors performed for her amusement. 'It's dinner again then,' Mum said. 'Come on, Edie. Supper for you, gel.'

There was a lull at home when Elsie had gone to London on the train. There was a scent left behind of the violets she wore in her fur collar, there was a swirl of cool air from her flying skirts. The kitchen, especially in the gaslight of wintertime, shrank small for a while.

The following morning she might give me the violets

33

but often they had been suffocated by the luxury of the previous evening, although Elsie herself wasn't tired. She sang the songs of the theatre, she bought the record which played the music and found time to sing to it before she ran from the house to the office, and while she sang she danced herself ready. It was the playing of gramophone records first thing in the morning which annoyed my mother.

'I'll give her Chu-Chin-Chow! I'll give her Rose Marie!'

She accused Elsie. I received the accusation. 'When she gets home tonight I'll tell her good and proper. No breakfast. No lining to her stomach. I don't know.'

We both knew that when Elsie came home she would sing her songs while she washed her bouncy shingled hair, which was as bronze and as glossy as my mother's, and nothing would be said. To the tune of 'Golden Slumbers' Elsie sang strange words; with a sideways glancing at Mum she sang so sweetly, 'But he so teased me, he so pleased me, what I did you must have done.' This version was much more interesting than the one which we were singing at school: 'Sleep pretty darling, do not cry. And I will sing a lullaby.' There the teacher snarled through bitter lips not – repeat *not* – to slush away at 'Kishyeroyes' but, with a hiss, to sing 'Kiss-sss-your ayes-ss'. I sang at school – 'What I did you must have done' – without either slush or hiss as my sister did as she darted about the house in the early morning. Whatever she did or said was marked out because she was doing and saying it. I wanted a heroine, perhaps I wanted a villain also, and all I dreaded and all I understood was that she must soon leave home.

Mum said, 'How can she talk her big talk? She can't save, and it takes cash to sail across the sea. Canada indeed! The New World! What's wrong, I ask you,

34

whatever is wrong with the old world?' But she didn't ask my sister, who was biding her time.

Meanwhile she was a torment and a delight and altogether without parallel. They forgot to criticize her on Sunday evenings for we, her family, could all be proud of her when she took turns with Auntie May at the piano in the downstairs front room. Auntie May relied on tricks for applause; she flourished her crossed hands; her veined fingers pirouetted, long nails rapped on the keys; she swooped from one end of the white notes to the other; she was enthusiastic about the loud pedal in 'Poet and Peasant' and terribly restrained with the soft pedal at the commencement of 'The Lost Chord'. Elsie scorned such manoeuvres but she did, it was true, play music that was above the taste of her audience. And so would I if I could play the piano, I thought. Still, I wished sometimes that she would hear how restless the aunts and uncles grew during the strained 'Goodbyes' of Tosti.

It wasn't so much that they didn't care for sad songs, for many of the songs of Sunday evening would be sad, but the sorrows were hearty, like the deaths of little children or mothers or heroes in battle. Those sung by uncles or by my dad were chock-full of dramatic incident, and made brilliant pictures, but Elsie's pictures were delicate, wreathed about with hints and allusions to grief itself without a clue as to the reason for that grief. And Tosti's 'Goodbye' took such a long time to sing and I tried to sit up and not to like my dad's 'Shipmates o' mine' so much. Yet the lingering fall of her music made me shiver. It was an invitation she suggested, to sorrow.

Of course she did sing brave and bright songs. 'I am Chu-Chin-Chow of China . . . dum-didi-dum-dum- . . .' And this with the loud pedal pressed hard because at last it was proper to press it. And 'The Rustle of Spring' she played with verve; it was Mum's favourite piece, for

35

which she closed her eyes and occupied her face with a listening-to-good-music expression. She kept them closed after the last note had died away before the clapping. Then she opened them and sighed – loudly. Elsie played 'The Rustle of Spring' less frequently as the time drew near when she would tell us that she was going away.

There was something I might do to prepare for her departure and I made up my mind to learn to play the piano. I gave up playing up and down on the black notes as Rene had taught me and sat brooding over the sheets of music in the front room until the message was received. I was sent to a teacher in Brocklebank Road.

The teacher dribbled over me, her long nose dribbled too so that I cringed at the keyboard ready to dodge at the precise moment of fall. From the first lesson she paid more attention to my weekly sixpence than to any signs of musicality which I might let slip. Paid even more attention to the paper which wrapped the sixpence. It was tissue paper from the laundry packing room; sometimes it was beetroot pink, sometimes it was blue, but whatever the colour my teacher seized on it and wandered about the room twisting her tissue prize into flowers and birds and butterflies, which she pinned to curtains or to her drooping cardigan or balanced saucily on the sour old aspidistra. All the while keeping up a recommendation to – 'Keep it going. That's right, dear. Oh! If I had some twigs . . . then I could – you know – prop the flowers on them. Like almond blossoms, you know. Yes – keep it going. A bit more . . . life, dear!' And, with a mouth full of pins, 'D'you think that Mummy has any yellow paper for next week?'

In spite of my lack of facility and her indifference to anything between us but the coloured tissue paper, she pushed me with fresh supplies of sheet music until one arrived with the encouraging title of 'A Winter Sleigh

Ride'. The publishers strongly advised the purchase from them of wristbands to which jingle bells were fixed. A performance enhanced by these bells would provide all who listened with the sensation of a jolly ride through the snow. Of course it would. I saw them all. Aunts, uncles, my family, Elsie too if I was quick, all rubbing their frosty hands, inescapably there – in the sparkling snow. I wanted those jingle bands.

For hours I practised in the frost of our weekday front room to deserve the bands; I practised the facial expression also, for my teacher had said, 'Now, remember it is varry, varry important to get the mood.'

How could I have ignored Mum's recurring penny-pinching? She listened when I put the case for the bands, and listened, really listened, when I played 'A Winter Sleigh Ride' to her. Hopes of a second musical daughter died; I saw them go. The weekly sixpence was withdrawn and the tissue flowers and birds grew dusty in the Brocklebank room. I returned to a snail trail of black notes and my piano teacher gave up teaching the piano.

She took up dressmaking. Perhaps it was guilt which prompted Mum to ask her, instead of Auntie Annie, to make a summer dress for Edie.

'You must have been the straw that broke the camel's back,' Mum said to me.

Week after cold springtime week Edie shivered, being fitted. Once I saw her tucking a fold of laundry tissue in her bag. Finally she appeared in the dress. Mum's eyes opened, but it was no surprise to me to see the bows. Edie was covered with bows, she looked like a sturdy apple tree. They fluttered, the bows did, they flew; Edie was philosophical and had a kind heart.

'I'd better wear a cardigan. I asked her not to bother with bows. Still, it's a pity to cover up her work, the bows are all picot-edged. She must have worked really hard, Mum, she says she's giving up dressmaking.'

37

Chapter Four

Book families were obliged to quarrel out loud and in front of everyone, including the reader. In Number 29 two sisters carried out a silent guerrilla war. Edie struck out from shadows at Elsie, who was forever moving and for the most part ignored the attacks as irrelevant. Except that when Elsie hit she hit hard.

Certainly it was difficult to come to grips with her, for she was as restless as the lace-curtain light of the bedroom windows. Edie did not reflect, she was as far from moonshine as the kitchen table and as the kitchen table was an indispensable part of our home, so was she. From time to time I came across her but I didn't have to think about her, not until I grew older; no one did, except sometimes the aunts gave her a poke and my mother tried to shield her and in doing so, poked and prodded Edie herself.

It seemed that Elsie's days were streaming torrents of happenings while our days, mine and Edie's, were a wash of ripples, circular, turning round and round, repeating and repeating sights and sounds. For example, my sister Edie's voice.

'You're supposed to be fond of me. I'm your sister.'

It would whisper again. 'Love me? You do, you've got to. I'm your sister. You have to. Always.'

And the first reply was the last reply. 'Of course I do. Oh, all right, Edie. I've got to go now.'

Yes, you have to love your sister, there was no reason not to. And – it was one of the rules. Oh, but I didn't want to be bothered by it. Poor Edie. Nice, kind Edie.

'You'll have no worry over Edie,' the aunts told Mum.

Sometimes, though, I gave Edie my full attention. No doubt about it, she had made the mistake of being born too soon after Elsie. She said as much in one of her brief and drastic outbursts: 'Mum had me too quick. Elsie had all the best things . . . Mum's time . . . all that. It's like a sale at Arding and Hobbs – first come first served – all the bargains go to the pushy people. Elsie had the bargains. Nice nose. Eyes. Hair. Mouth.'

Then she went red and said not to let on to Mum what she had said. I was interested and wanted to continue the revelations, but she remembered that she was a lot older than me and told me to go out to play.

I would have told her that she should have changed places with me. Both Elsie and I knew about ourselves in our different ways, but Edie had no idea. She searched herself out in a hunt-the-thimble game, now hot now cold, and apparently getting colder all the time. As the youngest sister she might have stood a chance; certainly she would have enjoyed praise for errands run willingly and without dawdling or complete loss of memory. She would have been a docile and understandable little girl. Without guile, the wet brush of moustached uncles would have been as welcome as the sixpences which those uncles nailed into her palm. I became more excited by my invention of young Edie. I saw her standing bravely in the starched agony of petticoats, not grabbing them and stamping them soft. I saw the way she looked up at the visiting lady, even at her necklace, which swung its large beads towards her as the lady bent to kiss her. They were like eyeballs, those large round glassy beads. But young Edie didn't shudder; she didn't, without warning and on the lady's silk lap, throw up.

I moved on to my position as contemporary of Elsie. Edie's complaints, which plodded through their shared childhood, had warned me.

'She had us all running about for her, didn't she, Bill?'

'What? Yep. I suppose so.' But Bill was busy forgetting his meek boyhood.

'D'you mind how Elsie made us give her our pocket money?' And, for my benefit, 'Such as we had, that is. She said – d'you remember, Bill? – she said we'd go to Clapham Junction on the tram when we had enough money.'

For a second Bill looked back and was curious. 'What happened to that money?'

'Well. Of course we never went. That madam! In the end she did give us a bit back to buy Christmas presents. And – she chose the presents, being the oldest. Shame! Bill, don't you remember anything?'

'We had a great time once, when we went on the tram to see London. Charlie and Muriel came too. Elsie said we were not to tell about it but just to save money and sweets, and when the right day came to just slide off. She would leave a message for Mum not to worry. She would know the right day.'

Edie was remembering too, and in spite of herself she couldn't prevent the smile of recollection spreading across her face. 'We had a whole day in London. Walked and walked!'

I was enthralled and wistful as Edie and Bill turned to me, eager to share the day.

Bill said, 'Elsie showed us everything – the River Thames, Big Ben, the buses . . .'

Edie said, 'She didn't know where to get off the tram or which bit was London. And we were starving. And when we wanted to feed the ducks she pulled us away to see Buckingham Palace. She said that we should see the King and Queen but a man told us they weren't in. So she didn't know everything. And I had a blister. And Muriel was sick on the tram going home.'

'I don't remember that. Muriel was always sick.'

'And when we did get home we copped it. Mum was

worried to death. Elsie had put her note in the front room, and it wasn't Mum's day for the front room, she did find it but only by a stroke of luck and only late in the afternoon. By that time she was worried to death.'

'Mum was always worried to death,' said Bill.

'Funny thing.' Edie pursed her lips. 'Elsie kept quiet about the man – '

'What man?'

'Oh you! You and Charlie never use your eyes. The man who sat next to Elsie on the tram, we couldn't all sit together. He wasn't half gassing to Elsie, smiling and nodding, and looking at her. A posh man, good-looking. Didn't you see?'

Bill was bored, and so was I. Edie murmured to herself.

'I asked her what he said, and she told me it was the usual stuff – about how pretty she was and that and when she grew older she should go on the stage. I asked her if she thought he was trying to lure her. Mum had warned us about being lured but Elsie said she wasn't afraid. She wasn't afraid either, of anything. That madam!'

It was pity which Edie nourished in me as I grew up. Often I wished to ignore her feelings; she had more feelings than the rest of us, yet few appreciated this. Clumsy people upset her, hurt her terribly so I would have to pay out my impatient pity, coin by coin until the puzzled expression left her eyes clear again. There was no escape from pity and if that was my way of loving Edie it was uncomfortable and I hoped to grow out of it. It would have been better if my sister had been really nasty, spiteful, dishonest, lazy. There was no chance of her performing a proper crime, no chance at all.

Long before I was old enough to appreciate her difficulties she had perfected a few tricks, a few evasions. Finally her own ill-health rescued her. She returned from dances where Elsie had dragged her for her own good, alone and pallid, complaining of headaches or sore feet.

'She wasn't on her feet,' said Elsie. 'At least only in the Paul Jones.'

During our parties at home or in one or other of the family houses the fun and teasing were too much for her; then she came over all anyhow, then she felt like chucking a dummy and would slip out of the room to be quiet among the heaps of cold coats laid out on beds, or at home, where there weren't many doors which might close firmly, she shut herself into the outside lav, preferring the company of spiders and beetles to that of joyful cousins and bright-eyed aunts.

'She's got to learn to take some teasing,' Mum said.

Teasing was supposed to be another thing that was good for one. I hated it but made faces and vowed silent revenge, not wanting to watch beetles crawl across the cobbled floor of the outside lav.

When Mum remembered Edie's absence she would roll up her eyes, shrug her shoulders, and disappear also and perhaps an aunt would go with her, both returning to the warmth and light with faces solemn and wise, nodding their heads over poor Edie.

Out of this hide-and-seek grew the rumour that Edie might have consumption. It would explain the funny turns, they said, and I heard them saying so. Edie heard too. Everything changed. She saw herself clearly, as a victim who carried some kind of distinction. She was made much of, she sat up straight and smiled. Bravely. I was glad and proud of her while she was with us. If she did truly have the consumption, if she wasn't putting it on, why, she would be such a good patient and I would sit with her and be good too. It occurred to me that I had considered the part of Beth for myself after reading *Little Women*, but I willingly gave up all claim

42

to it in favour of Edie. In any case Jo's character was far more to my taste. Beth fitted Edie like a glove – if Edie did have the consumption.

While she went to the doctor to be examined, while she waited for medicine to take effect one way or another, I considered the business and listened to the change in tone of the aunts discussing her. There were no more remarks about what they called Edie's lack of 'go'. They had always polished off those remarks with a comment on Edie's comfort to her mother when all the birds had flown; now they had to drop that virtue. I thought that the whole idea of Edie's decline was beautiful and after a little rearrangement of her appearance – thinner perhaps, shorter if possible, though when she reclined on a sofa covered with shawls, surrounded by flowers, height would scarcely be relevant – she would be a thing of grace and reverence in our kitchen. And she wouldn't suffer, not half as much as she suffered from mocking words and from being Elsie's sister. Beth didn't suffer, she was merely tired and sweet on her sofa while she got ready for heaven, and before that – the marvellous sorrow of adoring relations. I would help her to be brave. What a sight she would be. Together we would show them. I examined Edie every day with hope fading as the roses came back to her cheeks.

'That's right, my girl. Tuck in,' Mum said to my sister.

'What's up with you?' Edie asked me. 'Know me next time?'

So there it was, the shape of the world was already decided and the rules of it were made; until I was older I must make the best of it, invent a little and disagree with almost everything, especially with aunts and uncles. Mum had escaped from Peabody Buildings but she couldn't and wouldn't escape from her sisters and brothers or from the tangle of my dad's family who had married so many of them. Elsie tried to explain the relationships by drawing out a family tree; she wrote Dad's relations in blue and Mum's in red ink, but soon they puddled together in violet.

Swarms of aunts and uncles came on Sundays, vibrating with conversation, and it wasn't sweetness they hunted but the zest of reminiscence, to revive one another after the week's work in bubbles of talk. Words ran parallel, how could they understand one another? Below the table I listened to the cry of – 'Sparrer!'

Sparrer? They called one another 'Sparrer', and with reason, for the notes of their conversation were as shrill and as incessant as the chirpings of the sparrows in the gutters under the roof. There were no baritones until the uncles grunted their way upstairs to be fed, for on arrival my dad's hand waylaid them and they disappeared into the front room. While they drank and smoked my dad held up a page of yesterday's *Telegraph* against the mantelpiece to bring up the flames in the fire he had just tried to light.

'It's got no draw, this hearth hasn't,' he grumbled. 'Ah! Now we've got it' (as the paper singed a perilous brown). 'Now we've done it' (as the paper flared into the mantelpiece). He was never put out by the grumpy puttering of the coals for most of the day; I suppose, after his weekday chore of fuelling the laundry boilers, the front-room fire must have been a joke. But it took Mum only a minute with the poker to bring the black coals to orange and green and gold.

Downstairs the smells were of tobacco and beer; upstairs they had names like Ashes of Roses and Eau de Cologne. Auntie Florrie and Auntie May competed with scents, Auntie Lizzie didn't feel the need, Auntie Annie smelt warm, Mum smelt of gravy.

Because Dad's sister Hepsie had married Mum's brother Will, and dad's cousin Jack had married Mum's

44

sister Lizzie, Mum had a double responsibility to provide Sunday dinner.

'It's a proper swizz,' she confided to Auntie Annie. 'Mind, I'm not getting at you, you're out of it, your rightful turn comes once in a while. But – see what I'm driving at? Stands to reason the others should take a turn more often. They can't see it.'

'Don't want to.' Auntie Annie knew well her part. She and I both waited in sympathetic silence.

'Florrie ought to, not just at Christmas, or on her birthday. And there's May. Don't see why not – '

'May isn't married.' And Auntie Annie clinched the argument.

All the same, Mum gloried in her Sunday turns. It gave her a chance to prove she was the family's best cook. She was on trial, not only to maintain that position but to show her home, her children. Bill had to answer up; Elsie had to show willing when it came to clearing the table; Edie – well, she showed willing anyway but it was for her to perk up. I had to be quiet and not poke my nose in.

As for the visitors, they also knew their parts: for the first few minutes an initial politeness, the parade of best clothes which was made more delightful by comparison with the pinafored haste of the cook of the day; the freshly powdered cheeks more exquisite when sharp eyes observed the cook, rosy-red as she lifted the joint from the oven.

In our house the kitchen was the dining-room, there was no hiding place and Mum had chosen it to be so. When she had moved her young family into 29 Inman Road the kitchen had been a bedroom, the cooking had taken place downstairs at the back, where a door led into the laundry. And into Grandma Thornley's office.

Mum recalled those days. 'I wasn't going to have that old faggot bossing me about! Sharing a kitchen with the

45

likes of her, no fear! Don't know how I had the pluck to stick my ground, though. Cor! You should've copped eyes on her. Not that I should talk about her like this to you. You forget what I've said now, ducks.'

Her defiance was a thing of the past, like Grandma, but from whatever viewpoint our upstairs kitchen was agreeable. It was a playroom (not that we used the term); it was a studio when we dabbed watercolour pictures from scrubbed paintboxes; it was where I read, and wrote stories on old envelopes; it was a theatre; it was a quiet room where a convalescent was allowed to devote herself to being poorly; it was all mine when I frowned from the window and shivered when I came back to Inman Road from daydreams. On Sundays the kitchen was a dining-room, and suddenly all its other functions were inappropriate, like knitting in church.

The roast! On Sundays the roast was in its prime. It would descend through the week through cold to shepherd's pie, even to curry in the long run if Mum felt up to the grumbles. But on Sundays the scent of it overcame those imported fragrances of aunts and uncles and clung to the walls and curtains and clothes of all of us who licked our lips in Number 29.

Chapter Five

FROM the top of the bus on a winter evening you saw
how the street lamps paced out the darkness, illumi-
nating only a circle on each pavement but marking the
way from the Common down to Garratt Lane. Our
Sundays were like that, they didn't throw light into the
week ahead but pointed the direction of it. It was winter
which shone for me, coloured by the rainbow, amber-
jellied, apple-cheeked, red-nosed winter Sundays, and
the most recordable were those when Elsie was still with
us.

On Sundays Auntie Annie took off her overall. She
was the first to arrive, being just round the corner.

'Anything I can do, sparrer?'

'Yes. Talk to Lizzie when she comes. I've got to make
the gravy and she puts me off.'

I loved Auntie Annie, perhaps they all did because she
wasn't a blood relation. Blood relation. The words
curdled.

If Auntie Hepsie was coming she came early, puffing
from the walk through the Shoot on the way from
Southfields. She brought Uncle Will as far as our
hallway, where my dad whisked him into the front room
for a beer and a smoke. She brought her children, one of
whom mattered – my cousin Nora, who was only a little
younger than me. One day she brought Vera, her baby.
A surprise. Vera was put into the bedroom among the
coats and hats of the visitors and was occasionally
circulated to be admired and criticized.

Auntie Hepsie was known for her size and for her
intelligence and for being a good sport about both

distinctions. Like his brothers Uncle Will had become a printer, until his hand was caught in a machine. I kept my eyes from his hand but knew by heart the gloss of skin stretched tight across the stumps of fingers which were left to him. He was a joker was Uncle Will, as thin and springy as his wife was fat and ponderous. He wore glasses with one eyeglass missing, and he winked a lot. When he left The Print he bought a corner shop in Southfields with the money they gave him for the loss of his fingers, and because of the shop he and Auntie Hepsie couldn't always come on Sundays.

There was an aura of the eldest sister about Auntie Lizzie, a certain formality which insisted on her coat being hung up behind the bedroom door and not dropped on the bed with the rest. She was kind to me and I was careful of her. Auntie Annie hugged, Auntie Hepsie patted my head with a weighty hand, Auntie Florrie asked questions about me as if I hadn't a tongue in my head. And when her husband, Uncle Ernie the dentist, gave me his sixpence she could hardly wait to say, 'Well, speak up! You've got a tongue in your head, haven't you?'

I wished she would make up her mind.

Auntie May didn't notice me.

There was another aunt, Mona. She was the wife of the uncle who had coaxed from Mum the glad eye, Uncle Charlie. They lived too far from Earlsfield for the regular Sundays, and they were distant from the rest in other ways. Uncle was a clerical worker in the LCC. He wore best suits every day and took sandwiches to the office. He had two daughters; one was elegant, not as fair as Elsie, but graceful all the same. I was sad that she didn't come to our house more often, for she was fun and played games with me. Her sister had gland trouble and was as pink as a blancmange.

Last to arrive, except for the scamper upstairs of

Auntie May, were Auntie Florrie and Uncle Ernie. They drove their car from Clapham Junction and came late to give us the pleasure of their arrival. Auntie Florrie honked the horn to make sure of it; it was her bit of driving. She smiled like a queen at the children in the street who buzzed around the car. After they limpeted all over the bonnet she called them street Arabs and shouted at them to clear off, but they knew better.

'You go,' Mum said to me. 'They're your friends. You know how Florrie is. Go on! Tell them to hop it. They're your friends.'

'They are not! They're from the top end. Some are from Wilna. Some are from Bendon Valley!'

I went too far. 'Come off it! Not from Bendon Valley! Not in the daytime! I don't know – can't ask the simplest thing without this . . . this . . . You go, Bill.'

And Bill, embarrassed because of the jeers which would follow him indoors, went down to shout at the boys and to wipe them off the car.

'Frankie Finbow was one of them.'

Frankie Finbow was my friend.

Auntie May slipped into her seat at the awkward corner of the table beside my dad, who sat at the head. She timed this to coincide with the sharpening of the carving knife. Sometimes I gasped at the sideways glint of Mum's glasses as she flashed and clashed the blade against the steel, but her hands never faltered. The moment was upon her, the carving of the roast commenced.

Why May was late was a wonder for her excuses, though inventive and seldom repeated, were never credited. My dad enjoyed them, however, and he teased her under the cover of the general conversation. 'Poor old May,' they said when she was out of the room, and sometimes when she was in it. She was the youngest of the family and therefore too late to take advantage of the male relations; as husbands they were all used up. Naturally she was 'poor old May' as she had no husband and no possibility of one now that she was in her thirties; in spite of this fact she hadn't realized that she was too old no matter how often Auntie Florrie told her.

'Still going to dances at her age!' Auntie Flo shook her head. 'Still on the lookout. What a hope!'

'She goes to dances at the Home,' advised Auntie Lizzie. 'Poor old May.'

The Home was where disabled soldiers stayed, those who had been injured in the Great War. Somehow the dances there were to be looked down upon, but were the most that women like Auntie May could hope for. So there she went ferreting out a husband with her black liquorice eyes and found no one. Never mind, on Sundays she had a place, an important place, and a part to play; she was an entertainer, a piano player, a sauce-box, and above all she was a fortune-teller for the aunts and for Mum and Edie, and in such ways quite made up for her spinster state.

Grandma and Grandad Peggs rarely appeared at family gatherings; they needed a bit of peace and probably the absence of Auntie May gave them some. She, as the unmarried daughter, was available to care for the old folk, but it was difficult to see how this was carried out since she didn't cook, she didn't clean. 'Mustn't,' she admitted, 'because of my piano hands.' The piano hands were the means to a small livelihood, for she gave piano lessons to the children of Camberwell.

'She keeps the money,' said Auntie Florrie, her nearest and dearest sister, 'and, I mean to say, she doesn't have to spend a penny on rent or on food. It's all found. What she takes from tinkling the ivories is all in her pocket. And what does she do with it? Buys herself Russian boots!'

Auntie Flo could never forget the Russian boots. They

had swaggered into our house one snowy Christmas and proved the most dashing items in the festival's display; Auntie Flo's fox fur was limp by comparison, which was unfair as she had had to remind Uncle Ernie for months past about the necessity of one for her comfort. Auntie Lizzie hadn't minded too much about the Russian boots, for they were only what she would expect from May. And she was rather amused by Flo's indignation.

'Anything that Flo wants she gets,' muttered Auntie Lizzie to my mother. 'It's there for the asking. She leads poor Ern a dance and no mistake.'

Still, May had stood over a few children and watched stubby fingers prod the piano keys . . . and . . . lo! Russian boots! It wasn't fair. Auntie Florrie bit her lips and brooded and Uncle Ernie bought her some fur-backed gloves like the paws of grizzly bears and of course he would have bought her some boots but she stopped him. 'Copy her? D'you think I'd stoop? Ern! Don't you know me better than that?'

She told Mum this one weekday when we went to Uncle's surgery for my teeth to be examined, and as she reproduced both words and reproach we were as moved as Uncle must have been and appreciated the sensitivity which prompted him to buy her, instead, a real leather handbag with a golden clasp which snapped at her fingers.

Auntie May made money with her piano hands; Uncle Ernie made his from other people's teeth. He was the family's dentist; he had to be. Auntie Florrie was proud of him and of all our smiles; especially was she satisfied by the pink and white click of Auntie Lizzie's false teeth. She was the first to wear false teeth. She was very brave as well as being the eldest sister. She developed a skill in bringing the plate of teeth down from the top gums for an instant of comfort; she achieved this with a supple twist of the tongue, then, resolute as always, she raised a handkerchiefed hand to push the plate back again. Once, seeing my eyes on her, she nodded to me as if to a friend, not as an aunt to a child, and said, 'Hang on to your teeth as long as you can, Een. Let Uncle take one tooth, he'll grab the lot when you're under.'

And she was right, for he had shown me the gas apparatus when I sat in his chair. On Sundays Uncle Ernie's brown eyes were deep and gentle but seen from below, from the depths of his dentist's chair, they were pincushions set in bristled eyebrows; and his nostrils were furry; and his fingers gripped my jaws wide open so that my throat couldn't swallow and in that strangle-hold he said, 'And how is your mother?' and, 'Do you like school?' He was horribly eager as he bent over his tipped-up chair.

My teeth were all Sir Garnett, he said sadly. But I was young. The rest of the family were growing old nicely, however, and one day, set after set of false teeth would gleam around the Sunday table and create a crocodile paradise for Uncle Ernie.

Meanwhile Sunday dinners were safe, except that I had to eat them. The smells were delicious, but . . . there it was . . . the meat which would do me good. As a lure the first cut of the roast was put on my plate, as I was the youngest.

'I'll tell you for why,' muttered Auntie Florrie, who expected to be offered the outside edge herself as she was a cut above the others with a dentist husband and beginning to attend, nowadays, the Masonic dinners in a long dress with a fox fur strung nonchalant. She could have taken my piece; as it was I had difficulty hiding the meat under the greens and gravy. 'I'll tell you for why. She's faddy. And spoilt.'

My sisters and brother and the cousins sat separately

at a table made from a card table with a board on top; the whole construction was concealed by the starchy white of a laundry sheet. When they had finished eating they were allowed to leave as they had things to do, larks to get up to, and they were only young once. I was surprised at the indulgence shown to these young people. Edie stayed behind.

When they had gone my dad took out his false teeth, his eaters, wrapped them fastidiously in a handkerchief, and inserted his talkers. He was the second one in the family to go under Uncle Ernie. Argument was the nub of after-dinner-time, while my dad and the uncles were sitting around the table.

'The seventh day shalt thou rest from thy labours,' one uncle would say.

'Except for the women!' That was one of the aunts.

Off spluttered a familiar firework until a more explosive one was produced. 'What about . . .' the government? the miners? the French? There was a rhythm and a ferocity which was soon lulled by food and warmth and by the women too, who were impatient to get on with their own particular part of Sunday. Long before the arguments I had submerged beneath the table, to my place in all this, enclosed by the tablecloth, among the forest trees of legs. Some legs were planted into the lino, some wavered. Auntie May's glistened in peach rayon, crossing and recrossing, as snapping as the dangling legs of flamingoes in my *Wonders of Africa*. Auntie Florrie's legs were puffed over her new patent leather shoes; she wore taffeta petticoats, palest beige, and made a giant toadstool. A lump of custard dropped on her lap as I considered her and a finger came down to wipe her dress furtively clean; up above she was eating a second helping. Uncle Will, as usual, was tapping his feet, wanting to dance with his Hepsie. Who was not made for dancing. But – she might float though, yes, he might hold her and pirouette, gently balancing her pleasant bulk as if she were a balloon. And I closed my eyes, smiling at the sight. As for the rest of the men up there, soon they must drag themselves up by the roots, by their thick-soled boots all black and Sunday-shiny laced tight and nose-wrinkling with Cherry Blossom boot polish. Words pattered down to me like acorns to lie dormant, perhaps to strike roots into memory until – 'So that's what they meant when . . .'

Into the cloth cave came the echoes of chairs dragged back, the upheaval of legs and the clumping of feet downstairs to the chill of the front-room fire. There was no mercy shown to the men by their wives, for this now was their time, at last. I was forgotten. They spoke up about boring things like prices and neighbours and, from deep-grained habit, lowered voices to tell the rest. I was forgotten. They giggled, then they were all creased up with laughter, it was agony, pain. 'You'll be the death of me, May!' My mother's groan, and I was afraid. Beneath them I sat cross-legged, superior and grave, until the cloth was pulled awry by their tormenting laughter and I was remembered.

'Little pitchers have big ears. She's been there all the time! Gordon Bennett!'

Hands reached down to shadowlands to pull me out. I wanted to tell them that I knew, I knew all their stories, all their silly rules, even the incomprehensible ones like . . . for example . . . 'Breast' was singular and decent – as mentioned in hymns and in poems; 'Breasts' were plural and indecent – as mentioned sometimes in whispers by the aunts when they supposed they were alone together.

'Quick as you like! Off to Sunday School!'

It was off to the washing-up for them while Mum changed her frock. The scullery tumbled with aunts who were desperate to finish so that they could begin. The

54

kettle lid blundered on the kettle, Edie clattered the tea cups on the tray and . . . 'What?' the aunts screamed. 'What! You still here!'

What did the sparrows talk about when I had gone down the street with Rene and the others? They had finished with talk of past things during and immediately after the meal – there was always an awful lot of the past above the table top on Sundays, they threw the past from one to the other like a game of pass-the-parcel – and there didn't appear to be much left for them to discuss, yet they were so eager to be alone with one another. I put the problem to one side as we ran the cold streets to the church. There we were urged to confess our faults; I scrabbled around for something to satisfy both God and the Sunday School teacher and told about the scraps of fat meat which I hid under the gravy and to judge by the relief I felt my confession, a repetitive one, seemed to have gone down well. We giggled and chased all the way home.

Upstairs in the rosy kitchen the aunts and Mum and Edie sat round the table spread with its everyday chenille cloth. A thicket of women.

'Strewth! You've brought in the cold air!'

A haze of tea fumes hung about them, of cups and cups of tea. Auntie May put the cup the right way up on its saucer and pushed it across to Edie, who smiled deep into her reflection in the blue twilit window.

'All good things come to an end,' said Auntie Lizzie. 'More work for the wicked, Emma. The men'll be wanting their tea.'

Nothing had changed, everything had happened, and I must not be told.

Chapter Six

Sundays – an equable progression of steps, like those
in the dances which Elsie could take or leave and to
which Edie was dragged. The quickstep of the morning,
followed by the waltz and languorous slow foxtrot of the
afternoon, succeeded by the brisk quickstep once more
of preparation for the evening romp when each one had
found his partner, the one he would go home with. I had
not been taken to a dance but had gathered information
dropped by the sisters, and for the time being our
Sundays were a connection.

Every family had developed its own style. Auntie
Annie's Sunday was known for the way in which Uncle
George, not a domestic creature, spent the afternoon in
fishy abstraction in the scullery, shelling the shrimps for
tea-time, poking winkles from their shells. Because
Auntie Annie had more boys than girls there we played
rough and wild. They had a blanket for tossing people,
me especially. The ceiling rushed down to meet you,
you were terrified and brave – afterwards. They tossed
Auntie Annie because she was small, and they grabbed
Edie because she was big, but her eyes bulged, she went
pale and her upper lip was sticky and she ran away.
They didn't touch Elsie. One of the boys was in love
with her.

The boys in Auntie Lizzie's family were more polite;
there we pulled aside the connecting doors between
sitting-room and dining-room and played charades, and
balanced treading on upturned jam jars, and Auntie May
taught the cousins to dance the tango and the charleston
and the black bottom. In Auntie Florrie's house it was

the furniture which had to be respected, and avoided if possible. Uncle's dental surgery was in the next room, we felt uneasy and I for one was relieved to run downstairs, through the beaded curtains in the hall and out into Clapham Junction High Street. At Auntie Hepsie's there was the shop, endlessly fascinating, and cousin Nora, so much of grown-up behaviour was ignored.

In every house and on every Sunday Auntie May appeared, late and breathless and full of comic excuses, loaded with her bundle of hairdressing equipment and her cards and her ouija board.

'What a gun!' they said. 'Poor old May.'

The curling tongs burnt hair. Auntie May said, 'Don't worry. Hair grows quick in this family. And thick.'

She persevered until heads were hot and crisp with corrugation. My straight bob and fringe didn't tempt her so it was rags for me the night before a party and a bumpy sleep before I shook out a curious entanglement of curl and tuft from the rags.

How else might she do penance for being a spinster? Well, there was the piano; well, she kept them in fits round the table. What Auntie May gave was magic. Gradually I came to this knowledge; it was what happened on Sunday afternoons in our kitchen. She told fortunes. Cards, the kind we played Snap with, under her fingertips revealed all. The women swilled fortunes down with their tea, were bound together, were equally excited by promises or warnings made to others as to themselves. Tea leaves pitter-pattered their destinies up the side of the cups and into next week.

'She never had no tea leaves in her cup, May! You've been telling her all that stuff and she never had no tea leaves!'

I was in time to hear the squeal of distress; the fortune must have been particularly welcome, but now – ?

57

Auntie May rose to the occasion. 'There are times when I don't feel the need of tea leaves.'

Faith in her powers was restored. Yes, they would keep a lookout on Tuesday for a well-disposed stranger; yes, they were prepared for the encounter on Friday with a dark lady. The dark lady was a proper terror and as they let me into the afternoon that dark lady walked about in my night dreams, though unpromised to me by Auntie May. She smiled, her hand held out, but if I ever touched that hand it would pull me – it would pull me down into the cellar. But the others would rather have the dark lady than nothing. Auntie May never let them down; there was always something. Mum didn't care for the ouija board, or the cards with strange and sinister pictures on them, but she enjoyed the tea leaves, and the palm readings. Once my dad forgot himself and interrupted the afternoon. I was there, having a bad cold. (It was my colds which released me more and more frequently from Sunday School and admitted me to Sunday afternoons.) In whispers Mum had been told of her future. As he passed her Auntie May caught my dad's hand, turned it over. For a long time she stared, then, as sweet as an apple, she smiled up at him.

'You'll outlive poor Emma, Joe. Live for ever, you will.'

I believed her. The words sank into my mind, and I hated her.

Refreshed by bad and good fortune the women were ready for the evening, and once the men had removed the Sunday papers from their faces, once they had stretched and groaned and lit a pipe or cigarette, the men were stirred by the idea of it too.

Serious to begin with, then – Elsie playing 'The Rustle of Spring' especially for Mum, who closed her eyes. She waited a long moment until the last note died away, then

58

sighed and thanked Elsie. Sometimes Elsie was persuaded to play 'In a Monastery Garden', so that ever afterwards the word 'monastery' rose cool and leafy in my mind.

The serious part over, it was 'Come on then, May! Give us something. Something for Ernie to sing.'

'I've brought his music,' called Auntie Florrie. 'And mine,' she added.

'You sing for us, Auntie Flo,' begged the sons of Auntie Lizzie.

'The young devils!' Auntie Annie spoke to Mum behind her hand.

'They only want to take the micky.'

She didn't like Auntie Florrie – from her conversations with Mum I had discovered that – but on Sundays, all of them together, all one big family, liking didn't come into it. The thing was – to be together, to keep an eye on one another, to keep on keeping on they said, not too slow, not too fast either. Behind them the spectres of Peabody Buildings. Ahead? Not glory, at any rate not for my mother, she wouldn't have felt comfortable with glory; no, what she wanted was – a nice respectable house with a bathroom and a neat green garden and in the front room, which she would then call the drawing-room, a nice clean husband who stayed at home in the evenings and occasionally made things for the house.

'Fat chance,' she would say, 'but chin up. Make the best of it.'

They all made the best of it, kept together. They were an army singing on Sunday evenings.

One day Auntie Florrie heard a little bird. She trilled like the bird and ignored the photograph of Grandma Thornley on the wall above the piano. Auntie didn't care, she was a specialist in birds – brown birds, mocking birds, the naughty little bird in Polly's hat. She sang 'Goodbye' to a yellow bird who would rather stay in the cold on a leafless tree than a prisoner be in a cage of gold. Auntie May accompanied her on the piano, but accompanied was not the word to describe how she plunged beneath her sister in a whirlpool of crossed hands and through a rainbow of arpeggios. However, Auntie Florrie won, for finally she exploded in top notes, opening her mouth wider than seemed possible. We clapped her, the devils clapped the loudest and deserved the exhausted smile she gave them as she sat down. Uncle Ernie patted her hand. 'A lot of stamina has Flo,' he murmured to my dad, who agreed.

Uncle Ernie's voice was as rich as mincemeat. He rolled his 'R's' and he rolled his eyes and sang 'Marquita'. If repeated requests could be made, he and Auntie Florrie would sing a saucy duet during which she would tap him on the shoulder with an imaginary fan, and he would wag a finger at her. Unfortunately they had a trick of forgetting the words and then their gestures became fairly violent. But the ensuing quarrel added spice to the evening and as the two were very fond of one another their frowns soon changed to tender smiles. In conversation they supported one another absolutely, in fact right through the sentence, hand in hand, lip to lip as it were, one speaking aloud, the other mouthing the words, utterly in unison until the final word when both voices were heard, triumphant.

My dad's deep throated songs told stories and demanded a response: 'Tommy Lad'; 'Shipmates o' mine'; 'My old shako'. And one lovey-dovey song, 'The sunshine of your smile', which Mum relished in spite of her embarrassment. My dad didn't have to fidget with his music sheets to get them to ask for more.

'Give us poor Bessie,' they shouted.

'On the damp ground I must now lay my head,
Father's a drunkard and mother is dead.'

No one noticed my crossed fingers and scowl.

Elsie accompanied herself; she was set on bidding us farewell. 'Goodbye – for ever. Goodbye. Goodbye. Goodbye. Goodbye.' In her clear small voice it sounded like an invitation.

'Time for you youngsters to do a turn.' They didn't include me in the youngsters but my brother and the cousins who leant over Elsie and shouted their songs.

'It ain't no sense' (*thump*) 'sitting on the fence' (*thump*) 'all by yourself in the moonlight.'

Excited by their reception, they sang another about a certain party. 'Does she have eyes of blue? Yes' (without a moment's hesitation) 'she does have eyes of blue – that certain party of mine.' The questions got sillier: 'Does she like fish and chips?' and so forth. Eventually the demands bored all of us except Bill and Charles, and the cry was for May to give us some of the old tunes, and I agreed. We were back to the streets of wicked old London.

'Please sell no more drink to my father,
It makes him so strange and so wild.
Hear the prayers of my heartbroken mother,
And pity a poor drunkard's child.'

'What's up with you, duck? Miss Straight Face, look at you!' Sadly they misjudged the child they sang so loudly about, and they misjudged me.

There were sheaves of songs about the plight of poor children, and I placed myself into each one of them.

'Won't you buy my pretty flowers?'

I would! I would! You hopeless, lucky girl!

But we had touched the bottom of melancholy and

rose to the music of 'California, here I come!' We crooned lullabies to piccaninnies underneath the silv'ry Southern moon. We left America for Scotland and praised Bruce as he took the example of the spider to heart. 'Where there's a will there's a way. Tomorrow the sun may be shining although it is cloudy today.'

Puzzles they were to me but not, apparently, to the aunts and even the uncles – songs like 'Just a little bit off the top for me, for me' and 'Ta-ra-ra-boom-deay!' got them all up on their feet to dance in a sedate, skirt-lifting, feet-crossing manner while they sucked in reminiscent smiles.

Mum didn't sing on Sunday evenings. She couldn't sing, she said: 'You know I can't.'

I didn't give her away, or tell of the songs she sang to me on weekdays. She ironed and sang her worries away at the ironing table. We squeaked together, Rene and I, as we skipped about the kitchen chanting: 'Daddy wouldn't buy me a bow-wow, bow-wow.' 'Sing Polly!' we pleaded with her. And waving her flatiron, she sang: 'Down the road away went Polly with a step so jolly that I knew she'd win' – and with a voice that was so irresolute in the front room but so hearty in the kitchen she pulled at Polly's reins: 'Whoa there! Whoa there! You've earned your little bit of corn.'

'Sing a sad song,' begged Rene. 'About the crossing sweepers.'

She was aware that crossing sweepers were gone now, but in Mum's songs they remained, barefoot in the London snows.

'Now a funny one,' Mum suggested. 'One of Nellie Wallace's. You laugh at this,' she instructed, 'it's a very funny song. Uncle Will saw Nellie Wallace in the Music Hall. It's very, very funny.'

We were uncomfortable and polite. Mum was right – not to sing in the front room.

She didn't escape entirely; maybe she didn't want to. It was time to slide to the door to prepare supper, but –

'Give us the Two Rats, Emma. And Will. Where is he? Come on!'

'He was a rat,' and Mum spoke the first line because the verse required her to. Somewhere in childhood she and Will had learnt to mime, so – a long sweep of the hand to point to the sumptuous rattiness of her brother –

'And she was a rat –'

This exchange was all they needed to become actors. The story continued although each word, each gesture, was accounted for and all the lips in the room moved the lines along. However familiar the verses were through years of telling, no one would have presumed to take the places of Will and Emma. It was their piece, fair dos.

Its climax met with the correct silence, the end of the rats received a collective sigh, Mum resumed her bashful self and ran upstairs to the kitchen, with Edie, who hurried out too lest she should be asked to be a sport and do a turn. She needn't have feared this. Not everyone performed. Auntie Annie didn't because she had once been The Beauty and Edie because she never would be one. I volunteered. It was a disaster. The row of pantomime Babes had inspired me and I yelled, because they had yelled: 'Dinah! Is there anyone finer? In the State of Carolina?' After only one line I knew how awful it was, and how awful it would continue to be, and Auntie May was playing too slowly and Auntie Lizzie was muttering something about 'a little swankpot'. I faltered through the endless jerking of notes until, utterly ashamed and swallowing my misery, I ran upstairs to the bedroom.

There were years and years of Sundays, tables and tables of dinners and teas, and suppers luminous with crimson jellies and with celery, like flowers in a glass vase, and with the sound of the piano from the front room and the sparrow chatter from the kitchen. No end to it all. Only an end to each Sunday, when there were games played after supper, cards, Newmarket, gambling with the tin box of buttons on the table, or now and again a game entitled 'Winkle's Wedding' which was kept in the cellar for some obscure reason and was dredged up odorous with cellar smell. One person read aloud the story of Winkle and paused at each dash mark on the page. In turn around the room we had to read one of the slips of paper we held in our hands. 'Winkle's bride was a lovely' (dash) 'pig's trotter.'

'You laugh,' Mum whispered.

When the best card pack was produced, for whist, it was time for me to go to bed. It was the end of Sunday for me, but the others carried on with it and from the bedroom where coats humped my sister's bed like basking seals I heard the sounds of Sunday dwindle into my sleep.

Chapter Seven

I was clothed, fed, made better when ill. Thus far Mum conformed to literary mothers and after such requirements were met she left me alone to rummage through the environment of home and Inman Road. Her neglect was a blessing, the more so as she was ignorant of it. Only now and then did I ask, 'What shall I do?'

She produced The Album.

The Album was portentous. It was locked away like treasure in a desk with business papers, not like the Bible, pushed under the bed. It was heavier than the Bible and was fastened by brass clasps; its pages resisted turning; a smell of mould stole from it when the clasps were undone; it was a vault where lost relations waited. On guard, I opened it.

At once there was anticlimax, for the first photographs were of stony-faced, sepia-faced soldiers unknown to my mother. 'They probably died in The Great War. Fighting for you.' Children were accustomed to that kind of accusation.

After the soldiers The Album went further back to a time before wars when men dressed in tight coats and wore antlered moustaches above which they glared at women with firm braided bodices and blank faces. They turned their backs to the highland glen and dreary cattle in the lake, preferring to stare the camera out. By some grim misdirection my mother's parents, who were still alive, had found in the cardboard pages a recess among the dead, close to their own parents. By comparison the latter were debonair, younger, looser in limb and in dress, benign in the far reaches of the years. My grandad sat alert in a wooden chair, Grandma stood behind him, a palm tree stood behind her. It was hard on her to stand while he sat, for he was considered a sprightly man while she had bad feet, which gave her gyp. Grandad was up to the tricks of the photographer and pointed his beard at the camera; Grandma's features were indicated rather than presented, her face was broad, shiny with a lot of space left over from her nose, eyes and mouth, the emptiness accentuated by the dragging back of each strand of hair flat to her skull, yet there was no sign of pain on her, merely a disengagement. From everyone, even from pert Grandad, even from the photographer. Why, she was barely in the photograph, tired Grandma Peggs with her tight hair, her tight bolster chest. After a lifetime of hard labour she was trapped into idleness and had grown out of her clothes and skin as I tried to grow into mine. I knew these grandparents from their photographs; they seldom visited and when we went to Camberwell to see them it was the aspidistra gloom of their front room which I recalled.

I was never quite prepared for the first confrontation with Grandma Thornley.

'She was Mrs Chamberlain when that photo was taken, quite young she must've been.'

But – she looked the same under the next name of Thornley. She would have looked the same as a baby.

'We had a photo of her as a girl, when she was Hephzibah Ralph. Don't know what happened to it.'

Grandma Thornley's likeness was all around the house, there could be no escape from her, not even for her poor husband Thornley. Husband Chamberlain had not had time to have his photograph taken before he was killed, but Mr Thornley hung beside Grandma in the front room. He looked tired and the sunlight had bleached him grey. Sometimes when I played with the

66

shepherd and shepherdess on the front-room mantel-piece, or held the tiger tooth, or poured imaginary milk from the black-and-gold china cow, I would turn suddenly to catch Grandma spying on me. Her sliding eyes marked me wherever I moved but when I faced her, her eyes were as dull as pebbles. One room in the house was safe from her, and that was the kitchen where two Queens, Elizabeth of England and Mary of Scotland, were together in an oil painting. Mary knelt to Elizabeth, into whose ear a dark adviser whispered. The picture was valued for its frame, and was polished with Ronuk regularly so that every bump in its oil paint glistened.

'Why does Grandma have to hang in the front room and in the hall and in the office?'

For half a second Mum and I were conspirators and plotted Grandma's comeuppance.

Mum said, 'Where shall we put her then? In the lav?'

She went too far.

Household gods or household terrors, the photographs of Grandma remained on the walls of Number 29 to share our lives, and only within the locked Album was she under our control. So long as the page was not turned. Once exposed, however, she burst forth, challenged the camera to tell a lie, was indifferent and unsubdued by the constructions of fans and wickerwork and mountain scenery with which the photographer attempted to appease her. I thought her ugly, wide of face and figure, bright-eyed, but was entranced by her as I was entranced by Elsie. Excitement, that was what Grandma and Elsie had in common, and – a sort of delight which struck hard. One beautiful, one terrible, and both meeting somewhere inside me.

Mr Thornley hadn't lived long with Grandma and her four children. William Chamberlain had been a baker, a grocer, and was a Superintendent of Peabody Buildings and the rent collector when he was attacked and robbed and left to die in the gutter. Passers-by supposed him drunk and when his injuries were discovered it was too late for poor William, father of four. His wife was left with a baby of a few days, two young boys and my dad, aged seven.

A shuddering story, but when I told it to myself the adult faces and habits of those children interrupted and dispersed its dramatic possibilities so that I was forced to re-create them, drawing my own pictures of the pathetic little brood. Grandma, however, refused my rearrangement.

'Say what you like,' Mum declared, 'you've got to admit she had a lot of spirit. How she managed with that young family I don't know! 'Course, strong she was, a fine chest and good legs. And a worker and no mistake. She took in washing, no help for it, no choice, not for a woman of spirit. That or the workhouse.'

She glanced at me for argument; when I offered none she went into one of her thoughtful postures. Mine were called dreams. Mum's reconciliation with her mother-in-law never lasted long and sooner or later she recalled how young Joe had been deprived of his opportunities for a better life. 'Someone must've helped your grandma, she couldn't've bought two houses in Inman on the money she made from taking in washing. She was a cook in the house of a Harley Street doctor before she was married, I say it was him who lent her the money, not that she told us so. Still, she did well,' (a return of admiration) 'and she owed no one nothing.'

'What did she do to Dad?'

I reminded her of her indignation, for her conversations with me were subject to many distractions; she was cooking and the pans boiled over, she was mending and she sucked her pricked finger, she was cleaning windows. The perils of her cleaning windows were more than a distraction to me, but she smiled and talked through the pane while she sat on the windowsill, her back to the yard below, anchored by the window frame and polishing with all her might. This feat demonstrated her inexplicable courage, which took strange paths to show itself. Timid with spiders and mice and with Auntie Lizzie, she was brave in our cellar and could rummage in the clammy darkness there for ages.

'What did she do to my dad?'

'Oh yes. I was in the middle of telling you, duck. Just let me change this iron . . . Well, some gent, the same one who helped her p'raps, liked the look of your dad, nice-looking boy he was and clean and had a good singing voice then as now. He put him to a school in Kent, where they wanted bright boys who could sing in the choir. Your dad said as how he would've dearly liked to have stayed at the school. He was quick with figures and his handwriting . . . Well, you know how good it is – and you'd do well to copy your dad, young Een. He'd worked so hard, he said (and take note, duck, that nothing comes from nothing), and thought that if he tried very, very hard he might just get a job in an office. Like your Uncle Charlie did. Only Charlie was lucky, being younger and things better by then.'

She used the iron to punctuate her story-telling, to pause at the brink of happening, to emphasize the climax with a crash of iron on stove. Now Grandma Thornley came into her own as the villainess.

'What did the old faggot do? She dragged – *dragged*' (thud of iron on ironing blanket) 'young Joe from the boarding school as soon, just as soon' (bang of iron on grandma's remembered head) 'as he became able to work in her laundry.' (Goodbye office, goodbye clean shirts and suits and sandwiches packed in an attaché case.) 'And that was the end for your dad.'

I went along with her all the way until – afterwards – a puzzle. Hadn't Dad met my mother, married the sunshine of her smile, had the blessing of four children, five if the gravestone in the cemetery spoke the truth? Winifred was buried there, the first child, two years older than Elsie. 'She was taken from us when I was in bed with Elsie. I had to stay in the bedroom for a month, well, I was supposed to, having a baby, see. I did what I could. Peeled potatoes on a tray in bed. Did the ironing on a board across my lap. Mended socks. Auntie Annie cleaned the house – in a manner of speaking.' Mum sniffed. 'Then Winnie got the measles, she got them bad and I expect she moped, not seeing so much of me . . . Elsie was fine.'

So, Elsie had stamped her authority from the beginning.

Winnie was taken. Grandma was dead. She had done her best to resist death, by leaving her portraits to keep an eye on her sons and on the laundry and on the family who enjoyed hard-come-by 29 Inman Road. She had branded her formidable name, Hephzibah, on her daughter and on her daughter's first child. I ran down to the front room and glared at the hanging woman. She gazed back as steadily as I wished to gaze at her, and for a second her beaded bosom seemed to lift in breath. Along the wall Grandad Thornley shrank into his glass case, kept his sights straight ahead. It was the best way – with someone like Grandma. I touched the piano keys and glanced over my shoulder at her. She heard, she saw, didn't much care for what went on, didn't think much of me either.

I wanted to ask, 'Shall I always look over my shoulder to you? Shall I always do things just to show you? But – don't poke your fingers into my life! I'm not like the rest.'

I clenched my fists, stood square before her, and she lost interest. We had come together in a shared moment, now I was dismissed. But I had faced her in her front room and giving the highest praise, I found her . . . I found her . . . irresistible.

In childhood we took sides: Oxford or Cambridge; Royalist or Roundhead; Cowboy or Indian. The continual presentation of heroes and villains built the struts of our evolving world, and they were simply identified by deeds or style of dress or colour. For example, no friend of mine until I went to the Grammar School would have been taken seriously if they expressed a liking for Cambridge blue.

Ah, but doubts did arise. Take the tale of Dad's dream of becoming a clerk in an office – was that his dream, or my mother's? Didn't either of them understand how brave it was to see Dad lording it in his laundry, clogging up the top at midmorning, sparks flying, pavements clapping, applauding the Head Man of Inman? I worked on the stories told me or overheard, and often made little sense of them.

Not all family photographs had found a permanent sanctuary in The Album; among the excluded were the wedding photographs and I knew them by heart: the rows of relations pressed firm about the bride and bridegroom in order of merit, the less familiar and replaceable friends at the far borders of the group. Children sat cross-legged in the front; Elsie was unmistakable, pouting, dark-eyed, dark-curled and turned haughtily away from her cousin, the boy in a wide straw hat. The baby in my young father's arms was my sister Edie. Grandma Thornley and Elsie demanded attention; certainly the small bride was content to give place to them.

'There she is, your Auntie Annie,' they told me, and it was hard to believe them. So pretty she was, and sober and anxious, half buried in the hats and flounces of the wedding guests, close-set by Grandma's satin elbow, that lady being as powerless to efface herself as Royalty.

71

The brides in each picture wore no bridal veils, but hats. There were many hats, many feathers, best clothes all round which would do for other weddings. The same clothes, the same people appeared in all the wedding photographs, but were shuffled so that the bride and bridegroom were different. They took turns to be the happy couple, for the two families of Peggs and Chamberlains were intent on marrying one another until supplies ran out.

Now it is the turn of Auntie Hepsie and Uncle Will. He strikes a pose, head on one side, grinning. He is known as a card. She is thin, Auntie Hepsie is thin! Thin and earnest, taking Uncle Will's comedy seriously. On her head is a hat like a tray, a tray of flowers. Elsie stands her ground at the front, Edie is entrusted to the arms of an unknown old woman. When I was considered old enough to hear it, the tale was told of Auntie Hepsie's wedding. It seemed that the photographer was so tipsy that the business of hiding under his black cloth affected him. He collapsed in hysterics, and was sent home to return the following week to take the wedding photograph. Guests resumed their best clothes and lined up for a repeat performance. Perhaps this explained Uncle Will's unseemly flippancy and Auntie Hepsie's straight face, and also the air of theatre in the picture. It was a performance after a parenthesis of a week. Somehow a very old woman had slotted herself into the rows of guests, she appeared in no other photographs, she was as inappropriate in that company as a tattered book pushed between smartly bound volumes. Mum didn't give me her name so one day, pushed too far by her upper hand, I said, 'It's Granny Warren.'

I waited for the cry of 'How on earth did you guess?' Waited for the recognition of my sharp eyes. Did not expect mockery.

'Well – it's nice to hear that you don't know everything.

No, that's not Granny Warren. It's Granny Warren's mother. There.'

Granny Warren was old, the oldest person that one could reasonably expect to be around, therefore – her mother? Even in an old picture? Yet it suited the mystery of Granny Warren herself.

I knew that she was a member of our family, no one denied it, but didn't understand why she was not included in Sunday meetings. I gathered, in the way children do gather such prohibitions, that I was not to bring her into the conversation, that I was not to speak to her although she lived in Inman Road. Naturally I did go to see her, even without the embargo I found her interesting, probably because she was so frank with her interest in me. She crouched on her front step, head forward, eager to listen to whatever I had to say, almost a caricature of attentiveness she was. She didn't mind or comment when I stared at her old puckered face. It might have been sewn together, carelessly. Skin like calico, eyes like buttons, the whiskers on her chin erratically inserted, there was nothing of natural substance left to her. But from that assortment darted a smile which pricked out from behind her eyes and ran off as fast. My father smiled so slowly that you forgot about it, he laughed in similar fashion, silent, deep down, shoulders shaking until the laugh exploded. Mum's smile was lovely and sad. Elsie's was a lure to other people. Edie's was a surprise, saucy, mischievous. She should have smiled more.

Granny Warren sat on her doorstep and talked to me. Just as it was always winter when I thought of Sundays, it was always summertime when I thought of Granny Warren's front garden. She had no hedge, as we did, so the sun drove straight into her narrow plot where marigolds and cornflowers grew. She let me touch and pick them, marigolds so sticky and petalled so gold, and cornflowers . . . The first lines of Hans Andersen's 'Mermaid' – 'Far out at sea the water is as blue as the bluest cornflowers' – struck blue into my mind that was the blue of Granny Warren's cornflowers. I would not go into her house, becoming suddenly prim and obedient to Mum's wishes; also the passage to her room was dark and smelt of lavatory. She and I belonged together out of doors and only there, and in our shared passion for flowers. Before she died I could have brought her a bunch of flowers but the thought, like the possibility of her dying, didn't occur, it was a small regret, and one which remained. Wherever she went I wished her well, I wished her fields of flowers.

They did their best, for the sake of the family, to bury the disgrace of Granny Warren, but eventually I learnt that she was Mary Ann, sister to Grandma Thornley, both village girls from Charing in Kent. No one was certain who was the father of Mary Ann's boy, and his grandmother brought him up as her own son. This grandmother – Charlotte, who had been born Clover, descendant of the de Cloviers – was the ancient wedding guest in the photograph. It was assumed that Hephzibah had provided rooms for Mary Ann in Inman Road – at a safe distance from Number 29. She married a Mr Warren, who had disappeared, thus assuring her continued distance from her sister and her sister's family. She was intended to live out her life as a penance; instead she persisted as a merry old soul, independent among her marigolds and deep-sea cornflowers.

Was it the Huguenot blood which insisted on survival? I was, the doctor found, anaemic. If this was the Huguenot stuff I had inherited it was nothing to boast about but Mum, having no particular blood of her own, was keen on the idea.

'See these spoons?' she said, polishing them. 'Real silver. See the handles? D and C twisted together? De

74

Clovier. She's your great-grandmother. French. There you are, duck. There's your little drop of French blood.'

That was as far as she went, and as much as she knew. From Elsie I discovered that the Huguenots had fled from France because they were persecuted and because they were brave and skilful. The combination of qualities was irresistible, and they belonged to the past as far back as fairy tales. Grandma Thornley had transmitted their blood to me and I might have known it of her. Delight with my fabulous ancestors opened my eyes to the absurdity of the pretence of aristocratic birth and I walked as tall as I could, proud of the inheritance, proud of Grandma Thornley whose chest, I saw it now, throbbed with the blood of Huguenots. What Creatures those old Frenchmen must have been. 'A bit of orlright,' said my mother.

Chapter Eight

Now I was growing up and observed my mother with a critical eye. For her interview with the teacher on the school Open Day she had dabbed at her nose with powder, she had put on her best lisle stockings and her brightest smile. Worst of all, she fizzed with chatter. Some of the mothers were glum, some were stern as they mooched around the books laid out on desks. My friend's mother shook hands with everyone who offered with forceful and continuous vigour. The atmosphere was feverish; teachers, parents, children knew it was a performance; the trouble was no one was sure of her part. Nevertheless until that moment I had dreamt through schooldays, they had been no more than an interruption in real life, but now school became integral to my promises to myself.

Out of school, home and Inman remained, however, my place. There were complications, being one of the wealthy Chamberlains was a hindrance. As usual Mum was turned into a skinflint at the mention of our riches. 'Wealthy! Don't make me laugh! Look at the hours of work your dad and I do. Just because we've a business they suppose . . . d'you think we would live in this – this hole – if . . . ? Making and mending – making and mending – skrimping and saving . . . ? Listen! We should be off like a shot to one of the new houses in Morden.' The threat was sufficient to silence me. Elsie's yearning to quit the street also lay waiting for moments of gloom.

Out of doors too the situation had to be dealt with, for I was forced to play rougher, shout louder than any other child to rise above the purity of my underwear and to try to efface the stuck-up image of my sister Elsie. Also we were the only family in the street with a car parked outside on Sundays. Yes, the laundry possessed a van, but yes, that was OK. I found that the car was not in the end a grievance among my friends in the street; in fact it brought to Inman a touch of distinction. Auntie Florrie said it gave 'a bit of class'.

Sometimes in the summer Auntie and Uncle took me and my cousin, Nora, and Mum and Edie out into the country. Nora and I were in the dickey seat and the folk round about waved us off without envy and with some excitement. The dickey seat was great, we shouted to other cars on the road, we sang and lolled back, very worldly, with our hair stinging lips and eyes. The people inside the car were poor fish, shut away from the open road where all they could see was the unwinding of the road ahead.

'We'll go to Newlands Corner, or Epsom Downs. What d'you think, driver?' It didn't matter where we went for we didn't stop and the driving was the thing and the country which Auntie said we should see was a blur of greens and browns, but with more sky than above Inman. It was a background to the triumphant clamour of the engine and our voices.

Until my brother Bill grew into a job and an umbrella and a bowler hat and joined The Imps we made no trips into the real country. Once a year we went on the bus to Hampton Court, saw fields at a distance but spent the hours encompassed by old brick walls and dark trees and brilliant flowers.

'Lovely,' said Mum, closing her eyes, breathing deeply, 'better than the country.'

I didn't know.

The Imps was short for 'The Junior Imperial League', an association of young men and women who were what

Mum described as 'nice'. Most of the parents were members of the Conservative Club and all at once the Club became, in Mum's eyes, nice also. The Imps didn't talk about The Empire – not half as much, anyway, as did Miss Jones at school – but they got excited about dances, which they called 'dos'. Cars called to take Bill out in the evening.

'Bill's getting like one of those Bright Young Things in the papers,' Mum suggested.

Elsie, who made her car driver friends drop her in the Earlsfield Road, said that The Imps were nothing like the Bright Young Things.

'Those folk belong to the upper crust. They hold parties which last all night, into the next, or the next. Wild parties. Nothing spared.'

'What about their jobs then?'

Mum wanted to know, she was sincerely interested, but was cautious with Elsie because of her increasing impatience with living in Inman Road.

'They don't have jobs. They have money.'

A girlfriend of Elsie's had spent a night with us. There had been a great fuss about preparations for her stay; Elsie had wanted the bedroom we shared to be left free for Elaine, her friend. Where she would have swept us all I had no idea. As it was Elaine was given my bed, and I slept between Mum and Dad, so I was pleased.

Elaine was very near the upper crust herself.

'She speaks beautifully,' my mother whispered, 'makes me realize what a proper Cockney I am, duck.'

'Her fingers are all brown,' I whispered back. 'Not like yours.'

She shook her head at my comfort, looked down at her hands, idle for once. I loved her hands, polite and folded, listening to the posh girl and Elsie fooling at the piano. Mum listened with her hands, almost spoke

78

through the tips of her fingers. Cockney or not, her hands were eloquent.

'You awful bugger, Elsie C!' screamed the visitor. 'It was my turn to play that twiddly bit.'

I was shooed out of the room, and Elaine was not to stay with us again.

'I'll say this for Bill's friends,' – and Mum did – 'they talk clean.'

Edie nodded and made the most of Elaine's bad language.

'You see,' explained Mum, 'Elaine's mother is an Honourable.'

There was no question of shocking behaviour when The Imps and their parents invited us all up to Ranmore Common for a picnic – they came from houses at the top of the hill, from families who lived out respectable lives behind their ivied walls.

We must have enjoyed the day, for everyone smiled in the snapshots taken; everyone was eating too, eating for the camera, all facing the same way naturally, smiling, grinning, or rather grand and indifferent.

'Come on, young Een!'

But the call comes from a distance, for I have wandered off alone.

Have I been alone before? Only in bed. Which sometimes is good if I tell myself a story, or doleful when the laundry noises slide through the walls. I shouted out once, when I was quite young, and my dad ran up from the kitchen. He said, 'It's the machinery cooling. It's nothing. You're not scared of a heap of old machines getting the shivers in the night, you're a big girl now.'

Alone on Ranmore Common in the daylight and blown about by the wind is different. I jump over dead leaves crusted like broken biscuits. Hairy bracken elbows out from them. Some has grown tall and spreads as high as my shoulders, shines as clear as glass. I stop, am stopped by bluebells. Bluebells!

One bluebell for each child, that is the rule at school in the springtime. 'Mind you don't snap the stem because there is just one each and one for me to take to pieces. Paint costs money, so use pencils. Be tidy with your drawing, that's the thing.'

It's too late, all about the teacher stems are snapping. The stem is a temptation, its glue drips white and the teacher's face is red on bluebell-drawing day. I should know a bluebell when I see one, single blooms or bundled blooms, they are familiar signs of springtime, for boys on bikes ride through the streets of Earlsfield with great bundles of the flowers tied on the bike racks, stems flashing. The Collins boys bring them to their mother, who is glad of them and dumps them in a bucket in the back yard, in the narrow passage between our houses where the sun never reaches. One day, when she requires the bucket, she remembers the bluebells and throws them away.

Over the fence she tells my mother, 'They don't keep, not the wild flowers, not like the daffs from the shop.'

Now, and caught unawares, the bluebells are too much for me, I'm bewildered by the fume of scent and by the deep violet distances and don't know which way to turn. In the hollows of the trees birds are calling so I walk into the woods, slowly, treading between the blossoms, then faster, running to get to the distances.

'Look. The stamens. Look. Anthers. The pistil.' The teacher had slapped the dissected flower on her desk, dead, drab with the chalk dust.

I was finally overwhelmed by the sights, the first sights of wild flowers in a wood, gloriously alone, drunk and happy. I was stretched out on the moist earth, abandoned, sensual. Gradually my heart made quiet and in the wood it was quiet too. The birds had flown higher and the wind was gone. I was alone and this, then, was silence. I was alone. I was alone and lonely. After a long circling through the bracken I began to shout. And my dad called my name. 'You've missed all the fun,' they said.

But back in Inman I had nothing left of the country – nothing to tell, that is, only something to keep, pushed back inside. Inman was a territory to hold to, where friends were, until new friends were met at school. We were children, circumscribed by our childhood as we were by our street. Because of this we were well alert to the flavours of other streets. The long thoroughfares which ran down from Wandsworth Common to Garratt Lane had little interest, they were meant for traffic, for big houses, but any child, blindfolded and set down in Brocklebank or Winfrith or Dingwall would, on sniffing the alien air, know precisely the position. Superficially the streets were alike in style, even in direction, but the eye of a child perceived the distinction between them. Women gossiped, arms folded, in every street, but the Winfrith women stopped at once when you passed by, the Dingwall women yelled at you to clear off, the Inman women yelled at each other, taking no notice of children, and that was all right. Inman women had fights, proper ones, with hat pins, but at the other end of the street.

'They're drunk,' Mum said. 'Take no notice.' And she thought of Morden, where nothing ever happened.

In Dingwall they pushed at one another when they were drunk, but quite soon one of them was sick, and that would be that.

No doubt about it, Inman was the place to live. We had the laundry. Above all, we had a witch. Winfrith and Dingwall, Brocklebank and even Wilna tried to push their so-called witches forward. We saw one of their impostors outside her door. She was only daft, giggled, didn't have a cackle in her. She was young too. Another

81

had a snub nose, rather like mine, and so was disqualified immediately. Later we heard that she had three children, all snub and runny of nose, who went to school in Garratt Lane so we didn't know them.

Our witch was true. Bent and old and hook-nosed she hid herself in her shadowy front room and rattled on the windowpane if we dared to play on her pavement. Hers was the other privet hedge in the street; the boys had left ours unmolested because of my dad, and hers because of the witch's curse. Ours was clipped, hers was left to grow until no light penetrated into the room. It bloomed in the summer, sickly and waxen the blooms were. She was a genuine witch and we were proud to have her.

She lived downstairs and upstairs she kept a lodger, an old man who was seldom seen in the street.

'D'you think she keeps him locked up?' asked Rene of my mother.

'Whatever next! The poor old chap. He's a traveller. Travels in sweets. That's why he isn't here much.'

Rene looked at me. Mmm . . . travels – and in sweets. More magic.

'And while we're talking, don't let me hear you shouting out "Witch! Witch!" outside her door. Understand?'

One thing – Mum didn't understand, nor would she have believed had we explained how we had seen the twisted face pressed to the witch's window, hungry she was and sick for children, we had heard her screech as we skipped out of her sight. We didn't tempt her too far; only when the need for a jolt of terror was felt did we edge along to her bit of pavement, where from time to time we had all listened to moanings and howls.

'Spells,' muttered Teddy Jackson. He had seen a bat fly out of her window.

'It's never open,' I argued, taking my turn to be the sceptic.

Other signs? Well, Rene, who was good with cats, a tamer of all the cats in the street but one, had no power over the witch's cat, the hump-backed, long-legged pitch-black cat who strolled up and down the wall with lighthouse eyes darting warnings at her if she advanced her stroking hand.

'Dare you to skip on her pavement. Dare you.'

I skipped, skipped in circles, skipped my best and prayed the rope would go on turning, and watching me, I knew it, the witch would pray her unholy and lonely prayer too.

One other difference Inman held in private, and that was the friendship between Rene and me. There was no other twosome like us. It was a pity, we said, that we weren't sisters, but as nearly as possible we shared our lives. All things conspired to help us do so, the simplest things, like the loose plank in the fence in the adjoining yards. The gap was exactly wide enough for either of us to squeeze through. Rene shared in my family, except on Sundays, and I shared in hers, chiefly on washing days and especially once a summer on the fête day at her elder brother's workplace. Her younger brother, George, worked for my dad, the elder worked in Van den Bergh's margarine factory in Somerstown and it was a matter of some pride that he was put in charge of the catering arrangements for the fête. The night before the event he borrowed a van to collect the food and we sampled it. The trays of shop cakes were astonishing, more dazzling than the cake-shop window, as brilliant as jewels. Mrs Collins kept some by in case the fête ran out of supplies. They didn't, so we ate them for days until the sponge inside the stiff red icing was as hard as a bone. On the day itself I ate little, it was too exciting, and there were races to run and games to play. At the end of the afternoon we sang . . . 'Let's all sing and make the rafters ring, Van-de-van-de-Blue Band margarine.'

'It's to the tune of the Stein song,' Elsie said, 'and please stop that . . . that . . . caterwauling.'

Six years, seven, eight, time was a circle, turning around itself, as contented as a cat making its whole and perfect resting place, and Rene and I were inviolate within that circle. Years afterwards I shall find a snapshot that has turned brown in some forgotten sunshine. The sun beats down in the photograph too, and on to the back yard where two girls in summer frocks stand on either side of Uncle George. Never mind the heat, his square sour suit is for photographs, his neck is gripped by a starched collar, a watch chain ties him up, across the chest his iron arms bind him tight. Around his elbows the tendril child arms are clinging.

The sun shines for the camera, it glistens on Uncle's forehead, it strikes into the girls' eyes. They have bobbed hair and fringes, cut identically because they are best friends, and the sun polishes identical patterns on each bent head. Behind them the golden privet shimmers, it is the bush which has survived the thin black soil of the yard. The soil is called dirt.

Three people smile. The smile of Uncle George is hard come by, he tries it on his face, a jolly uncle smile; it hovers, is almost – settling; the smiles of the girls are obedient, but wary. You have to smile at cameras. They all do their best, it would be a waste of time to coax and wheedle for the girls won't get any closer to joy, neither will Uncle achieve merriment. All three are as glossy as conkers in the sun. One of the girls is me, the other is my friend Rene. She is two years older than me; she is beautiful and lives a wonderful life next door with her mother, who is a widow and too poor and too tired to look after Rene carefully. On Saturday mornings Rene plays the piano in her front room and in her nightgown.

She plays 'Spring Song' by Mendelssohn. 'Your piano is out of tune, Irene,' Edie tells her in a voice she is practising to keep up with Elsie. Rene takes no notice. She looks like the infant Mozart in my book. Mozart has his amazed family to watch him. Rene has me.

What happened when the camera had snapped? Where did the girls go? They went nowhere, of course, but stayed behind with an uncle who tried to smile, and with a tough old gold privet bush which lived for ever.

Chapter Nine

AROUND Rene and me other children collected,
drifted apart, and reassembled. The regulars were
Daisy Stanbury, Frankie Finbow and the Jacksons. The
Jacksons lived next door to Rene and came in threes; if
one happened to join our game soon the other two would
be there, they turned up, emerged, at once were
absorbed; they were amiable, inescapable, and willing to
be the dogsbody, the corpse in funerals, the aunt or
uncle of the bride in weddings, near Christmas the three
shepherds. Frankie Finbow came and went; he was fun
and a nuisance and we let him in at our own risk and
because he lived next door to Auntie Annie in Wilna
Road. In spite of her living in Wilna Road Daisy too was
a close friend. I think my mother must have had a hand
in this friendship from early days, the ones when she
chose for me. Her mother was, as Mum said, 'a nice tidy
little body'. Mum would have preferred Daisy to Rene
as my best friend. Others tried to belong to our gang.
One tried and failed. She swept down upon us one day
in school holidays, claiming to be a bosom friend of
Rene. We drew back and Rene blushed.

''Lo, Dinah.'

Hm! Dinah!

'Now, kid' – no one called me kid – 'Where's this
laundry of yours? Show me. We can play there.'

I looked to where Rene shuffled up and down the
gutter. She had told! I said, 'We can't, only on Saturdays
when it's empty.' And, rigid with anger and betrayed –
'Only if I say so.'

'Oh well.' This Dinah flicked her satin ringlets as she

looked about her. 'Well, there must be something to do around here.'

Rene said, 'We're playing sevensies.'

'I know, Rene, you and me, let's go down Garratt Lane. I've got some dough.'

Dinah jingled coins in her pocket to prove her point. The Jacksons moved nearer her and Rene was on edge with indecision. She didn't look at me. Daisy and I stood side by side. I could wait no longer, moved outside the circle, and Daisy came with me.

'No,' said Rene.

She said, 'No!' That was all she said. Dinah stared, then bounced her ringlets out of Inman and up Wilna towards the top of Earlsfield Road, where no doubt she lived. On the corner of the street she turned and shouted, 'Wouldn't go down Garratt Lane anyway. Crummy old place.'

The Jacksons closed in again and Rene said, 'She's a new girl in my class. She's a bit bossy. She goes every week to the pictures.'

'Tried to take over,' remarked Teddy Jackson, who had a knack of brevity. 'Come on, Dais. It's your turn.'

And we stood close, closer, muscles tested, friends.

The Jacksons lived in a house which bulged with people. Mr and Mrs Jackson and the three children, Teddy, Evie, and Maurice, lived in the downstairs front room. In that room they slept and ate, washed and cooked; perhaps this constant coexistence was what made the three as one. They were all in the same boat; sometimes the boat was almost visible. Mum wondered about poor Mrs Jackson and her tight way of living. She wondered if they quarrelled and I assured her that they were invariably mild. I was very smug about the Jacksons' good tempers, especially if I had heard raised voices at home the night before. Mum was doubtful when I was asked to tea at the Jacksons', though I think she thought of the hazards of picking up fleas rather than any extra trouble I might cause.

Their hospitality was fine; we ate shop cakes and sat on the big feather bed together. Beneath the bed was a kind of trolley which was rolled out at night for Teddy and Maurice to sleep on. I never found out where Evie slept when her father wasn't working a night shift. After tea Mr Jackson sewed his fingers up, in mime of course, attaching them to his elbow, one by one and with excruciating agony if he thought the performance was going well. He made us laugh when the imaginary needle pricked his skin and he howled his silent howl. Always he was a silent man, he spoke more to us when he mimed than he did the rest of the time.

At the Stanburys' I was an important guest, for Mrs Stanbury admired everything I did: the way I drank tea at the end of the meal, not during; the way I held my knife, swallowed, everything; sometimes this esteem was too much to bear. So I did all the wrong things: left bits of crusts, sloshed tea, fidgeted, and Mrs Stanbury admired those too. It was probably the laundry that she thought of when she gazed at me so fondly. In spite of this burden I did appreciate the way she accumulated those items of food which I had boasted as my favourites, most of which I had never tasted because they were on Mum's list of forbidden things. Of course I went too far, came out in favour of celery. There it was, decorating the table.

'We got it specially,' beamed Mrs Stanbury, and she watched and listened to the crunch and crack of my jaws while Daisy and her sister Dorothy slipped quiet jelly down their throats.

But it wasn't the tea which made me accept each invitation to the Stanburys', ignoring the fact that they lived abroad, in Wilna Road, forgetting while it suited

88

that Rene was my best friend, tolerating Dorothy Stanbury; it wasn't even the heady elevation imposed on me by Mrs Stanbury; no, it was the garden, Mr Stanbury's garden. All subsequent gardens had to meet his in beauty. It was small, fenced on two sides and backed by a brick factory wall. Over and through this framework Mr Stanbury had thrown purple clematis, shining roses, honeysuckle and runner beans; he had laid a rug of turf, had built towers of delphiniums, minarets of lupins; bees and bluebottles and I went crazy with pleasure. His family weren't interested; the garden was a place for Mrs Stanbury to hang the washing, but only on Mondays, and she wasn't to pick the flowers. Daisy was not to play there; Dorothy had no intention of playing, she despised the garden as she despised most things, tossing her thick golden plait like a whip. (The plait! Its colour and solidity and length had once made her into a May Queen and she had been crowned with other May Queens chosen from South London schools. There was a picture of the moment in the front room.) When Mr Stanbury saw what effect his garden had on me he took me round it, told me the names of flowers, advised me what to do with our back yard. In return I let him call me 'Ena-Dena-Valentine-Emily', although I didn't understand why he never tired of his joke.

Above all I wanted to be left alone in his garden. One day Daisy was sent on an errand, Mrs Stanbury had to chat to a neighbour at the front door, so I slipped into the garden, didn't know what to do, which way to turn among its glories. Madonna lilies! Mr Stanbury had prepared me for something very special which was due to occur among the lilies, and as I turned towards them it happened: a steady splitting of the long buds, a stealthy revelation of – I peered closer – a long silken throat, filaments of stamens, golden anthers.

'Whatchu doin' in the flowers? You won't 'arf cop it!'

Daisy's yell jerked me back to fall, grabbing a lily stem. She screamed, Mrs Stanbury came running, followed by Dorothy. Daisy and I could not move, she with her mouth open, me on the grass clutching a broken lily.

If we kept our positions, Mrs Stanbury did not. Shimmer after shimmer of fright and anger passed across her face, ending with anger.

'Can't I leave you for one minute? You've done it now, Miss.' She shook Daisy's mouth wider, the pretty head flopped in a frenzy, her howls brought a smile to the lips of Dorothy.

'It wasn't her fault. It was me.'

Mrs Stanbury stopped, her hand poised above her daughter, exactly like the picture of the cook about to hit the naughty boy, but arrested by enchantment in the Sleeping Princess's castle.

'You?'

She wouldn't believe me; the torn lily in my hand, the pollen on my nose, the glare of righteousness on my face, the accusation of false punishment, she denied it all. And I saw for the first time that she was cruel and that her cruelty was reserved for Daisy alone, and that I had no claim to it.

'You – you had better go home. Of course I'm bound to tell Mr Stanbury.' After I had put the lily in water I told Mum. She sat down in the cane chair by the kitchen window. Underneath the cushion the old newspapers were kept, they rustled and the cane of the chair creaked, but not that time when Mum listened to me.

Then she said, 'You'll go to see Mr Stanbury yourself, this evening, when he gets home from work. You'll say sorry and mean it. And you'll look sorry, too. I know all about your sorries.'

She looked down into the back yard. 'You could grow

lilies in Morden,' she said, 'and bigger ones than he grows.'

At this point her yearning for a new house in Morden and my hunger for a garden met. I leant against her, set off the noisy chair, and she put her arms about me.

Mrs Stanbury kept me at the door, Mr Stanbury was surly and my confession and apology didn't help Daisy. She had to stay indoors for a week, wash and wipe all the dishes for a week, and not speak to me until they gave permission. However, they couldn't stop her attending school, and needed her to run errands otherwise Dorothy would complain, so we met as we jogged along with our shopping bags.

'Could've been worse,' she said. 'It has been.'

Daisy knew that Rene and I and the others would play games without much thought to her. She lived in Wilna Road and must make the best of it. And I had lost the garden.

Mothers made the rules, they allowed and forbade but I had not considered the power they possessed in terms of cruelty, not the kind which had been exposed when Mrs Stanbury smiled — as she found Daisy guilty. I wanted to ask my own mother questions which couldn't be put into words. Instead I told her about the time I had stayed the night at Daisy's house. For example:

'Daisy and Dorothy don't get up on Sunday mornings, they eat sweets and read comics in bed.'

This fresh slant on Sunday morning was offered . . . As I had expected: 'The very idea!'

'Don't you and Dad play games?'

'Games? What games?'

'Bed games. Mr and Mrs Stanbury play bed games. They made noises on Sunday morning and Dorothy said not to worry, it was their bed games . . . she asked if you did and I said – '

'You said – what? You said *what*?'

'I said, "No".'

I had told Dorothy 'yes' to wipe the grin off her face.

The pity which I had felt before was an illness, an ache and a stab of pain and would return, perhaps not for Daisy or for Edie, but wearing some fresh disguise, and I had begun to realize this. Now I was to be threatened by this uncomfortable sensation once again and once again, though not by design, through my mother's meddling in my affairs.

'My mum says you're coming to tea, Saturday,' Margaret Hewitt told me. She ran after me down Swaffield Road, and for once I was alone.

'Can't, not Saturday.'

'Why not? Mum says so. Your mum said.'

Margaret Hewitt lived in Dingwall Road, she wasn't allowed to play in the street, she was almost as clean as me and didn't mind, she went to dancing class regularly and didn't mind. I had gone twice, liked the glove-soft ballet shoes, hated the stumbling two-step that we suffered and refused to go after two attempts.

'It's such a waste,' Mum sighed, 'shoes bought specially, but I may be able to sell them back with a bit of a loss.' She shook her head with exasperation. 'Put it down to experience.'

'If you'd tell her that I must be a tin soldier . . . or . . . if you'd get me some tap shoes . . .'

I saw myself tapping, above all I could see myself as a tin soldier, jerking meticulously to the rapping music, with red circles on my cheeks, in a tight scarlet uniform and a black busby – what a picture sprang up before my eyes!

But the teacher had already smiled, with great effort – 'No two-step, no tin soldier.' And my mother did not pursue the matter. Margaret Hewitt had sailed by, two-stepping like mad, and without counting left-right-left –

'She would make a nice little friend.'

I could hear the words assembling on Mum's lips. To make sure of me Mum took me along to the Hewitts' on Saturday afternoon. Mrs Hewitt was tiny and candle-coloured; her pale wormlike curls jigged in front of me down the passage. Margaret's Auntie Hilda was already there; she had been promised as a source of fun, not that I could see much hope of that. She smiled a kind smile, the sort which disappeared gradually, in her face it was meandering around the fat folds of her cheeks for ages. Soon it became obvious why she was fun; though not so much fun as made fun of. Because she was fat.

'Auntie Hepsie's fat, and we don't laugh at her.' Then I had to remind myself that we did, sometimes. But not like the Hewitts.

Everything Auntie Hilda did or said was held up to ridicule; they handed her a plate of sandwiches and teased her because she took only one. She played up to them – saying she was watching her figure.

'And there's enough of that to feast your eyes on, eh, Hil?'

When I refused another sandwich they took refusal as a token of my joining in their game, and I could see the excitement kindling in Mrs Hewitt's tiny eyes.

'Why does she put up with it?' I wondered, and Auntie Hilda answered that one when she was dismissed with the children – 'while we clear the table'.

'Little love,' she bent down to Margaret, 'what have I got for you today? Tell me, how is my darling?' And she nodded to me, including me in her loving-kindness.

'Sweets,' the girl said, pushing her arm away, 'have you eaten any?' Turning to me, she whined, 'She eats my sweets so I only get half. That's why she's so enormous.'

With all the strength I could gather I pulled her ringlets until she squealed and struggled to bite the arm which held her. Auntie Hilda flapped over us, startled at first and then angry with me, and when Mr Hewitt came in we were all in a confused huggermugger of arms and legs and best dresses and furious but muted grunts.

'Now then, what's all this?'

You could tell he wasn't used to fights, only to spiteful teasing; alone with his sister Mr Hewitt was nice to her, called her his dear soul and soothed her, quietened us all as there was nothing else to do. I heard him mention the wherewithal and then – 'Just a few quid'. Auntie Hilda opened a handbag as large and squashed as a cushion and rummaged in it for the paper money, which she handed to her brother. As though she had waited for the correct cue Mrs Hewitt burst into the room, sparkling in her eagerness for games.

'We play a good game,' I began, but Margaret shouted, 'The tray game! That's what I want!'

I was the novice. They blindfolded me, whizzed me round about three times, shoved me on to something that was smooth and slippery.

'Hang on tight! You're going for a ride on an airyplane!'

I was in midair, I was touching the ceiling, I gripped at a head of greasy hair and bony scalp. I swayed around in limbo, choking in pipe smoke, smothered by a woollen scarf. I felt sick.

'Once more round the Broadway and . . . down . . . down we go. There.'

'Scared, weren't you?' Margaret poked her chin into my shoulder.

'Oh, look! Aren't they fond of one another! Oh, sweet!' cried her mother.

'You was only a little way off the carpet, cowardy-custard,' sniggered the girl.

Auntie Hilda patted the sofa beside her and her warm stomach embraced me.

94

'Come on, Hilda. Don't think you're getting away with it,' said Mrs Hewitt.

'But I know what happens.'

Just the same Auntie Hilda let herself be tied up and turned about, and, yes, in their hands, stooping and helpless she magnified, became monstrous. Bulging legs fumbled on to the tray and I was grinning a grin which was identical to the grins of the two who strained to lift her off the ground. One second and she was up; the next, a tearing of wood, a crash of bodies, and the pile of Auntie Hilda sagged on top of them all. All fall down! But that wasn't the game and the only one laughing was me.

Auntie Hilda was apologizing and saying she'd buy them a new tray.

'You better had, fat pig!' yelled Mrs Hewitt.

'Pig yourself!' My voice.

I stood almost as tall as her. Then I was sick.

Mr Hewitt took me home to let my mother know that they were surprised at me. I was sent to bed. Later she put her head round the door.

'I like Auntie Hepsie. She's nice.'

''Course she is. She's your auntie.'

'Mum, I'd rather live in Morden than in Dingwall Road –'

As she bent closer: 'Mum, I made myself sick.'

And as the door closed: ' – if we didn't live in Inman.'

Chapter Ten

MARGARET Hewitt returned to her life behind the curtains. Very thin-lipped, her mother explained that she had a delicate daughter, sensitive, quite unsuited to rough children and to this neighbourhood. For a short time the idea of her, pale as the Lady of Shalott in her upstairs room, was intriguing, but it was soon forgotten and when we next raided Dingwall I didn't glance up to see if she was there. She certainly was an odd one to have found in Dingwall Road. The Walls weren't fighters, only with abuse, and with that they were all above board, nothing subtle. Round the corner of our street we heard them.

'The Walls are coming!'

They knew each one of us by name.

'Flea Pit Jackson!'

'Bloody Chamber Pot!'

'Ringworm Collins!'

And the rest.

They started at our end, for the children at the far end were really tough, but soon the whole street was gathered, yet nothing would begin until the first brutal insults were done. Even then there wasn't much of a show, just threats: 'You try coming up our street!' 'Cor! Catch us!' Then lumps of mud would be thrown, usually at the laundry van if it was outside and if my dad or Big Ethel wasn't there. Mud-slinging brought the women though, to shake their fists and finally to drive the Walls back home, without victory and without defeat, for these were not the points of the exercise. It was the turn of Inman next, and the rule was strictly observed.

Rituals they were, these statements of territory, as unpremeditated as the seasonal games we played, like whips and tops which signalled the arrival of spring, to be succeeded by hoops and, for the duration of the summer, by skipping ropes. When the time was come, when indignation was roused either by the requisite insult or by the mere sight of an inhabitant of Dingwall or some other enemy . . . or by the wind in our ears, then came the cry.

'Where you all going?'

'Up Dingwall.'

There was no question, the army grew. Few were hurt, everyone was returned with dirty hands and glowing cheeks, marvellously satisfied. The Walls used words as stones to throw, we used them as swords, we had a reputation to keep up, and made it our business to find and strike at the weakest spots in the Walls's armour. It was called 'Going up Dingwall', or, with more cunning and by way of a reconnoitre, 'Going round the block'.

Other phrases conveyed a network of esoteric information. If we were going 'up the top', this meant we were going to the shops in the Earlsfield Road, which were commonplace shops, for everyday necessities; Gully's, the greengrocer's, the barber where my Dad had his daily word in private at the back of the shop, a word which licked his lips and refreshed like nothing else could in the middle of his long day. And there was the forbidden cake shop, the cobbler's, and a general shop which sold anything from shoelaces to newspapers, and on one blazing day in summer sold a bowl of loose ice cream to my reckless father. Loose ice cream, on a weekday, too much for us to eat, sumptuous and as yellow as custard. Dad and I gobbled as much as we could and so did Rene and Mrs Collins and Auntie Annie and the laundry women and the cat.

'Chucking money about,' Mum said. 'The idea.'

97

Chucking money about. And the way to live. I ran all the way back to school licking my sticky fingers, living the good life.

Alone in a no-man's-land between Inman and Dingwall in the Earlsfield Road was another shop, the post office where my sister Edie worked. Mr White, a friend of Uncle George, owned the shop; he was remarkable for snuff-taking. He called me dearie and pinched any bit of me that I was careless enough to leave near him, unless I took Rene with me and in that case he preferred to pinch her. I didn't speak to Edie, though she peered out from behind her wire cage, not selling things but writing on pieces of different-coloured paper, dipping her pen into the inkwell, stamping on her juicy stamp pad, stamping her papers and looking important.

Mr White had two daughters. The elder one was a civil servant and was not seen, the younger one was Winnie who helped out in the post office and was hoped for as a friend to Edie, although even I saw that Mrs White was more of a friend. Winnie had red hair which she wore in the style of a Norseman's helmet, with two protruding coils above each ear. Mr White boasted about her hair, which was curious because no one in our family was boasted about, not even Elsie, and she was really lovely.

'You should take a dekko at young Win when she lets her hair down,' Mr White told Uncle George.

Prestige attached to long hair. Look at Rapunzel. Look at Dorothy Stanbury, whose long hair had taken her to be crowned May Queen on May Day. Winnie White undid her red hair one afternoon in our kitchen, she shook it into a sea of waves and waited.

'Look at Ena,' she laughed, 'she can't get over it.'

I was standing below Rapunzel's tower, aghast as the prince took foothold in the rope of hair, biting my teeth at the agony of Rapunzel's scalp. Winnie took what she

98

wanted from my silence, admiration, just as a moment later she misinterpreted Bill's response. He had dodged into the kitchen searching for his football boots, until he caught sight of Winnie's hair. 'Crikey!' he said. Made a face. I had seen that face when the aunts tried to kiss him hallo, but Winnie hadn't, of course, so you couldn't blame her for going on about Bill.

'Let's see,' Winnie said, 'Bill must be only a few years younger than me.' When she had wound her earphones on again she went home, saying how much she liked to watch football. 'Shall we go and watch on Saturday, Edie?'

Later Mum said, 'What's that Winnie White dressed to the nines for? Boy mad. You'll be like that soon,' she told Edie, but doubtfully.

Edie wasn't in the end one of the aunts' secrets, for they discussed her when I was in the room.

'Who is this man?' asked Auntie Florrie. She wagged her silk leg at my mother and smoothed the seam straight. 'Edie said she was going out with a young man this afternoon.'

'It's about time too,' chipped in Auntie Lizzie. 'If she don't get a move on . . .'

They all glanced towards Auntie May, who was fiddling with her curling tongs, testing them on bits of singed paper.

'She's not very old. You go on as if she's an old maid.' My mother's best strapped shoes squeaked against one another in defence of her good quiet girl who was such a help and was no bother.

'She ought not to jump at the first one,' said Auntie May. 'I'll take her dancing if she wants.'

'Hasn't done you much good,' snapped Auntie Flo.

Edie arrived home fairly late in the evening, when they had reached the 'Ta-ra-ra-boom-de-ay' point. She

99

seemed hot, in spite of the rain which had pelted down for most of the evening.

'Nice time, Edie?'

Auntie May rested her hands on the piano keys. No one spoke.

Edie was the focus of interest.

'Well? Say something, girl.'

'Mum,' said Edie, 'I don't like sidecars. And,' she wiped her eyes, 'I'm soaked. I think I've caught a cold.'

And that was that, except next day Edie told Mum that Winnie had pulled her leg about the man with the motorbike.

'She's jealous. Give her half a chance she'd be out with him herself. Here's a bit of advice I was given when I was a girl: Never introduce your donah to a pal.'

Was Mum looking forward to a succession of young men courting her Edie?

Edie said, 'Anyway, I don't like sidecars.'

I asked Rene, who knew things. She wasn't as clever at school as me but had no need of cleverness, being beautiful. She pursed her lips. 'Edie's old enough to be going out with boys – well, a bit too old to start. You mustn't leave it too long. I shall go out with boys when I'm in the top class.'

I looked away from her.

'I've been asked already,' she added.

'Asked?'

'You know.'

I could guess. No one had asked me. I should punch them if they did. Still. I didn't want to be like Edie, not an old maid to be pecked at by the aunts. Again a forced acknowledgement of Rene's extra two years held me from her at arm's length.

'What about me?' I enquired of the wise person who sat beside me on her step. 'Shall I go out with boys when . . .?'

'Oh, I s'pose so. Yes, you will. I'll find one for you. Not yet, though.'

I sighed. 'Thank goodness for that. I hate boys.'

Changes were on the way; they were in the air, yet as I looked around everything was in place and so was I. It was like Grandmother's footsteps the way things moved at the edge of vision, and stopped dead when one turned. Sometimes I wondered whether it was me who was moving, for people weren't black and white any longer, sometimes I looked from my own eyes and sometimes from theirs, and all the time from the eyes of the book people. All the same there were fixed points, like my mother, my dad, and Inman Road.

The family waited for Elsie to get married. I had gathered from books that marriage was preceded by falling in love or, as the aunts put it, walking out, or before that – 'being soppy' or 'taking a shine'. Passion was restricted to books and magazines unless it was used to describe a bad temper. Not until the announcement of an engagement was the business of affection taken at all seriously and then the talk became excited, and was all about setting up the new home; as the older women spoke of crockery and linen they became girlish, and laughed a lot, but the young couple lost their smiles.

Elsie in love would be different. She would be ablaze with loving, and we would stand around and warm our hands and our eyes would shine in her reflection. That was how it would be. For the time being however, instead of marriage she chose travel and adventure, and I for one was content.

'I've cashed my insurance policy and I'm sailing with the Salvation Army, it's cheaper.' Elsie confounded them all. She had sung goodbye to us so often on Sunday evenings that we might have been ready for her departure.

'We'll give the girl a good sendoff,' said Mum and

entertained the visitors with tea or the glass of port, but it was difficult to know what to say, for it wasn't a wedding they celebrated or a funeral and some of those who came to say goodbye were curious, poked about for other, unstated reasons for her daughter to leave home. All the relations, except Auntie May, gave advice. For the journey they told her not to look over the side of the boat, on arrival they told her to wrap up.

'It's perishing in Canada. Eskimos eat blubber to keep the cold out.'

Elsie had already grown out of us at home; she smiled and was patient. I couldn't believe how patient she was. She saw my expression and winked.

'What will you do for a job?'

'I'll get a job,' she said. And we knew she would.

'What pluck,' the aunts congratulated Mum. 'What spunk that girl of yours has. A chip off the old block.'

The old block was Grandma Thornley, though no one mentioned her name, and Mum nodded and bit her lips in fear and in pride and was discovered by me, crying into the wardrobe because her eldest wanted to sail away from her nice home.

When Uncle Ernie warned my sister against the cowboys and gangsters in the USA Elsie said it was all right, that she really intended to get to the States, that Canada was only temporary, but that she had to wait for the Quota. The Quota, which sounded like a form of transport, nevertheless relieved Uncle's anxiety.

'Mind you do then. Mind you come back too. We'll miss you, and . . . come and see me before you go, we'll check up on those back teeth and' – looking round to see if his wife was near – 'there might be a little something to help you on your way.'

Elsie's dearest friend was sad. She came to say goodbye with her parents. I met them on the doorstep as I was running in from school and was prepared for the custom-ary teasing from Mr Cobbett. His kind of teasing I enjoyed, it wasn't spiteful and it was funny. But he nodded and hurried his family away. From the top of the stairs I heard Mum's voice: 'Get out! Get – out! Get out of my kitchen!'

It was difficult to pick out Edie's words from her sobbing, but they had something to do with it being her half-day and with who did the Big I Am think she was? And Elsie, as I walked into the room, was saying quite clearly, 'Don't you ever, ever – treat my friends – so – rudely again . . .'

They stopped, all of them, stared at me, hating me. Hating me? Then Edie drew her sleeve across her nose.

'Well?' she muttered. Her lips were bloated, her eyes puffed and she didn't care. 'Seen enough?'

'You're early from school,' said Elsie. She looked as sharp as a diamond, stood tall, shone like a knife. I was afraid of her.

Mum spoke. 'You should be ashamed. Both of you. I've never . . . never in my born natural . . . with visitors . . . Edie. Apologize to your sister.'

'You were rude to Mr and Mrs Cobbett. Apologize.'

'All I said – '

'You said,' Elsie interrupted, in her best clipped voice, 'that they had come like fools to say good riddance to bad rubbish and that they were doolally if they gave me a present for going because I would have gone anyway.'

Suddenly she started to laugh, and Mum, trying not to, gave up and began to splutter. And after that so did I, I couldn't help it, kept saying to myself, 'Think. Think of something to stop it.' And I was full to bursting and couldn't stop. And Edie was rocking with tears.

Exhausted at last, Mum said, 'Well, there. I'm sure you're sorry, though don't be surprised if the Cobbetts never come here again!'

Edie was a sight, she held nothing back, her crying was shameful, ugly, she dribbled tears, her nose was swollen, her hair, fallen across her face, was drenched with tears.

'You're enough to give me the pip, my girl,' Mum continued. 'And how would you feel if your sister was rude to your friends? If you had any friends. It was as much the way you pushed past them when Mr Cobbett tried to talk to you.'

Edie gasped, she was angry now. 'He didn't want to speak to me! Not me! He was only waiting till you all stopped making a fuss of . . . her . . .'

'Well, p'raps he was, but you shouldn't be so offhand when someone's only being sorry for you . . .'

I heard my voice then. It startled me, it startled them.

'Shut up! Shut up!' I stood below my mother, fists clenched. There were probably other words to stop my mother's wickedness. Going on and on with hitting and hitting Edie while she bowed down and while Elsie smiled.

'Cruel! You're cruel!'

This was the worst time for cruelty, the worst pain ever. I felt the burn of tears starting behind my eyes.

'Monsters!' I gave them a name.

'No!' I screamed to freeze them still, and they were. I bent over Edie who was hiding her head against the table. I tried to put my arm round her but she shoved me off, all elbows and hunched shoulders.

'You have got friends,' I said, peering under her hair. She was soft and as moist as grass. 'You have got friends. You've got' – Oh God! Send me some names! Oh Jesus! Just one – 'You've got Madge' (dumpy Madge). 'And Winnie White.'

It wasn't enough, was it?

'And me,' I said, and committed myself for life.

Edie blew her nose and hugged me back. 'Dear little

sister,' she whispered between sniffs as I wriggled free. I escaped to the front room where no one went on weekdays and stood before Grandma Thornley. What would she make of my sister, Edie? And sister, daughter, granddaughter, aunt one days perhaps – were these the only names Edie was ever to claim for herself? Grandma Thornley stared down at me, indifferent, implacable.

The heat of the emotional disturbance cooled in the busy days before Elsie's departure; already she was credited with a blaze of exaltation; she was a star, a shooting star, they all were aware of her now in her approaching splendour of life. If she returned it would be to show us how fame had not changed her affection for us. Quite how she would be famous wasn't yet clear, it would happen, that was sure. Mum didn't understand, she was the only one who didn't, as she frequently explained away her puzzled grief; it wasn't as if Elsie was getting married, that was normal, one of the stages of life, and you knew that she would be home again to visit, and there would be the visiting of her in her new home, all her new things and so on. Going off like this wasn't what she had expected of her daughter, or of life come to think of it. There was a great deal of talking about life at this time.

'I'll certainly miss her goings-on,' Mum said.

'You'll still have me,' said Edie.

Only Mum and Dad waved Elsie off from Southampton. I was sent to school, and Edie gave me a cold dinner at midday, and my heart broke just like my mother's.

Chapter Eleven

ELSIE had gone, and there could be no replacement. She wrote from Canada; she had a job, had turned down a couple. 'It's because I'm English. They like the English over here.'

But it was because she was Elsie. She sent snaps and later a photograph. In letters she was more affectionate than she had been while in Inman Road and my mother searched for signs of homesickness, and found none, not even between the lines where she hoped to find them. Elsie had whisked herself into a magic land where parties of Anglophiles lit bonfires on the shores of Lake Ontario and in the gloaming toasted marshmallows and ate buckwheat cakes and maple syrup and swam in the lake shadows to the jazz of ukuleles. I tried hard to keep her real and avoided the photograph because by looking there I might lose her altogether. But very soon there were two of Elsie, one smiled from snaps, one from memory; and while the latter was full of faults the other was being washed of all her sins and before long would be as white as snow. Pictured as she was, this girl in Canada, against a background of lake or the suds of Niagara, she couldn't fail, she was as pure as her smiles. She smiled all the time in her snaps.

'It's the air, sparrer,' Mum explained to Auntie Annie.

'Sometimes,' she said, 'it comes all over me how I wouldn't half love to hear her play "The Rustle of Spring".'

'May played it last week,' Auntie reminded her.

'She means well . . . I do wish she'd get her fingernails

cut short. Click-click they go. Gets on my nerves. There, I'm all on edge lately.'

'If Edie could get hold of some nice young man . . .' proposed Auntie Annie, my mother's best friend, 'would take your mind off . . .'

A man had waited for Rene and me every day for over a week outside Swaffield Road school.

'I've an idea,' I said to Rene.

The man was thin, weedy, but clean as Mum would wish him to be, and polite. He hesitated before following us, didn't mind our nudging one another, he smiled when we giggled, and didn't get cross when we skipped fast near home. He was outside again, waiting for us.

'What d'you think, for Edie?' I asked her.

'A bit . . . a bit thin.'

The man smiled and nodded.

'He could be a bit . . .' she tapped her forehead. Seeing my disappointment, she relented: 'Well, not much . . . well . . . OK.'

We walked sedately all the way home, no looking back, and the man came closer, we heard the shuffle of his shoes. At the bend of Inman Road Rene turned and smiled at him. He stepped forward, right up to Number 29. I knocked hard on the door and Edie stood there. I hadn't planned it but congratulated myself that it was her half-day, and now was sure that fate was working with the plan.

'He wants to be your friend,' I said and beckoned to the man, who had turned to run.

'Come in,' I said.

He tried to run but fell over Rene, who was guarding the way. Edie, being kind, ran to pick him up. He had cut his head on the coping. 'You stupid girls! Oh gosh! He's bleeding! Let me . . .' and she waved a hankie at him.

'What's your name?' I asked; some kind of fact seemed called for.

'Ian. Ian Anthony.' He was at the corner, hunched and bleeding, and thin. Very thin.

'And now, Miss,' said Edie, 'you'll come in and tell me just what you've been up to.'

We told her. The man was for her. We had examined him, nice clothes, washed, nice name now we knew it. Moreover – he was looking for a friend: hadn't he proved it? He was lonely. Edie had no sympathy for him, or for us. She laughed when she told Mum the tale, and a month later she was angry. Ian Anthony's name was in the paper, arrested for molesting young girls. 'So. Ta very much!' Edie snapped.

At this time one of Mum's old yearnings revived, stimulated by both the loss of Elsie and the advertisements in the papers. The Morden housing estates were expanding and becoming more strident in their claims for the dream houses. They were labour-saving, they were unused, they were cheap, they were set in green fields with modern sanitation. Inman Road wasn't set anywhere, and as to sanitation –

'Guess where we're off to?' Mum held out my coat.

'We'll have a treat. Go into Joe Lyons on the way back.' Because I was sulking, suddenly anxious to go to see Rene about something.

Mum said, 'We're going to Morden. Don't tell your dad.'

The Show House door opened in a great tide of warm air, we were sucked into the hall and into the presence of a man in a navy suit, all navy cloth and white shirt, impeccable. He waved us to look around, to feel free. 'Best take off your shoes,' he said, after a quick inspection of our feet. (The road outside was furrowed in wet yellow clay.)

In bare feet we walked humbly up and down over

carpeted floors – 'Right up to the skirting boards', whispered Mum. Now I shared her thoughts. She kept wiping her eyes, taking off her glasses and putting them on to see more.

Small exclamations came from her lips, died on them. 'Fitted car—. Curtains – oh my lor'.'

She went out of reach. Grabbed my arm: 'Look! Windows, casement windows! Not your old sash!'

We tiptoed about the landing.

'The – oh – the bathroom. Taps and all! Chromium they are. Duck, fancy having a bath in this bathroom.'

She had said the wrong thing at last. There could be nothing to beat the way I bathed in front of the kitchen range, with the firelight on rosy skin, in a tin bath which swayed and gulped at every scrub, hauled out of it to a cloak of furry towel, laundered legs and arms and wrinkled crinkled fingers all curious and beautiful – though I didn't say so. Mum was dreaming, the way she dreamed of new clothes and I recognized the dream for what it was and was not threatened any longer by an exodus from Inman. Now Mum walked as straight-backed as a lady and as her hand came up to sleek her hair she furnished a new home, her unused new home in the desirable suburb – with velvet and silk, perfumed it with bath crystals and filled up the empty spaces with smells of perfect sponge cake baked in a white and chromiumed oven (for she was free from the slavery of the range). Her youngest daughter ran indoors to cry, in well-bred accents, which were not at all a surprise to her mother, 'Mummy, I've been asked to tea with the Grangers, who happen to live in the quite detached chalet house with garage on the corner surrounded by green and sanitary fields.'

We sat in the tube and she said nothing; we sat side by side in the bus and she was silent. Perhaps I had been too confident about her mere fantasy, perhaps nothing

109

would stop her now and if she won and we moved I would lose, and if she lost, the quarrels with my dad would be tremendous. As it was the night noises were sometimes loud enough to wake me, if they broke into the day there would be nowhere to hide. On the walk home from Garratt Lane her silence was beyond bearing, and feeling sorry for her in spite of all she might do I put out my hand to hold hers.

She looked down, came to life and said, 'Well, that was all very posh. D'you think those colour curtains would go all right in the front bedroom? And what would you like for tea?'

The following day she moved the furniture in the front room; she hung Grandma on a different wall, facing the mirror over the fireplace. 'Let her look at herself for a change,' I heard her mutter.

I was safe. If she spoke of Morden again it would be to Edie and not to me; I was too young to understand. I used childishness as a protection, at least indoors when Mum and Edie closed in on themselves. Bill, once locked away in homework, was now either gone to London to his office or to football, or to dances. My dad was as overalled and as greasily tired as ever. The sparrows arrived on Sundays in flutters and chatters. Across the Atlantic Ocean, past seas which heaved and ice floes which reared against brittle skies, past forests and lakes and great rivers Elsie worked and played and was given tributes to her beauty. I lived my own way, with friends, or, when alone, went underground, submerged into my own private place which had to do with Inman, began there, but was not confined at all.

Inman had its pattern which regulated all those who lived there. For example – the eel man. He came once a week.

'Listen! Cats!'

From Wilna and Dingwall and beyond in tail-twitching anguish the cats followed the progress of the eel man. He stood outside Number 29 waiting, dumb and patient, encircled by the revolutions of lusting cats. He paid no attention to the pitiful mewings, kicked out at the coaxing of furry heads which attempted to rub his trousers. He didn't answer Mum though she chattered hard, saying that it was always a nice day, that she knew he would be coming today because the sun was shining first thing, wouldn't he like a glass of water, or perhaps . . . a cup of . . .? He shook his head.

'It's my hubby, you see. He does relish his eels. Eel pie. Jellied eels . . .'

Not a word from the eel man; he gave only the eels.

The eel man was one of the fascinating horrors of Inman. It was impossible to escape him; once he was there we had to stay, to watch. For he chopped the eels alive. They glistened, they twisted, and he chopped them for my dad's supper. Hands which slipped with slime and blood were precise with the knife; the knife slashed, segments jerked, quivered as lively as before. Whistling was what the eel man did while he chopped and chopped at the eels. Mum held out her white enamel bowl for the pieces. She forbade Grimm's fairy tales, she cared for my insides, she made me scour my nails, teeth, everything, but she soaked the eel stumps in a bowl in the scullery so that the water swirled red; she cooked them and served them up to my dad, who knew no better.

More cheerful threads ran through the week. Carters rattled by, cracking whips behind them at boys who clung to the backboards like strings of onions, teasing drivers with the customary yell of 'Cut be'ind, guv'nor!'

As regular as the eel man came the rag-and-bone man, the milkman who served milk from a churn into brass-trimmed measures. As reliable, if less frequent, came the man who pulled a cart of plant trays every springtime. The trays were all flowers, daisies, chubby and pink-tipped, polyanthuses and bloated calceolarias which Mum bought to put on the grave in Earlsfield cemetery, where they died. In the winter it was the coalman who groaned his 'Co-o-al!' A bizarre apparition he was, bent double under the weight of sacks; he wore a leather helmet with a long leather tail.

Gossip was the background of these pictures, and the women supplied it. 'Gas bags' Mum called them, shaking her duster down at them where they gathered on the pavement, their hands folded under sacking aprons. But she asked me what they had been debating when I came indoors. A wedding, a funeral, an operation, and always before the participants had breathed a word of the event, and perhaps before it had actually occurred to them – these were meat and drink to the gossips.

They were taken quite seriously in the street, and indeed they acted as impresarios for our entertainments; they were as alert to perform at funerals as they were eager to gasp at weddings, and their reward was simply the successful outcome, as they were seldom invited guests. Inman Road was famous for white satin brides and for saucy bridesmaids as pink as seaside rock.

'White! White brings 'er colour up, don't it? Talk about a treat!'

It was a funeral which brought out the best in the women. A funeral in the street was an inspiration: everything sooty black, widow buried in veils and black-clothed relatives, black gleaming horses nodding plumed headdresses, the final splendour of the black coach. The poorest folk afforded a good funeral, it seemed a pity that the dead man could not be there to join in the knees-up later. It was always the men in the street who died, and always the nice ones too, as we listened to the chorus of wailing women who lined up outside the bereaved home. 'Underneath all that – y'compris? Not a bad old stick, old Bert. Liked his drop o' course. Split up with most of his folk, still, they're all here to give him a sendoff, ain't they? Nothing like a good funeral to bring families together.'

As children we couldn't add to the obituaries but nevertheless we stood on the pavement in solemn attendance, and later scavenged for silver horseshoes from wedding confetti or petals from wreaths. We would make our own weddings and funerals at a suitable interval and in our back yard. Weddings were easy, using sheets from the laundry; funerals required a certain cunning in order to smuggle black coats and scarves from the house. We covered our faces and giggles in net and Maurice Jackson was the corpse.

Even before Elsie left home I was aware that my family thought we were surrounded by foreigners; their habits were foreign, they spoke in a foreign tongue, they stared at my sisters and brother as though they were the strangers, but my dad was admired and I was accepted. My mother also: she belonged to my dad. I had to admit that the children who lived at the other end of the street didn't have much to do with my friends and me unless war had been declared between Dingwall and Inman, and then they followed us like anything. We couldn't have played with them, they didn't want us and we didn't want them. They went to Garratt Lane school and apart from that journey they didn't leave the street. Like their mothers they truly belonged to it. The husbands drank. Especially did they drink on Saturdays, paydays.

Mum said, 'That poor little thing, Maudie Singleton. She tells me that her husband drinks most of his wages before he gets home on Saturdays. Then he falls asleep, hands in his pockets to prevent poor Maudie from getting what's left. Which she would do to buy the kids some-thing to eat. Men!'

Edie and Mum scowled at the lot of them. Men!

'Ah! But you listen to this. When he wakes up shouting for his dinner she tells him he's eaten it. For why? Look at the gravy round his lips and the drips of it on his shirt. Don't he remember?'

'Does he?' asked Edie.

''Course not. There wasn't much anyway and he was blind drunk so she had given his dinner to the family and wiped the gravy round his chops. Serve him right. She said the kids had started to giggle and he gave them a look. But his kids are a bit soft in the head and snigger a lot just to pass the time, you might say.'

'Don't try it on too often,' Mum told her, 'he might twig.'

'All the same,' she said to Edie and me, 'good for her. Men!'

On Sundays the watercress and winkle men came by. Each one had his own tune, both were loud and urgent. Roused by the greenness of watercress and the saltiness of winkles, we bought both for tea.

'All very nice and fresh. Winkles! Wy-ink-ulls!'

The singer reached our street as we returned from Sunday School; he was a sad man with one sad song and in our poor street few pennies were thrown at him.

'Becorse I love you,' he stretched out the soft toffee words. 'I've ter-ried so hard I can't forget – becorse I . . . er . . . miss you. You linger in my memory yet – becorse I-er-lorst you. I ter-ried so hard I can't forget – it doesn't matter dear – thank yer Sir – thank y— – souvenir – thank yer – dum-de-dum-de-dum – becorse I love you.' His lament wasn't disturbed by the coins falling and he kept his temper and continued to sing, with hardly a break, into Wilna Road.

Rene and I were shamed by the flippancy of my

brother and his friends, who attempted feeble imitations of the song. The man's heart was broken, wasn't it? Why would he traipse winter streets if it were not so? How would they like it? One Sunday Rene and I followed him along Wilna Road, noting how he had to sing the song twice to make it fit the length of Wilna, and admiring the skill with which, with a bit of a tug, he had timed it into Inman. We were prepared to go the whole way with him, along Garratt Lane, but he turned round on us and muttered, 'Shove off!' And when we gaped at him he pushed his elbow at us and shouted, 'Bugger off!'

Summertime expanded the street, winter contracted it into hollows of darkness and disguise. Our privet bush was golden in summer and hairy with frost in winter. Paving stones struck sparks – that is if you were lucky to have shoes tipped with blakeys. My shoes had rubber tips.

Mum said, 'Blakeys are for boys. They're common.'

'They make sparks,' I whined. 'That's what they're for.'

Winter held children to wild games which made us gasp cold air into throats which burnt; at dusk it gathered us into a circle, closer and closer to the lamp-post. One by one we were called indoors, in from the tingling cold and off the starry pavements, to leave the last one, one child alone kicking at the kerbstone hands in pockets, waiting to be called; finally, for want of something better to do, wandering homeward, unclaimed.

Chapter Twelve

WINTER was my mother's season, and winter evenings especially were to her taste.

'Let's draw the curtains,' she said when she felt the pressure of the dense blue November dusk against the kitchen windows. 'Let's shut it all out, shall us?'

Narrower and narrower our family circle contracted – Elsie gone, Bill out, or studying downstairs in his bedroom, my dad never at home, though Mum hoped against experience that one day he would look about him and find the company of his club friends as stale as the smell of drink and tobacco in the Conservative Club. It was his perpetual association with the laundry women which drove him from home to find a welcome among the men, but one day he would realize, he would stay with her, stay close. She would see to it, Joe would be as tame as a cat, ever after.

On winter evenings I was sent to bed alone in an icy bedroom, where I lay flat, pinched between starched sheets straining to catch the cheerful talk from the kitchen four steps down off the landing. Carefully, testing the air of my room, the flutter and wince of the cooling laundry machinery penetrated the walls. Next day I compared dreams with Rene and Daisy, trimming them up a little, giving them a positive ending, because dreams were like that, you could do anything, say anything; they were your dreams, surely. Nightmares were taboo, they were beyond telling, they followed no story, only lifted me up into terror and – the worst thing about a nightmare – it was a visit to territory familiar from earliest childhood. Up and up, floated horizontally out of bed into the heart of a snowstorm, flakes spinning around and down on to me, but the flakes were warm, the warm flakes filled my mouth and blinded my eyes. Then there was no more me, all that was left was a mouth to scream with. Even then no scream came as relief until –

'Ssh! Oh, for the love of Mike! Ssh! You'll wake Mum and Dad. Oh all right, come on then, come in with us.' And I pattered across the cold lino to lie safe between the generous limbs of sisters until I melted into sleep.

'Now,' said the teacher, 'I'll read the story of Joseph and his dreams. No one can remember a dream she has had for more than a minute after waking up, but in the Bible people did remember, long enough to describe the dream to a person like Joseph who could explain its meaning. Yes? What is it, Miss?'

She didn't care to be interrupted and aimed her glasses at me from the edge of the Bible.

'I can remember. I can remember a dream I had when I was four.'

The glint of the glasses was not friendly.

'You would, clever dick,' murmured the girl behind me.

Knowing that she had the rest of the class with her, the teacher said, 'Much as we should enjoy hearing you tell us about it, and astounding as it must certainly be, we haven't time now, for we must talk about Joseph.'

She droned on about the fat and the lean kine and the bowing down of the sheaves and I returned to my own recollection. I could date it. I had started school at four years of age and to calm my feverish running up and downstairs from bedroom to kitchen Mum had advised me to dream about school – not the wisest counsel. I dreamt about burglars. Words came. 'The burglars are over the hill.'

A small girl looked out of her bedroom windows and

saw, instead of the houses opposite, a line of hills, along which moved a file of grey shapes. It would be best if they kept marching across, right to left, and she clenched her fists, not daring to take her eyes off them. As they drew nearer she saw that each one carried a jug in front of him. Now the sweat ran down the girl's body. Now it was happening as she had known it would. One of the burglars broke free of the line, trod steady, trod slow, and the small girl could see herself and that her face was wiped clean away. The burglar was near, his body blocked the light of the window and he paused. He stopped on the brink of her room, somewhere out there, suspended. Then he smiled, gripped the girl with a smile like a claw, moved back to the line of his companions and passed, like them, over the hill.

Where was Joseph, the teller of dreams?

Winter was all kinds of things to all kinds of people and in the wintertime my friends and I made a place of our own in it. The kitchen was our theatre; Mum and Auntie Annie and Edie were our audience. We gave them comedy, poetry, Shakespeare, and Elsie missed it all. Although Rene and the Jacksons and Daisy and I were in different classes we had all seen the top class perform a scene from *A Midsummer Night's Dream*. It wasn't Shakespeare who had so enthralled me in the school hall but the girl who had played the part of Puck. Her name was Hazel Bray. A name to wonder at. Hazel Bray. Rene was the nearest in age to her.

'She's stuck-up,' she said of Hazel.

Quite right, and so she should be. I didn't want her for a friend but just to be – posh – and stuck-up.

Hazel Bray pulled me into a passion for Shakespeare and for a limited period (while I was eight or nine) and in a certain place (the kitchen) and in front of a picked audience (Mum, Edie and Auntie Annie) she made my friends and me into actors.

The scene we named 'Puck and the Fairy'. How we learnt the lines is a mystery; we had no book of plays, we were considered at school either too young to learn Shakespeare or, in the case of Rene, better equipped to learn to sew run-and-fell seams. But we recited the words and they were the ones Shakespeare had written. Puck was the illustrious role so we took turns to play it – that is, Evie Jackson was allowed the part only when she sulked in a determined way; her brothers were content to be the trees in the wood near Athens. Having announced the play, we retired to dress up. This took a long time, though it usually resulted in a rolling of scarves about our heads, and a rolling up of skirts into our knickers as we did when we went paddling in the pond on the Common. We faced the audience and waited for silence.

'How now, spirit! Whither wander you?'

From that moment the audience was forgotten – or rather, it was changed from three into one corporate body to whom we brought enchantment. Right through the scene we went: Puck, the Fairy, and four trees, aching branches outspread. 'Here comes Oberon,' back to a firelit kitchen where three people collapsed before us, torn to bits by rocking laughter.

'Oh! Oh! Oh! You'll be the death . . .'

Puck, the Fairy, trees, gazed at them and at each other, shrugged shoulders and accepted the sweets. But – wiping eyes and blowing noses, the audience recovered and clapped as they had clapped at the Wimbledon Theatre and as they hadn't clapped at our singing. They wanted more, always. Daisy would do her funny monologue (the audience liked that, they knew where they were with that); Evie Jackson did Walter de la Mare, because we all had a great deal of Walter de la Mare to learn at school. For some reason his name was enough to –

'De la Mare – Walter – Don't set us off again! Oh duck! The pain!' Then, sniffing and snorting, 'Go on, duck, don't take no notice, we're listening now, see?'

Faces composed, they would listen though it hurt, knees together, straight backs, while I dared them to laugh at Evie Jackson, who was easily put off and might cry at any moment.

'Silver,' announced Evie.

Our glares made a wall around her while she lifted her arms ready to begin the actions. We were taught to recite with expression but while standing on one spot, as too frenzied a motion might well distract the listener. Evie did her best; flung out her arms as in drill sessions; she pointed high, to the moon, rose on tiptoe, like the rising moon, good old Evie. Then she wobbled, lost her balance and her words.

'Walks the night – '

'Oh yes, walks the night – '

'In a – '

'Yes. Yes. I know it now . . .'

Our lips moved in silent unison – our arms too, for we had learnt the actions from our teachers; rather stiff-limbed they were, and so were our reflected ones. Yet in spite of flapping arms and her over-long peering into moonlit pools, the words made a circle about us. Evie was deep into the poem, speaking now in teacher-modulated accents, folding her hands with soft grace to indicate the sleeping dog, staring moonstruck and taking the poem gently down with 'Silver fish in a silver stream'.

'Very nice, Evie. Thank you.'

Rene was the first to refuse to perform before my family; there was never any question of doing so in anyone else's house, although we were not so restricted in summer back-yard concerts. Rene had made up her mind, it seemed, and had stepped back the few yards from stage to auditorium to join the adult audience.

When it was my turn to give up we were reading Tennyson at school. 'Can't you recite to Auntie and me? Go on. Like you used to. Oh, go on.' But – tell them of a hand 'clothed in white samite'? Tell them of Geraint riding into the castle court? It was too great a risk, and I could not share the words. Nor did I need to speak them out loud, for by that time my teacher was Miss Howard.

Learning by heart was just one of the tricks which were the prerogative of school. Learning to read came first.

'I can read.'

'Now don't make a fuss. Sit there like the other new children and we'll all go through these letters.'

'But I . . .'

'Now listen – dear. You're here to learn to read. Sit down!'

Fortunately the learning to read stopped for me quite abruptly and before I became tiresome. I was free to graze on the meagre supply of books in the classroom. Out of nowhere came the paints. How fat the brushes were, how lusty the worms of paint that we squelched on to saucers.

'Careful! Careful, children!'

I expected to hear my mother's voice: 'We're not made of paint!'

Oh but I wanted very much to do what was required, to please, to make petals . . .

'Load your brush – ' (delicious! Did she see me lick my lips?)

'Now, lay your brush on the paper, and – take it off, without dragging – see? Like this. Stop! Watch me! Like this! Now I've made a petal.' And so she had. And so did we, or most of us in the bent-over, tongue-biting class, rows and rows and, getting the idea, circles and circles of petals. Orange for marigolds, yellow for butter-cups, red, and blue, all the petals of the rainbow; sometimes they wobbled on the surface, sometimes they dribbled colours into one another, all of them glowed pinpointed with light until the paint dried. We loved that teacher, she was the first one of them for me to love.

Usually there was no question of teachers being flesh and blood, they belonged to the school, they were the creatures of the cold, door-slamming building and were not controlled by the laws of the world outside, and most of them gave evidence of this. Because I was a reader and enjoyed writing, which was restricted to handwriting and copying for many years, I took little notice of teachers – until I came to Smiler's class. Smiler was all for Arithmetic – and I was not. I blamed my failure in sums on my frequent absences from school and those sick absences on my scar and thence, by progression, on my culpable mother. The heaping of excuses was of no use, vital information had been lost. It was too late. Smiler had a reputation; she was a real strict teacher, she broke rulers across knuckles. All the time.

She was not named in fun, for her smile was inflexible, it was worn through the days of the week, through the hours of the day; it glistened through sneezes and blazed in the droning summer afternoons.

'What's she got to smile at?' There was hardly time to put the question to one another, she kept us busy, and out of school we promptly forgot her.

My friend in the class said, 'She got stuck with that on her face when the wind changed.'

Yes. Smiler's face was dark and hairy, like a flushed gooseberry, and its natural expression would have been a scowl. Adults had a way of interfering; to poor old Smiler one had said, no doubt, 'Cheer up. Take that look off your face.' And Smiler had done so but at the

'Everyone said what a dear
little girl you were'

She might have been a
queen, my mother

(*above left*) Auntie May
didn't notice me

(*above right*) Elsie . . .
beautiful and clever and
captivating

(*left*) 'You know where you
are with Edie'

My mother's parents

My parents

Two girls in summer
frocks . . . either side of
Uncle George

The wedding photographs . . . I knew them by heart

Earlsfield Station, *c.* 1914

wrong windy moment, and she was fixed with a skeletal smile for ever.

Her pleasure was in mental arithmetic. The fascinated observer caught the faintest change of expression in such periods of her delight; a fraction of curve of lip met the quick calculators, a softer gleam was bent on those whose hands shot up instantly, if they were accurate and not merely guessing. I was one of the stutterers and had I looked up from mouth to eyes I would have been turned to stone. She taught me to be afraid; she didn't teach me humility or perseverance. I concluded that after all you were either good at sums or you weren't and there wasn't much you could do about it. Numbers, they danced around your head like jugglers' balls and some could catch them and I could not. So – I was contemptuous of figures and withdrew to safer ground: reading . . . writing. Smiler had no time for stories or poems. We had recitation because it was the rule, and we wrote our compositions but I didn't bother for her. I gave nothing and was no longer the clever girl at school and became the dunce at home, causing Mum to shake her head and ask Elsie to write to me, urging me to try, just to try.

'Whatever's come over you? You're getting to be a real old madam,' Mum said. 'And where've you been? Rene was looking for you.'

'With Margery.' Glaring because she knew, and I knew, that Margery and Margery's home were almost down to Bendon Valley standards.

'You've been playing in her house. I can smell it! Take off your clothes. Scrub yourself till I say stop.'

What freedom bad behaviour opened up. I scrubbed because I chose to – true, there was a smell – and knowing that now I didn't want to be liked, I didn't care to please, and if and when I did, why then Mum was bound to feel blessed by my effort and hope for future repetitions.

Smiler was the first teacher to emerge from the chalky

background of schooldays; she was the first teacher to disapprove of me and the first one to receive my dread and my fascination. Because of Smiler I saw myself and other people with a fresh perspective.

School was a headquarters for teachers; it was also a kind of zoo where subjects waited – subjects like History, Geography, Arithmetic, English – labelled for our attention. We 'did' subjects. For example, we 'did' History. History was about Man, but chiefly about his clothes, which were called costume. It was about a frieze which lined each classroom. We were told to read the stories of History, which were random scatterings through the centuries, which were about kings and queens and battles, but we lived alongside the frieze and knew which way History marched – from the classroom door Man marched around the room at eye level until he reached the door to its left. By this time Man had disposed of his furry chest for the red coat and beaver hat of a soldier. The truth was that we never got further with the story of Man than accounts of Old Stone Age Man who crouched and looked dismal. With some teachers we hurried to catch up with the more upright and aquiline New Stone Age Man, but in a new class, back we went to the Old One. Ahead of him Ancient Greeks stood about among columns of white marble; they looked blind and thoughtful. Before them marched the Romans, ready for a fight. And so, on and on went Man in a follow-my-leader progress, seeming to move more briskly with each change of clothes, aiming for better and better things. I was wistful about the Tudors, felt I had a connection as we hung the portraits of Queens Elizabeth and Mary in our kitchen. I longed to know about the Tudors, they were so velvety and so raised up above their ruffs. However, our place was to tag along behind the procession carrying our weapons and tools of flint. We drew pictures of these things until we were equipped to build the circle of stone on the skyline of the first section of the frieze. It was called Stonehenge.

Botany and Geography were other names for Drawing. For drawing neatly, both plants and maps. That was all, except in Geography the lesson of History was repeated: that Man was walking uphill, that the view was growing more sumptuous each decade, and the especial edge of Geography demonstrated the fact that Great Britain was the ruler of the world, the British Empire corseted the globe. Weren't we lucky though?

English was easy and I enjoyed it, chiefly because I enjoyed being top. Compositions had nothing to do with the stories scribbled on the backs of stuck-down envelopes at home, any more than reading at school had to do with books I read at home. Reading and compositions were both intended for the teacher and I knew what she wanted..

'Describe a room in your house.'

I gave her the room of her life. I invented a room in the same burst of enthusiasm which prompted the Morden builders to invent their dream Show House, though I didn't go so far as to invent, as they did on the posters, a dream family to inhabit it. My room was too smart and shiny to contain people. Some of the furniture came from the shop in Wandsworth High Street and some from pictures of Buckingham Palace. I wrote of carpet, not of lino, of lamps and not of gas mantles, and I wrote this on the kitchen table while Mum lit the gas lights, while I listened with one ear to the plop and glop and hiss of the mantle, and I looked up to wait for the light to unfold and bloom and spread about the room and scoop shadows from the ceiling. I gave the teacher what she wanted and I was top.

She wanted more: 'The Flower Shop'.

This time it was carnations she required, or a bunch of red roses and a bit of gyp. What would she make of the flower stall in the Shoot? Where fat blue hands grabbed wet daffodils out of buckets, where gypsy primroses were exchanged for pennies under the dragon flares of kerosene lamps? She had her florist flowers all wrapped up in white shop paper. And I was top.

Until Smiler Arithmetic didn't worry me; it was a matter of chanting, like most aspects of school lessons; the tables had a rhythm which carried us along together. Keep with the others, that was the thing, don't race ahead or lag behind. The same with written work: if we had finished we would just have to wait for the rest, it would do us good. Goodness was as important as smartness – better, as it was in short supply.

Other lessons were acquired, not taught. How to shut eyes on ugly things. 'The Dirty Heads', for example. These belonged to children who suffered from ringworm or from lice, and some were guilty of both. The Dirty Heads sat in the front of the class, removed as far as possible from the teacher and the clean majority – too far, anyway, for a flea to hop or a louse or worm to crawl. We saw only the backs of their shaved heads, half-covered by caps of calico. Outside in the playground they kept to their shady corner by the wall. Only once did I glimpse the face of a Dirty Head; her eyes had no lashes and were red-rimmed. Each morning in Assembly we prayed for the Untouchables in India and for the heathens everywhere, and, at a safe distance, the Dirty Heads prayed also. We learnt not to be like the Dirty Heads. It was a lesson for life.

Chapter Thirteen

Boys and girls began school as a huggermugger of bodies named infants; after a few years, the secret was out and they transferred to their separate departments, Boys and Girls, labelled and segregated to avoid contact. Not that the teachers need have worried, for the girls dismissed boys from their minds more drastically than did those averted doors, or those walls built high between playgrounds. From the moment of separation all we knew of boys were the shouts of their play, the skidding of their boots on the other side of the wall.

It took time to grow accustomed to the school playground, even for children who had grown up into street play, and of course the girls' playground was absolutely distinct in character from the one over the wall. An empty playground was quite another place. Once when I was an infant I was late for school. I remember looking back to the gate where my mother hovered; perhaps I was a very new child as she came with me as far as the gate. Parents were unauthorized persons except on Open Days. She waved to me across a continent of asphalt, she waved and nodded me on, I looked back again and she was gone. The loneliness of that moment settled, would always remain. Not a sound escaped from the cliff walls of the building and I was stuck like a fly in treacle to the endless surface of the playground. I tugged one foot and then the other to reach the stone staircase, to push into the clanging doors, to be shut away like everyone else.

Now — the satisfaction of being an old hand, of knowing the habits of the place, of being known, of becoming a cynic, hardened by the practices of school. It was a good thing, being a Girl.

As a rule school was peaceful; the ripples circled by visitors served to accentuate the steady peace of the place. The nurse was one visitor, and she had her own routine, a whip through heads with her steel comb, dip in the bowl of Lysol, and grab the next bent head. In my case she put down her comb in order to concentrate on my interesting neck. Regretful about the lack of swelling, she examined my fingernails for relief, for I was famous for fingernails among the teachers. It was the problem of cleanliness again and this time it was my fault, as I was fussy about stickiness on my hands.

'Filbert nails you've got,' said Mum, 'and it's your Grandma Thornley, you take after her nails.'

I spread my fingers, wondering. Rene had told my mother about the inspector who had ordered me to do so.

'I thought he was going to give you a tanning,' Rene said.

'He just wanted to look.'

Mum was quick about it. 'It's because she's got lovely hands,' and sharply correcting herself, 'Clean hands.'

But the subject brought her to sit down in her remembering position.

'D'you know,' she paused while the light came to her eyes, 'a girl in the restaurant where I worked – '

'Stewarts',' prompted Rene.

'Yes, that's right, Stewarts' on Ludgate Circus. Well, this girl, Iris was her name, she was a plain girl and no mistake. But – her hands were lovely. With all the rough work she did and all. Lovely hands and a lovely nature to go with them.'

Mum glanced at me.

'Tell us about Molly,' said Rene, who had already chosen her part.

128

'Oh yes, Molly, one of the waitresses. Molly – wotch-ermacallit – oh, what was her name – I'll forget my own next – she was a real beauty. Like a dream. Not common, mind, quite the lady to look at, until she opened her mouth. Now her hands! Ugly! Ugly's not the word! Molly used to go on about them, asked Iris what she did to her hands. "Nothing much. Just wash them."

'Once she pulled Molly's leg, told her to cover her hands with cucumber slices and stay like that for an hour. Well, for a start cucumbers were too expensive to buy on our wages, so Molly went around sneaking bits until she had enough. Poor girl, she did hate her hands. "I can't see my face, only in a mirror, but I see my hands all day long, especially when I'm serving my gents. I must give them the shivers." I'm sure her gents didn't take their eyes off her face, but there you are. We always want what we can't have. Molly wanted Iris's hands, and I daresay Iris wanted Molly's face, though she never let on. "I'd give anything for your hands," Molly used to say.'

I narrowed my eyes at Mum, aware of the inference in her story. From books it was clear that poor old Iris's life would be dreary, though lit dimly by her lovely nature. Poor old Iris, perhaps her life had already ended, had dwindled, and stopped, her lovely hands a sieve unable to contain any drop of gladness. As for beautiful Molly, she no doubt still danced through the years wearing gloves.

'You've a good mouthful of teeth as well,' approved my mother.

Assembly. We began the day by being Christians to the crash of piano chords and the scowl of Miss Jones, the headmistress, who faced us from the dais. Accustomed to see her thus raised up and at a venerable distance, I was shocked at last to stand by her to receive praise for some work I had done. It was her whiskers which were unexpected and when she told me, 'Well done. Now, quick about it, off you go,' her speech was slippery with false teeth.

One Assembly stood out for ever. We faced Miss Jones as usual; also the large picture of Swiss mountains on the wall behind her. It was sunrise in Switzerland, the snow-covered rim of the mountains kindled and Miss Jones announced: 'The roseate hues of early dawn'. This made a composition nothing could destroy – Switzerland, God, and Miss Jones. She pointed her finger at the piano, our mouths opened – and closed. It was a chilly morning, our breaths puffed into the air and hung there. From the stairs beyond the hall echoed the cries which had stopped the piano. Miss Jones's finger wagged again, we opened our mouths again, but the cries came closer, through the glass doors behind Miss Jones. She pointed her finger, this time at a teacher in the front row, who leapt to the doors; another teacher was pointed to the scuffling on the stairs. The tiled walls out there bounced with cries; then – a gruff voice – the caretaker had come. Step by step feet and cries were dragged down and away. Was it all over? So quick? But – no! The clatter was coming back. Right back this time. Into the hall! No messing about this time!

Two women staggered through the doors, teachers reeled after them. The women's hair sprayed from under felt hats; with battering chests they advanced on Miss Jones. They rocked against the dais but Miss Jones stood as stiff as a breakwater – we were all of us lines of breakwaters.

Teachers hovered. 'Please! Do you mind – oh please stop it – '

Meek and mild the teachers were, even Smiler's grimace was uncertain. One teacher tugged at the skirt of the bigger woman so that she jerked her elbow and knocked the teacher off balance. She collapsed against her class of small children and tipped them over like rows of dominoes. The rest of the children in the hall were aghast and blissful; there was one wish. More! Please more! On one side the action was that of a slow-motion film. Miss Jones's hand, for instance, descended slowly to the Bible on the stand. On the other the film was speeded up. 'Cow! You up there, cow! You! You! Bugger you! Sod you! Bitch! Cow!' Gosh!

'Me gels! Our gels! Bloody gels! Me sister – ' she introduced her sister, a lesser character, with a wave of the hand to include all the school. 'She'll bear witness, may I never move from this spot, as 'ow these gels never did nothing. No they never.'

We wriggled, settling into the business, it was turning into words rather than actions and we prepared for a long performance. But we hadn't the measure of the women. The big one was reaching up to the dais. Would she pull Miss Jones down? The dais wobbled. What next? Knock her to the floor as she had knocked the other teachers? Tread on Miss Jones? In front of the whole school? Yes?

But the women had carried on too long, they had lost the initiative and the teachers all came to life and the caretaker galloped in with his wet mop and a bucket of disinfectant. He heaved and the teachers pushed and the women were bundled out of the hall and down the stairs, shouting pitifully, a retreating wail of 'Cow! They never! Bloody buggers!'

Afterwards it would have been fair to tell us of the crime the girls had committed but we had to find out what we could for ourselves, or what was left of it.

It was too late to discover the extremity of their sin, for when our class were passed the word and we rushed out to the lavatories the caretaker had been busy with the green paint and all the messages that the girls had painted were lost. All morning it seemed the bladders of those in the know had been exercised in trips to the lavs, where no one went if they could help it – as a rule, that is. They were cabins where no sunshine entered, a cold place, and the doors banged like gongs. Teachers called them WC's and when I told Mum this she was impressed and stopped using the word lav at home, but only for a while. The caretaker had had to burn some of the words away where they were carved with knives. Two doors of words! The girls had worked very hard. For the rest of the day they were kept behind screens, and separately, in the hall. At the end of the afternoon they were expelled. A teacher brought them their dinners on trays, I heard her hushed voice as she went behind the screens; they were like important invalids and the teacher was cross with me, not with the girls, when she saw me watching her.

There were no more invasions from the mothers, the girls just – went. They were old enough to leave school and one of them came to work in the laundry.

'A good little worker,' said my dad. 'Very willing and very strong.'

By the time I had made up my mind to ask her what words she had scored in the school lavs she was wearing light stockings and tiny gold earrings twinkled from her long hair. She was grown up and I couldn't ask her after all. Anyway she didn't write rude words in our downstairs lav.

Nothing ever matched that morning for excitement, although the day when Miss Jones showed us her legs was memorable. They were displayed once and never again, before and after they were sheathed in boots, not the fashionable Russian boots which Auntie May wore but old-fashioned boots that laced, crisscross all the way up to the knees. Miss Jones chose to appear before us stripped of her protective leather covering. She marched up to her platform in shoes and stockings, rayon stockings, shiny and flesh pink. She had kept her legs a secret, and now – It was as though she stood there naked. Our eyes were fixed on those legs. Legs? They were Mabel Lucie Atwell legs, pudgy and straight all the way down to where they lapped over her new patent leather shoes. Pink sausages, fine on Mabel Lucie Atwell children, but for a headmistress . . . we gave our verdict and looked away from the poor shamed limbs. Miss Jones wore boots next day. Her legs would not escape again and it was for the best.

Friends made at school were kept for school hours, they didn't meet old street friends with whom I spent out-of-school time. However, there were birthday parties. Street friends had only teas, but birthday parties carried a seal of popularity and my increasing vanity kept me on edge until I received an invitation, in spite of not actually enjoying the party itself. Mum joined in like anything, for party-going, especially to the houses at the top of the hill, opened your eyes, she said. She didn't understand about Violet Buckling.

Violet Buckling had asked me to her birthday party. She was pretty and fat. Not so fat that she had earned a place in school by way of the fame of her fatness; maybe she was merely plump. Girls pulled her hair, pinched her creamy cheeks, and she went home with her pretty frock as clean as it had been when she came to school in the morning. She didn't mind any of this, being innocent about things. Nobody took much notice of her except to pinch and pull bits of her, and this in an absent-minded way. Yet Violet wished to be liked. She wouldn't be choosy, and liked everyone just in case. The thing which made me uncomfortable for her was that she never was chosen.

By the time Violet came into view we had started to play team games as a proper lesson. Some girls already had a reputation for skill in games and were chosen immediately by the captains of the two teams. Others, like me, relied on the claims of friendship to be rescued from the huddle of waiting girls. The perils of waiting to be summoned were real; at any time I knew that I might stand cold among the unselected few, horribly conspicuous, derided, unloved. The power of those healthy, gamy team leaders was appalling. Would they recall that I had a habit of dropping the bean bag in relays, that I started to run too soon, that I went off into an uncontrollable dream in the middle of a ball game? As Uncle George said all the time, 'It isn't what you know, it's who you know.'

Uncle George was a wise old man, and I had friends in the team who chose me before I was disgraced.

'If I was standing like Violet Buckling, waiting – I'd die,' I whispered to the girl next in the team, which was now, and heartily, my team. 'It's her own fault,' she whispered back and danced up and down in a frenzy to begin, and I danced up and down too looking down my nose like the others at smiling Violet, who was being forced by the teacher on to the other team captain. Of course it was Violet Buckling's fault, it must be. Oh, come on, let's start! We were all jolly games girls, no nonsense about us once we lined up in our parallel teams.

Did Violet apprehend my reluctant pity? There was no way of telling, for she maintained a smiling blandness whenever I looked in her direction; at any rate she invited me to tea. As I hunted for a way out she told me that it was her birthday. More of a party really. As birthdays were sacrosanct, to refuse would be difficult and besides, birthdays meant several guests so she couldn't claim me as a special friend. The attraction was, of course, her dog.

For ages I had asked for a dog. At first openly: 'Why can't we have a dog?' Then obliquely, in sly letters left around to Father Christmas mentioning the gap in our lives, or to Elsie in Canada asking out of a mild interest about the huskies which abounded in that country, being awfully reasonable about such large dogs, which would naturally be out of place in Inman Road, but – a smaller dog? Didn't she think that a smaller dog would look after us well? There was no response from either side of the Atlantic, although I left the letter around for examination. Violet had a dog.

I was the first to arrive at the tiled porch in Earlsfield Road and was relieved to glimpse through an open door a great pile of party food laid out on the dining table. Mrs Buckling hadn't quite finished setting the places, but the plates of sandwiches and cakes and jellies were banked ready. Her panicky welcome reassured me as to the numbers of guests expected. I wondered who they would be. It was strange that no one had mentioned the party, but then no one would brag about it. I hadn't.

'I've been cooking all morning.' Mrs Buckling drew me in to the front room. 'I've heard all about you. I feel we're friends already, dear.' Being fat suited Mrs Buckling, but she carried her head in the same begging slant as Violet, she would do anything I wanted. 'Sit yourself down, lovey. Tea is almost prepared, won't be a tick.'

This wasn't the way to do it. Birthday parties began with games, quiet games with giggles and pencils and paper, which were followed by rowdy rushing about, with someone, usually the birthday person, bursting into tears, and accusations of 'Cheat!' and 'It's not fair!' Didn't they know the routine, these Bucklings?

Violet and I sat ourselves down in the brown shade of the front room. A slow clock ticked on the mantelpiece.

'Where's your dog?'

And where are the other party guests?

'Here's Timmy,' faltered Violet, crouched beneath my scowl.

135

'We call our cat Timmy,' I said, and she brightened.

Timmy was a cat's name, all our cats were called Timmy, they were always black. One Timmy after the other they drank the cream I slipped them out of my compulsory ration, without a lick on my hand of gratitude; they grew sleekly out of kittenhood; laid one mouse at Mum's feet in payment; and escaped to grow wild among the coke piles in the laundry yard. From nowhere a replacement kitten would be set down by the fire to have butter put on its paws, to be trained by having its nose rubbed in its messes, to be praised for acceptance of houses rules – to be lost. A pride of Timmys prowled and howled in the coke piles, until the gloss of their cream-nourished coats dried to brown. A star shine of green eyes contemplated secrets out in the yard.

'Timmy isn't really a name for a dog,' I explained.

Still, there he was, and he didn't wrinkle his muzzle, or twitch an ear at his silly name. Just lay in his basket. Good dog. Violet was watching me closely, she tried to rouse him: 'Timmy – look who's come to see you,' in a voice I had heard used towards invalids. I hated it, hated the way I was feeling. I wanted to smack the pretty soppy girl. I felt the pang of cruelty as sharp as excitement, a poisoned apple came into my head. Apple. A word to curve itself around a picture of perfect redness, perfect roundness, and, as immediately, around wickedness. I forgot Violet as I looked upon the apple in my head.

'You aren't 'arf a scream – with your mouth open like that,' she said. That was better, much better to be cross than to feel so cruel and – sneaky. All the same, she made me mad, and my cheeks were burning.

'When are the rest coming?' I asked.

It was her turn for an open mouth. 'What others?'

'It's a party. Isn't it?'

'Oh, you're the only one.'

136

There was the dog, though.

Violet tried to tug him out of the basket. His broad back heaved, and sank. She patted him and his nose wrinkled.

'You pat him too,' she said.

I put out a hand, and as I did the dog let off a mighty stink which made me put my hand back under my arm.

Violet thought it a joke; I had not seen her laugh so frankly before.

'He does that,' she said, 'he's awful. It'll go away soon and then you can touch him.'

Touch that sticky coat, that flat wide back? My stomach gave a lurch, it was going towards its inevitable reaction.

'I – don't feel well – '

Mrs Buckling must have been listening, I think, because she bustled into the room.

'What's the matter? Oh dear! You mustn't say that! You've all this tea to eat, and it's ready now.'

She held out her hand to pull me up. My face was shrivelling into green.

'Mind, Violet!' she shrieked. 'Keep clear!'

'Run!' to me. 'Out in the kitchen! Oh! Do mind the carpet!'

After I had thrown up I had quite a nice lie-down on a cold eiderdown with a pot beside the bed and I could hear the clatter of plates from the dining-room where Violet and her mother were tucking into the birthday tea.

I told no one at school about the visit and with a certain degree of dithering Violet attached herself to Eileen, who was better equipped to control a slave. All Violet required was a minimum of attention, and Eileen gave her that in return for regular tributes of sweets and adoration. Violet did more than this service. When it came to the choosing of the annual May Queen, Eileen

137

and I were favourites. We were the correct age and it was our class's turn to choose the girl to be crowned on Hayes Common on May morning. No girls in our class had long hair. Eileen and I stood together, equals in bobbed hair, in friendly rivalry. I thought she understood the rules as I did. I voted for her. She voted for Violet Buckling. Eileen won by a single vote. Mine. Violet was delighted that someone had voted for her.

'It was me,' Eileen whispered, and that was how I knew.

When Mum knew how I had cheated myself she was glad. 'Eileen's mother is able to dress her proper. She's got a draper's shop so she can get stuff cheap.'

And as I fumed, 'It wouldn't do for you, duck, you know how shy you are, standing up in front of everyone.'

'Not with a crown on my head, I wouldn't be.'

Chapter Fourteen

I HAD paid for my generosity in voting for Eileen and felt the lack of that May Queen's crown and the grace that would alight on me when I wore it. Then I looked to Dorothy Stanbury and her golden hair and saw that no such ceremony had touched her, that she remained as stubby and as spiteful as her plait. Something had happened to her all the same, for I listened when Mrs Stanbury lowered her voice in the greengrocer's when she talked to my mother.

'It's happened early to our Dot. Isn't it a shame when it does – one of the drawbacks in being a girl – there you are, though . . .' The two of them stroked the stems of early rhubarb, considering.

Daisy said, when I asked what had happened early to her sister, 'Oh, I suppose it's when she hurt herself, there's a pail of blood and cloths soaking under our sink.'

We were soon bored with Dorothy's accident, and with my lost crown. Anyway, I thought, Eileen would look silly with her bobbed hair among all those Rapunzel girls.

Birthday parties I learnt to take like sweets and in the end I chose the ones I enjoyed. Like Pearl's party. She lived in an enormous house near the Common, the garden was endless, and wild. The family possessed a wireless, a sign of affluence, and during the birthday tea a voice from it, in 'Children's Hour', told us to go into the garden, Pearl's garden, where we should find – well – surprises. Then the voice said, in a hearty shout, 'Happy Birthday, Pearl!' Under a fern I found a bar of chocolate. I loved Pearl, she was frail, too slight a girl for a wide-skirted mother and a ponderous tweedy father who indulged her enviably. She was blown like a leaf out of Earlsfield into the country to grow strong, and quite out of reach she wrote me pining letters which I did my best to meet. Until they stopped.

Dad's Conservative Christmas party was like medicine, tasted awful but did me good. Moreover it was an annual event, tagged on to Christmas itself. Really it was Mum's party, for she was one of the helpers and more laughter blew out of the kitchen than from the party hall itself. My dad had thought up an additional hurdle for me to jump: I was not given a ticket like the other children; instead I was to beg to be let in.

'Just you say to Mr Sibley at the door that you're Joe's daughter, he'll understand.'

I recognized Mr Sibley from past years and from similar messages delivered by me in whispered embarrassment, but he didn't remember me. Neither was it easy to whisper, as he was so tall. Folding himself down to my level as I shrank back, he said, 'Speak up, young lady. I'm a bit mutt and jeff.'

Pushing his ear towards my lips, he pointed to it and waited. It was not a moment for speaking, the ear was inescapable, it became as I stared a disembodied feature, I said nothing. He turned his head and mouthed, 'Speak up' as though it was me who was mutt and jeff, and twisting his ear even closer to my lips, waited once more for my message. Other children queued behind me; desperately I faced the sinuous gristly maze of bone and skin which led into Mr Sibley's brain and finally shouted, 'I'm Joe Chamberlain's daughter. I haven't got a ticket but I've got a place.'

The ear didn't flinch but Mr Sibley did and, unfolding himself, he gave me a push into the hall.

There children were arrayed at sheet-covered tables. I knew none of them, no friends of mine were allowed and we were ordered to make pals with one another, and to tuck in. No one did. We stared blankly across to the person opposite, until a scream, a ladylike scream from one of the hovering helpers, relaxed our party manners.

'You naughty boy! Fancy taking a cake before you've eaten a nice jam sandwich!'

In a panic, adjusting the paper hats we had been kitted with, we set ourselves to eat before it was too late.

Out of the corner of my eye I saw how the churning of jaws had brought Mum out of the kitchen door to find me and try to encourage me with nods and funny faces. She wasn't one of the ladies in smooth frocks who supervised the party food, she wore her best overall and had a jolly time washing up. To my distress she crept up behind me to murmur, 'Your dad's handing out later on.' She winked and was gone.

The party continued. It would continue through the performance of the marionettes, hideous creatures with large old orange faces with tiny cloth legs which jigged about on a stage like a mantelpiece. The heads were asking and asking whether we were having a good time. We shouted, 'Yes!' but it was never loud enough for those creatures until we had yelled 'Yes!' three times. One year I didn't shout and one of the heads said, 'There's a girl in the blue frock who isn't having a good time. Oh! Dearie me! What shall we do with her, boys and girls?'

And someone called out, 'Chuck her in the dustbin!'

I was the only girl in blue, and plain for all to see. After that I shouted as fervently as the rest.

It seemed that every entertainer was anxious to learn about our good time.

'Having a lovely time, kiddies?'

'Yes! Yes! Yes!' We had been rehearsed by the marionettes.

'That's the ticket! You lucky kiddies. Now, give the

ladies in the kitchen a cheer. Come on! One! Two! And *Ther-ree!*'

Mothers' faces clustered like paper flowers at the kitchen door; it was true, the Conservative ladies loved their kiddies to distraction. The high spot of the party was the conjuror, always. Children loved a conjuror. Ours couldn't stand long on the stage by himself, he demanded help from his audience.

'A boy – well – a girl, then. Come along boys, you're not going to let the girls show you up? Righty-ho – you, sonny.'

I watched from low down, screwing myself tight down behind others' backs lest the conjuror should discover me as one year he had. I was pulled out. He had to wrestle with me, though, for I was strong in my shyness and he got angry, the powder started to bubble on his nostrils and his lipstick was smeared as he tried to grin at the children. By this time I wasn't shy but as angry as the man.

He said, 'I can see that I'll have to tie this young lady up, I can see that or she'll run away, won't she?'

'Yes! Yes! Yes!'

He tied me to a large boy in braces, who waited as surly as me but tamed, and we were tied up while the conjuror played tricks with brilliant silk scarves. The boy stuck out his tongue at me so I put my thumb to my nose as best I could with roped fingers and everyone sniggered. By this time I was the entertainer, making faces behind the man's back, mimicking his fancy ways. I was beginning to enjoy myself when he turned and saw me, muttered something, and said, 'We'll have to forget the magic rope trick today.' The boy and I were shoved off the platform.

The year when I helped the conjuror was a year to stand out from the rest, all other parties ran to a pattern.

After the entertainment a Conservative made a speech, and then there were games – with prizes.

'Now then all you winners. Up on the stage with you!'

And there, every year, was my dad! Handing out! Dipping his hand into his princely pocket and handing out real money, it shone silver and chinked. The Club was redeemed at last by the prizes of money and not by suspect packages of trinkets which no one wanted, not as prizes. 'It's not your dad's money, you know,' Mum said, but I refused such heresy. Up there on the stage my dad appeared in his true colours – magnificent and awful.

'Give Mr Joe a big cheer, kiddies. Hip-Hip!'

Oh yes! We knew all about cheering by this time.

The windows of the hall were blue with night. The party came to an exuberant and thankful end as balloons were released from the netted ceiling and floated down in a glimmer of rainbows. Streamers were flung, balloons were popped and we were making friends, making our own games, having a good time at last.

'Where d'you live?'

'Inman.'

'Oh, Inman. Can you come and play?'

'Where d'you live?'

'Southfields.'

'Oh. Southfields. Well, see you.'

'Yeah. See you.'

Father Christmas, an afterthought, made an appearance, handing out his chocolate drops and oranges, and Mum waited outside.

'Goodbye. See you.' Knowing how final our farewell must be.

'Did you enjoy yourself, ducks?' Mum asked me as we hurried home.

'Wasn't it awful when the conjuror made me go up on the stage?'

'I was busy washing up. Not bossing at you all the time.'

By her smile I knew that she had seen me and my rude thumb and had heard them all laugh because I had made them laugh. A sort of success, but no prize.

The Conservative party was a treat, for me. Treats were the primroses along the path, and while the dream of the Morden house faded Mum held firm to her treats of going up to the West End with Auntie Annie. Before these events could be relished there had to be the preliminaries of temptation and conflict, and the signs of forthcoming extravagance. Old phrases were produced. What had been termed 'good money' now became 'only money'. The frock which 'would do for another year' now was shown to be 'all holes'. She needed an argument and my dad wouldn't allow one.

'Go on, treat yourself.'

It was too easy. So she argued against herself.

Naturally she had the advantage of Auntie Annie as a fellow-traveller, and the adventure began lightly, with little suggestion that anything more than talk would come out of it. There was no mistaking the sense of wonder that hung about Mum and Auntie, though; when I ran in from school they turned to me as if I was the astonishing one for arriving there, when the amazing sights were still in their eyes. Tea cups, half full of cold tea, were by the fender and their housework hands had touched velvet and silk and cambric that afternoon. I knew it, I had heard every word of it before. It was material they would have spoken about and Berwick market they would have planned, oh – one day – to go to. Not the ready-mades, not the big stores along Oxford Street, seeing that Annie was a trained dressmaker, seeing that you paid through the nose for the ready-mades. Besides – just to feel the stuff – and shivers would come as they weighed the imagined delights.

The next stage was to find a necessity for new clothes and it was such a shame that Elsie was in Canada and was no doubt buying ready-mades at that very moment. They might have bought her a nice length of . . . and the hunt for the perfect cloth for Elsie's frock was on. But they didn't waste too much time for they were allies, the two women by the fire, and sooner or later one of them would come up with the idea that the other had a duty to buy herself some kind of dress length. From that moment the blood was up, Auntie was calculating yardage with a tape measure, muttering dangerously, measuring her very talk by inches and yards. And what fierce colours they let fall: emerald, cerise, purple, magenta; and what names: chiffon, crepe de Chine, georgette, satin, barathea, rep, and – nun's veiling. The two sparrows softened their voices, their eyes were shining.

It was too much for them, there must be a pause for recollection, it was not too late. But recollection soon persuaded them into a parade of past clothing.

'What about a nice cheery colour, Em? You looked a treat when you wore that rusty-coloured jacket. Quite lah-di-dah.'

Nothing was forgotten of former wardrobes, or of the ins and outs of alterations, or of the final dispersal to the rag-and-bone man.

'Know what? I found a piece of that jacket in the duster box. Makes a good duster, nice and soft.'

'Nothing goes to waste, sparrer.'

'Tell you what, sparrer, you did look just so in that pink, when was it? Three? No, four years ago. No – tell a lie – five years ago. Shell pink it was, Annie. You did look . . . ever so . . .'

Although they forgot I was there when the tape-measure talk raced its fastest, Mum came back to me to tell about Auntie Annie as a younger woman, and I liked to hear the tale, all over again. 'Your Auntie Annie, duck, was a lovely girl when I first met her.' Mum could say these things now and in front of Auntie, for she had saved them up until it was safe. Auntie Annie too would listen with great interest, smiling her agreement without a trace of vanity.

'When I first set eyes on her I said to myself, "She's a flower, all pink and white, like a rosebud."'

It was safe to tell of Auntie Annie's beauty, since it was all gone away. Wiping her eyes and her glasses, Mum would regard her friend gravely. I too wondered what had happened. Rosebud? All pink and white? Her skin was the colour of biscuits, it had the texture of a worn-out balloon, sinking into itself and into a hundred little puffs and crevices, and . . . my Auntie Annie . . . I put my nose to nuzzle her pliant cheek and sucked its looseness into a giant kiss so that she pushed me away.

''Ere, 'ere! Don't go kissing your young man like that! You'll have him all of a doo-dah!' Up she would jump and chase me screaming around the kitchen until Mum reminded her that she was a wife and mother and to go home to get her family's tea ready.

Auntie didn't grieve for lost beauty though Mum did, but only when we were alone. 'The most beautiful girl I ever clapped eyes on.'

Elsie would never be awarded so; for one thing her time was too close, for another Elsie was Mum's own daughter. Besides, Elsie's other qualities were more suspect – her charm, for instance. Charm is all very well, Mum said, but charm had precious little to do with niceness. It was character that told in the long run.

'Like Edie. A hard worker. Reliable. You know where you are with Edie. She's a good girl to her mother.' Worn old epithets, and as I grew older mine were, 'Sharp' and, 'She's got big ideas'.

146

'The most beautiful girl' label warmed the cockles of Auntie and Mum. It didn't occur to my mother that if Auntie hadn't been such a flower, Emma might have been awarded the crown. Her hair was luxuriant while Auntie's was as dusty brown as her skin. For a moment I was jealous on Mum's behalf, but of course she would have shrunk from the publicity. She could withstand Auntie's loveliness but her own, never. Also beauty, in order to qualify, had to be a passing thing, captured only in memory or in photograph. Well, we had Elsie tight in both.

After sufficient money and resolution had been generated, Mum and Auntie went up West. In the late afternoon they returned, barnacled by paper bags, all the swagger knocked out of them, dead beat, they were dying for a cup of tea, yes, they had had one in Joe Lyons and later they would show and later they would tell. Now it was duty that called.

By the time Auntie Annie slipped back to our house, a different mood had taken them. Two buccaneers told the tale. They hinted at adventures too daring for me to hear and instead made for me a West End of such glittering splendour that I believed every word of it, while knowing that tomorrow would come reaction and retreat.

During the following days and weeks the two of them wrestled to turn dreams of high fashion into reality; it had to be done and all of us, except Bill and my dad, were involved. It was slow torture for me, turning and turning while standing on the kitchen table, somewhere within a garment which stabbed pins with precision. The final trying-on was merely depressing. After all the splendid and romantic overflow of energy the results of it, the clothes, frocks, blouses, skirts, drooped from the hangers disconsolate, and gazing at them Mum and Auntie drooped too under the weight of the economies

147

which their extravagance had imposed. The programme was set for months to come and would end, as it always ended, in the turning. The turning involved much unpicking, begun in repentance and concluded in fretfulness.

Cloth and clothes, the temptation of remnants, the buying of the new paper patterns, Mab's patterns, where all the drawings were of the same pert girl, clothes as an incitement to wickedness, or old clothes as pledges of self-denial, clothes weren't far from Mum's thoughts or conversation. Even the paper patters were both inspiration and economy; she tore them up when she was done with them to use in the lavatory.

'Nice and soft,' she said, 'better than the *Telegraph*.'

If clothes were Mum's imperative, quite abruptly holidays were agreed to be mine, as a result of persistent poor health and also from the competition of other children's holidays as Mum's acquaintance widened to take in (though briefly) the more prosperous of my dad's Club families. Edie was more impressed than I was by my luck.

'It comes from being the youngest,' – she repeated an old complaint – 'when we were kids we never had a holiday. Never,' she gave me a push.

'It's not Ena's fault she's sickly,' Mum snapped, ignoring my sneer of distaste. I was to be alone with her for a week some time, somewhere, for Dad couldn't leave the laundry or the Club. Edie must look after Dad and Bill, it was good practice. Who was she intended to practise housekeeping for, I wondered? Elsie would be rich and have servants, Edie would have my mother always. All that was needed now were a few more urgent reasons to take a holiday, and of course we should go in the spring as then it would be cheaper in the seaside towns. Finally – 'A holiday will buck you up.'

But I was very well, in spite of the knack I had of

being sick at the least provocation, and in spite of the scar which worried other people more than me. I had survived all the diseases; also the cod-liver oil and malt which fur-coated my stomach, which glued tongue to teeth. 'Like eating slugs,' I moaned, trying to make myself vomit. Inside also was a curious swirl of tonics that would bring some colour to cheeks and, most gruesome of all, the scouring medicine. This was the weekly dose which all beloved children were allowed – Californian Syrup of Figs, occasionally interrupted by the pale and deceptively meek Senna pods. To scour was a verb, a verb was a doing word and wouldn't Mum love to have my insides out so that she might scour them gleaming white. As it was, the frequent bouts of sickness, which I took for granted, must have had a bright side for her.

'Cleaned you right out,' she'd say. 'Clean as a whistle.'

'You've gone downhill since Elsie left home,' she said when the spring came. So we took my insides and my anaemia to Brighton. The landlady served gravy glob-uled with fat, and fleas were waiting for us to get to bed. Mum and I sat up in matey horror pouncing on the tiny objects until neither of us was squeamish any longer but lusted for more blood. 'We don't 'arf see life, eh?' she winked at me across the bed. She found other lodgings and to rid us of the memories of the fleas and the gravy she booked for a Mystery Trip in a charabanc.

The trip was into the country, the driver said, the mystery was what we might find there and he didn't seem too hopeful. I was. This was the chance I had waited for. The country was the borders of the road which blurred alongside Uncle Ernie's car, it was also the single experience of the bluebell wood on Ranmore Common; the country featured in books but it was written as vaporous as the clouds and not half as startling as a sunset over Inman Road. In the winter the country shut down and gave itself an extended Sunday closing. Now we were going into it, to stop, to be there. And to find it out.

The charabanc stopped. 'One hour,' grumbled the driver.

'What we s'posed ter do fer an hour in this 'ole?' squawked an old woman.

'Walk about. Lots of pretty flowers to pick. Orders is orders. This is the stop for the mystery tour, it's just as bad for me, y'know. Never mind. Be a good girl and we'll stop at a caff on the way back.' And as he settled down in his front seat, put his feet up against the windscreen, 'You get off the blinkin' coach and leave me be.'

A few steps and the wood had opened its doors; running through it I was soon beyond the coach people and into a meadow where primroses mounded the banks and there were bluebells, not actual bluebells yet but blue-veined buds pressed against stems which prodded up through moist grass blades. Again the overwhelming of sight and smell and touch. (The floor of the wood was white with fallen cherry blossom.) It was not to be borne. 'Whatever are you crying for now?' asked my mother. 'Oh no! You're not feeling dickey after that coach ride?'

I hadn't the words to explain to her or, most of all, to myself. All I could have said was: 'It hurts – this.' And she would have shaken her head and called me a Dreamy Daniel and told me off for mooning around and no one would have blamed her.

'Pick a nice bunch, I know you want to, before the man blows his hooter, quick!'

Once we had a proper holiday in August. Auntie Hepsie and her two youngest children went with us because they had all been under the weather and I, of course, could be relied on to have been poorly too.

Auntie Annie joined in. We stayed in Littlehampton in rooms, which meant that the landlady cleaned when we were out and cooked the food which the mothers brought back from the shops in the morning.

'A nice woman.' Auntie Annie was quick to praise while Mum, always a fighter against her generous impulses, paused before she made up her mind. 'She'll stand no nonsense,' decided Auntie Hepsie, and this was taken as a compliment. After a day or so Mum's freedom from Inman exhilarated her and she became the most animated of the three, exchanging recipes and anecdotes with the landlady with a buoyant air that was embarrassing.

Perverse as usual, I refused to become her sunny daughter and nagged to go on the beach. Now! The landlady, by this time a trusted friend, assured her that Littlehampton was as safe as anything and we were let loose to run to the beach, and to stay near the jetty until they came with the sandwiches. We must make sand castles, that was what children did at the seaside. The wet sand was the best; we gradually moved down to the long levels near the sea and there a wind came down, a wind which didn't blow in Earlsfield or Southfields where my cousins lived. We didn't meet often, Nora and Vera and me, yet they were the nearest to me in age. Being on holiday like this together had seemed a marvellous idea, and so it now was, on the wet sands with the wind blowing. It was all elbows and shouting and giggling and turning like windmills. The air brushed our bare arms, it filled our mouths, it exploded in our ears. The mothers were waving madly, for they wanted us to make sand castles. We were at the seaside for that. As I trudged up the beach the wind hooked my red balloon from my hands and lifted it higher and higher until it lost its red and became a speck in the clouds.

Mothers met the sea in a different way, they walked

151

together on the sands at low tide, tight together, talking, always talking. We ran away from the talk, frantic to be out of earshot. Panting as we paused to assess the distance between them and us, we saw that they were stick people, even Auntie Hepsie; they plodded heads bent to the edges of the folding waves. It was not the way with us for we were giants under a giant sky and out of pity we couldn't see them so abandoned, creeping as they did on the brink of the earth. So we ran back to save the stick people. However, we would scare them before we served them, they were still obscured in their talking and were startled as we yelled and fell into the pools where they paddled.

'Does them good to run wild. They've got roses in their cheeks all right.'

We shivered in bathing costumes, navy cotton with sleeves and short legs; when they were wet the cotton flapped in the breeze. We wore rubber bathing caps. If the sea was too cold we bulged our frocks into our knickers and paddled until one of us fell right in, nothing was as good as getting soaked when wearing ordinary clothes, it was wetter and better than proper bathing. We called it bathing as no one could swim and the holiday made me determined to put this lack of skill to an end. Drying after the bathe was remarkable, rubbed in rough towels, huddled close to keep warm, we had not known such cherishing, there was a rivalry of cherishing. At last we were given a Wallsy or a Snofrute – so lavish were the mothers beside the sea.

As we children grew to fill the spaces by the sea, our mothers and our aunt sank down under them. Now and then they roused themselves, especially when the young men arrived on the sands and built the biggest sand castle of all. It was a pulpit, they produced tambourines and girls and shouted holiday-makers around the pulpit. After yelling about the Lord everyone must join in and forget their troubles. Our grown-ups had quite forgotten theirs already but they did their best to please the young men. They offered us, their children.

'You go on down to the beach,' they said. 'Stay somewhere near the Christians, might as well. We'll know where to find you.'

It was always a long time before they did find us; they were always merry and bright when they joined us.

'We're H-A-P-P-Y! We're H-A-P-P-Y! We know we are we're sure we are, we're H-A-P-P-Y.'

Some girls behind us sang, 'You're B-A-L-M-Y' – and so on. Perhaps J-E-S-U-S would do something about them. The effort put into the singing exhausted our grown-ups. They were slack in their deckchairs.

'Makes you think,' said Auntie Annie. 'This is more like it, eh?'

'A bit of life, that's what it is.' Auntie Hepsie wiped her upper lip.

Mum's voice spread like butter. 'All this sun and yet . . . those great white clouds . . . Annie – don't it remind you . . .?'

When Auntie Annie grunted in sleep I heard Mum say low down to herself, 'It's like the laundry yard, when they hang the washing out, when they can – in Inman Road, those big clouds.'

There was just time for us to enter the sand competition before we left Littlehampton, and because we were so practised at the art of grotto-making we were sure to win. For some unexamined reason a comic had to be displayed in or near the grotto; I was given *Tiger Tim* and arranged it in a frame of the thin bright green seaweed which looked like ribbons in a tangle, and decorated the whole with fragile pink shells. Then I sat by my grotto as we all did, awaiting judgement. I won a consolation prize, which was a stick of Sharp's toffee.

'Bad for the teeth,' Mum said. 'And the winner was helped by her father.'

Mum being so much on my side was nearly a prize. Our experience of grottoes hadn't counted. Of course in the street we had far more material to select for the construction: milk stones, fag cards, shrimp pots filled with daisies or privet leaves and snail shells banded like liquorice allsorts. Grottoes were one part of the sequence of summer events. For a day or two we sat beside our own patch on the pavement as patient as the beggars in Garratt Lane and were more inclined to show gratitude than the beggars were if pennies were thrown. Grottoes soon lost their attraction; just as no one ordered their making, no one told us when to sweep them away.

We came home from the seaside filled to the brim with fresh air and rowdy happy songs, and for a minute or so the Inman sky pressed hard down upon us. Edie shone.

'She's been a real good housewife,' said my dad. 'You're my little old woman, aren't you, Edie?'

A lump came to my throat. But – it was me – *I* was his little old woman. I blazed up at him, swallowed tears.

'Still, we've missed you, duck. So has young Rene, mopey she's been while you've been away, kept asking when you were coming home.'

Friends were loyal. Friends were better than relations – fathers.

Chapter Fifteen

Around my ninth year Dad looked out from Inman and made one grand gesture to the world outside. Again I was the excuse and it was my mind, not my cheeks, which were to be polished. He was a magician pulling silk handkerchiefs from empty sleeves when he spoke to our blank faces: 'Young Een doing all right at school. Elsie says we should show her the sights of London. After all, we are Londoners.'

It was a Sunday when he astonished us like that.

'We'll all go,' and Uncle Will pushed his family forward, for hadn't he got daughters and weren't they doing all right at school? It wouldn't do for one member of the family to push or be pushed ahead of the rest.

'Bother old school,' chipped in Auntie May. 'See, I told you, Flo, last week – in the cards – you're going to cross water.'

'You made it sound like the sea – abroad,' grumbled Auntie Florrie.

'Well, the Thames counts as water, don't it? You're too fussy.'

My dad stuck to his project; one night in the week he stayed at home to look up London in the encyclopaedia, and Mum had to be impressed by his resolution.

'We'll begin with Westminster Abbey, then we'll take note of the Houses of Parliament next door, then we'll nip along the . . .' (pause to check on the map of London) 'the Mall to pay our respects to Buckingham Palace. Then – '

'Whoa back,' interrupted my mother, 'what about food, where can we have our sandwiches?'

But my dad had an answer. Tracing his route on the map once more, he said triumphantly, 'In St James's Park, of course.'

After that we accepted that he knew his London, we were safe in his hands. He made all kinds of promises: the Tower of London, the Bloody Tower, the Crown Jewels.

'I don't know what's got into you, Joe,' Mum said.

'If there's time we'll fit in Madame Tussaud's.'

'If not next Sunday, we could go another time,' she said, but her belated enthusiasm had gone too far.

'Once is enough,' he said.

Younger ones were to be educated, for the adults it was a bit of a lark.

Following my dad's finger, I was excited. The names! In the Abbey – Geoffrey Chaucer was remembered, it was recorded in the book at school. Chaucer, Father of English Literature. The rest of the family wandered around the Abbey subdued and it wasn't a lark at all. I pulled Mum around Poets' Corner searching for Chaucer's memorial.

'We'll have to get a move on,' Mum urged. 'Your dad's thrown in St Paul's and you know Auntie Flo is wearing her new shoes. She would. Look! She's sitting down already! Sitting in the Abbey! What a neck she's got!' She shook my arm. 'You don't want to see old Chaucer. Anyway, there'll be another time.'

I did, and there wouldn't be. I knew all about another time. An old man in black was watching.

'Where is Chaucer?' I asked him. He beckoned me to follow and there indeed was the stone, a modest one for a Father of English literature.

'Have you read anything which Chaucer wrote?' he asked, bending down, though he wasn't much taller than me, as though he really wanted to hear what I had to say.

'No, not yet. I don't have a library ticket until I'm ten.' I felt that he, this small attentive man with his searching pale old eyes, would understand the injustice of such rules.

'I'm going to be a writer, you see, and I'm to be a poet too.'

'So you will be,' he said, 'and may I know your name so that I may recognize it when I see your books?'

'I'm Ena Chamberlain.'

He pulled a notebook from out of his black skirt and wrote my name – my name with 'Geoffrey Chaucer' beside it. 'I'm getting old and forgetful you see, my dear.'

'My dear'! People in books called one another 'my dear'. Not 'ducks'. Not 'Miss'. Not 'Ena-Dena-Valentine-Emily'.

We started to walk around the rest of the memorials together, the man pointing to some, ready to tell, and I was on air until Mum grabbed my arm. 'There you are. You bad girl! We've been looking all over!'

Her glares, though, were for the old man and I suddenly realized what she was thinking. From time to time she had warned me about strange men who lured innocent girls to wicked places, frequently abroad. She was not explicit regarding methods or destinations or reasons for the kidnapping and made, if she had known it, the business rather attractive. I had taken to it as to one of her stories but now, in London . . . Was my learned friend a kidnapper? At that moment another man in a long skirt came up to us, greeted my old man warmly, taking his arm. They paced up through the avenues of chairs, but not before my friend had turned to say, 'Goodbye, Ena Chamberlain. I shall look for you in the bookshops.'

'What a cheek you've got!' Mum said as she hurried me out through the great doors.

In one day we had seen everything in London, and that was it, it was a single and unrepeated exercise and Dad, along with the rest, returned to routine. Nevertheless he had given me a city; no father could have done more.

Next? We put in a thumb and pulled out – Mrs Collins's wedding. How she had kept the secret of her courting Rene and I had no idea. 'I'm bettering myself,' Mrs Collins told Mum.

'Bettering herself? The man is a widower with dozens of children. Bettering herself! Poor Rene!'

Before I could think 'poor me', supposing that Rene would move to the man's capacious home to be smothered by his dozens, I learnt that the new family were to live next door and that only three were coming, two of whom were getting married soon and would move elsewhere. The youngest girl was between Rene and me in age, I hoped in no other sense. Meanwhile I was invited to the wedding.

Tables were laid in the Collins's yard, the feast twinkled with the dot and dash of jellies and tinned fruit. It wouldn't rain. At night candles were lit and we held them in our hands and danced among the tables, lifting our arms high. They were very happy to be married, were Rene's mum and stepfather. And Rita, the new friend who came with the new father, was pleased. She was also sick and so was Rene.

Rene was never sick and because I was the regular invalid and because I detested being this, in spite of admitting the few benefits, I was comforted enormously by Rene's sickness. Instant sympathy demanded instant response and the next day, finding that she was still flattened into the bed, I opened my money box. There was a half-crown in it. I didn't stop to wonder where it came from; when treasure is discovered, don't question. Rene lay, yellow-skinned, in the room which she now shared, two to a bed with her new sister. She didn't like her, this Rita, which was nice for me but horrible for Rene. Perhaps if things got too bad Mum would say that she must live in our house and sometimes I asked if I really would enjoy that.

In the meantime the half-crown went shopping. With the Jacksons I went to the florist in Garratt Lane. For the first time drenched in cool flower smells I chose carnations, and cradled their long stems so that they wagged their blooms over my shoulder.

'What about sweets?' cadged Teddy Jackson. 'Sick people have sweets; I like raspberry drops.'

I bought a bag of drops for Rene and one to share with the Jacksons and because there was still money in my hand I bought a yellow paper book for myself, it was one of The Schoolgirl's Own Library books which other girls had begun to pass around at school.

'Rene will say Ta later on,' Mrs Collins said in bewilderment at my generosity. Exhausted by it myself, I left the Jacksons knobbly-cheeked with raspberry drops to go indoors to read my book.

Mum stood at the top of the stairs. 'Have you been to your money box?'

She was finding it hard to speak. 'Have you?'

She shook me. She didn't glare like that, not at me. 'Have-you-robbed-your-money-box?'

'There was a half-crown in it. It's my money box.' I was scared. Mum towered over me at the top of the stairs.

'Now,' she took a huge breath, 'just you listen! Listen! I was the one who put that half-crown in the box, just this morning. What-have-you-done-with-it?'

It was of no use to be defiant or to put on the injured look, or to sulk. She had taken all my defences from me, this fearful, awesome woman. For so long I had sinned in perfect peace, employing the knack of innocence, developing a spurious open style of manner to commit crimes more important than the spending of my own half-crown. Later I was righteously indignant, but at the epicentre of Mum's storm I could only cringe and suffer. It had to do with money. Which came the hard way. Which didn't grow on trees and – a pause – 'Let's see what you've got left.'

I told her everything, about the flowers for a sick friend. It wasn't worth lying.

'I . . . there's nothing in my pocket. I've spent it, all of it.' I tried to swallow.

'There's a red stain round your mouth, you bought sweets too.'

If she could only see, if I could tell . . . about the mouths of the Jacksons . . . I was saved from crying by her awful unfairness. And then, right on cue, from the next-door yard, Rene was shouting. 'Coming out? Ta for the flowers!'

Invalid Rene bounced up and down against the fence. She choked on the bunch of raspberry drops in her cheek and the red spit ran down her chin. I didn't look at Mum.

'What else did you buy? What's that in your hand?' She spoke very softly. 'Read it. Read it out loud.'

I read, 'Because she was a spendthrift.'

'Give it to me. Go to bed.' Every word an imperative.

I sat cross-legged on the bed. I had never been so angry, and by this time so justified in anger. Hours passed and still it was light in the street. Children were playing out there. My dad's footsteps came to the door, there was whispering, and then both parents came into the bedroom, they were quiet and repentant and formal and after a period of such talk we became friendly and then quite lively as Dad crawled under the bed and bounced the springs up and down so that I flew higher and higher. He hadn't had so much fun for years.

Rene's one and lightning illness had one other result. It seemed that her mother's marriage had upset Rene, that the girl Rita was a selfish telltale and that she, Rene, was anaemic like me. We were sent away together to Haslemere on a scheme got up to cheer the sick town children. We couldn't believe our luck! Together! And as it was September we should miss the first weeks of the new term.

Haslemere was green and golden in September. The grass sucked at our sandals there had been so much rain, but now the sun shone. We were given the Morgan children as friends to play with, they were let off school so took kindly to us and showed us how to cut turf and make houses out of the slabs. Then we sat inside them, right inside the damp root-and-earth smell. Trees were still a part of Earlsfield, in spite of the boys' destructions. Chestnut trees stood on the Common, they spread branches of sticky buds, they flapped palms of leaves, raised up candles of flowers, threw down conkers which were in no way adequate to supply the needs of the children of Earlsfield. Again, there were the may trees which we tried to climb although they were stunted and bristled. But here, on the downs outside Haslemere, there were great oak trees to climb. Climbing became an obsession. One old groaner claimed us in particular. We entered into the life of that tree, halfway up its branches we were leaves, acorns. I was a green man covered by leaves which were turning ginger and yellow, and rustling from perches above or below were the other children. It was a tree of children and I rode on an ancient bough and put my ear close down to it and breathed air which was about to change me, everything. It was beyond naming, and I slid down the trunk of the oak, fell into broken ivy and tried to hold on to the wonderful tree by sniffing and sniffing the bitter crushed ivy leaves. I was crying, I think, but when Rene and the Morgans

161

tumbled out of the tree I started to laugh so that they caught it and collapsed against one another without knowing why.

The Morgans had older cousins, even older than Rene. They took her away. This happened at school, though it had not happened to me, and while the business seemed painful for the girl left behind I had supposed that in some way it had been her own fault. Well, I hadn't given it much thought as it didn't concern me.

These older girls began by making fun of our turf houses. Then they told Rene about the rec and the fun you could have there. They winked at each other and at Rene when they mentioned this fun. They pronounced Rene's name to rhyme with bean, which I knew she didn't like, but she went to the rec with them just the same. She stopped at the bottom of the hill and called back.

'You all right?'

I wouldn't answer, watched them go out of the corner of my eye. The older girl had a pointed mouse face with a nose like a pin and a tiny mouth which nibbled.

'Come on then, kid. If you want to,' she yelled back at me.

I flung my knife on the turf and began to build the biggest turf house ever.

They kept Rene away for a week. Once or twice she and her new friends came back to the oak tree to look for me. Invisible above their heads I hung in the branches and listened to the mouse girl saying, 'Don't take on, she's OK. Our cousins are around, they're the same age, oh come on. She's only jealous.'

So that was what I was. Jealous. Jealous, an ache which didn't go away. I tried out the word after a bit on other people, on Edie for instance. Was it jealousy of Elsie which shook the life out of her? Perhaps . . . but the idea could turn the relationship between Rene and me upside down – Rene who was so serene and superior in the way of her beauty and her age and her poverty – perhaps Rene was jealous of the new friends I was making at school? There was no need, of course, for I kept them in their place outside Inman and would discard them at once if she said so. For she was one of the permanent loved ones, as secure in me as were Mum and Dad and all at Number 29. So I signed off my message to Rene as holiday postcards were signed, and refused to include Elsie in my meditations except as the sister in the photograph where she was – had to be – permanent. Rene wouldn't leave me, for Canada or for two stupid girls. I gritted my teeth and told her so, high up in the oak tree.

At the end of the week Rene said, 'Let's go up on the downs, eh?' She said, 'I've gone off that Joyce. Come up higher and sit on my branch. Look, a squirrel,' she said, but mildly and without much excitement. 'That Joyce. She's always on about things . . . you know . . .'

I pelted Rene with acorns until the branch rocked like a boat in high seas.

The last days in the country were as mellow and as content as the autumn itself. It was our last time together in close friendship and precious and held carefully by both of us. I think that we let go of one another, but gently, as good friends should. On returning to Inman, as brown and as bonny as anyone required, we did the same things together, Rene and me, but deliberately, and with a purpose as we had done, my cousins and aunties and Mum at Littlehampton on our final day there. One last look at the sea. One last dip in the water, one last walk along the shore. For old times' sake. As wistful as New Year's Eve.

Chapter Sixteen

U P and down and round and round; jump off the
roundabout or stay on. Choose. Grow up or remain
a child. Choose.

'Let's go up the Common,' said Rene. She seldom
took the initiative, so I went along.

'We've not been up there for ages, why not? D'you
remember the good fun we've had . . . ?'

I was made uncomfortable by Rene's reminiscence.

'D'you remember the way we used to go round the big
houses before Empire Day, asking if we could pick their
daisies?'

Remember? It was only a few months ago! Next year
no doubt we would ask again? But she had put the
picture into place, and I saw the two of us stepping on
the tiled paths towards great doors which were opened
after a long echoing time to caverns of hallways. I heard
small voices asking, 'Please, can we pick your daisies?',
recalling, too late, that we should have said 'may' instead
of 'can', as Elsie had taught me long since.

Daisy lawns at the top of Earlsfield were white as milk
for Empire Day and many of the rich people who lived
among them were glad to have them picked green. We
took them to school to celebrate the Empire. The word
had gone out: 'Gather daisies. The daisy is a symbol of
our greatness.'

Indeed it was. The golden centre of the flower was us
– Great Britain; the petals were the colonies, absolutely
inseparable and dependent on us. Miss Jones, as Empire
Day approached, brought one of her cracked and shiny
maps of the world into Assembly, forgot God for the

moment and tapped away with her pointer at the pink patches around the globe. She insisted on the Empire and in obedience we scalped the top lawns of Earlsfield. One year there was an additional reward when an old gentleman took us into his kitchen for a glass of lemonade and we moved on to other lawns with hope but received no other refreshment. Quiet roads made us walk slowly under the acacia trees and the leaf light reflected on Rene's pale face.

Empire Day was also notable because it was the one day in the school year when boys and girls were confronted with one another in the girls' playground. Registers had to be shouted in case any fool had decided to miss this jubilant day. Boys' names were shouted by surnames only. I heard 'Finbow' and the small answer – 'Sir' – and both Jacksons who shouted back, surprising me. After the name-calling we sang together in one boasting yell to God to bless the Prince of Wales; we stamped out the words of 'Men of Harlech' and the lament of 'Ye banks and braes o' Bonny Doon'. Finally we thundered that Britons never never never shall be slaves. Then a man in a dark suit got up and voted that we should all have a half-holiday. Then we went home.

But – 'Let's go up the Common,' Rene had said. On the jog up the road she started on her wretched memories again. 'D'you mind how you tried to drown Frankie Finbow?'

I had to grin; had to hold on to Rene, both of us twisting with laughter.

'Oh! Oh! His face!' Rene moaned. 'His face all dripping wet and weedy and . . . his mouth wide open! Oh! And yours! Busting with temper!'

That day the pond teemed with fish and frogspawn and children were busy with jam jars and nets. Frankie and I had lurched forward into the deeper water around the island in the middle. Here lay the fabled big fish. At the edge of the pond the Jacksons, Daisy and Rene were paddling but we took little notice of them, for we dipped and raised our piece of sacking, stumbling across the uneven bed of mud. Up . . . down; up . . . down – a smear of emerald weed, but no silver. Nothing. And again. Impatiently I yanked at my end of the sacking, telling Frankie to hurry up and move over nearer to the island.

'Look! There's one! A big 'un!'

He jerked his head. I pulled down on the sack, and Frankie went down with it. He was under, gone. He rose again close to the overhanging willow. And sank, this time with such a roundness of mouth and eye that a panic of hysteria threatened me. I told myself that three times were all a drowning man was allowed. Did Frankie understand this? Did his life flash before him at this very minute?

People screamed from a long way off. Later they patted me on the back for my prompt reaction, suggested that I had even risked my own life in plunging to pull him up; I had gone right under, and that was bravery indeed. In fact Frankie had dragged me down with him and it was my fury which had saved us. I trawled the shrimp to the round safe cement edge of the pond.

'You won't 'arf cop it! Your mum won't 'arf give you wot for!' That was our welcome, and – 'See what I caught.' Evie Jackson showed her tiddlers.

'I've got some frogspawn.'

'I've got weed.'

Frankie sobbed because of his mother, who would get him. I sobbed while I planned what to do next, whether to wring Frankie out in our house before taking him home to face his mother, a person we knew only by repute. Briefly I considered that I might be praised as the onlookers had praised me, but . . . away from the scene . . . grown-ups who knew me . . . and . . . with

Frankie shivering and steaming before them . . . there was no hope of praise. As it turned out, we were both punished in expected ways: me by the usual solitary confinement when I read from a store of books kept for such an event, under the bed, and Frankie by tortures unspecified but hinted at later when he had resumed his swanky ways.

There was a sequel as Rene, the patron of our younger selves, reminded me: 'Remember the island?

'We took our jam jars, didn't we?' she went on with the story. 'And waded out to the island.'

'Why didn't anyone see us?' I asked.

'Because it was early. We sneaked out before the others were in the street. Then we scrambled up the concrete blocks on the bank, and . . . there we were . . .'

'On the island. Go on.'

'What we should've done, to be proper, we should've separated, you go one way, me the other. To explore, d'y'see?'

I was full of admiration for her, but remembered that I had been afraid.

'But you were scared, so we stuck together.'

'Then we thought it was a boring island, nothing much after all, no caves, no valleys. Until – ' Rene hurried to tell –

'Look!' I shouted. 'Look!' I whispered. 'There was a heap of sticks, smoking hot.'

'We stopped – '

'And the bushes opened and a face peered out.'

'And it was all parcelled up in scarves and whiskers and his eyes were little orange scratches – '

'I don't know about that,' said Rene, 'but he grinned, the man did, and said –

'Morning, my duckies.' We spoke the key line in unison.

'He dribbled,' I added.

167

So much older as we remembered, we put hands to mouths as we had then.

It had been our experience, ours alone. Soon Rene would have forgotten it and the secret would be mine.

'It's nice, just you and me on the Common,' Rene said. She should not see my face and I turned away, shielding my eyes.

'Can you see the Keeper?' I asked.

We might make camps in the tattered bushes, we might pull and plait the reeds which grew only in one area, see who could squeeze in and out of the railings in the shortest time, play cricket on the bare patch of The Frying Pan, but to all these activities the Keeper supplied an essential edge. At the sight of his old figure bent over his prodding sharp pointed stick the cry went out, 'Keeper! Look art!' He didn't catch us, maybe he didn't try, but we fled from him and it was great.

Rene changed the cry to 'Boys! No. Don't look. Over there. See?' Two boys, apparently oblivious of our head-turning, put hands in pockets and surveyed the clouds. Rene seemed to know what to do and it wasn't as straightforward as with the Keeper. We mustn't make a quick dash from the boys for a start but must stalk around the trees where the boys deliberated. It was confusing, almost as though we were hunting, but did they know it, those absent-minded boys? One boy shoved his friend, jerked his head towards us.

Rene took up the challenge at once. 'Come on! Oh do come on! They're after us! Run!'

Thank goodness for that. From this point it was easy, just run. And to my surprise I could run faster than Rene, who wasn't trying, she was hanging about. Now she was taking off her shoe, shaking a stone out of it and the taller boy had caught her, he was standing nearby, kicking at the grass. I saw her grinning, talking, and she looked over to me and called out to wait.

'Wasn't it awful?' she panted after me. 'Why didn't you wait? They caught me because of that stone in my plimsoll. Cheek! That one said was we coming up later on.'

The Common had changed for Rene, but not for Daisy and me. All my friends collected on the Common; they collected fag cards or silver toffee papers or lucky clover leaves or wet-the-beds. We couldn't pick flowers at home, Daisy because her garden was forbidden and me because nothing grew in our yard except the privet.

Our earth was starved, and as thin as dust, though once for Grandma Thornley it had been rich; she had grown vines against the laundry wall; the nails which had supported them were still there, rusted into the mortar, and some had bits of calico attached. Once too for me, strictly for me, our yard had bloomed again. I had gone back into hospital, for nothing more than a minor exploration the doctor said, and when I came home, when I was told to look out from the kitchen window . . .

'She's overcome,' said my mother. 'Never mind.'

But I did. Mind. Minded with all my heart. I looked behind me at my parents, turned to look down at the yard.

'Don't you want a closer look?' my dad asked.

They had made a border around the dirt of lumps of clinker from the laundry furnace.

'It's a rockery,' explained Mum.

And – they had embroidered small plants throughout the rocks and across the middle of the yard, all kinds and colours and shapes of plants, pansies, rosy daisies, polyanthuses, lobelias, even one rose bush – well, scarcely a bush, more of a strand. They seemed to have been freshly planted, were pert and confident of survival.

'Better come in now,' said Mum, 'you've gone white. Time to lie down.'

169

Soon I was able to spend my time out there, to stare and touch and water relentlessly with the watering can, and (as the flowers dwindled and shrank from me) with my tears of frustration and remorse. Fathoms deep lay a source of nourishment which the roots of the privet had reached and where no other plant might penetrate. The bright flowers died, the yard became dirt; it held a few worms but it was only black sand. Dirt.

It took me longer than the sparrows to come to terms with our yard, for they made use of it simply as a dust bath; for food they relied on crumbs of bread and scraps from the street carts. Because I was used to sparrows, both as aunts and as birds, I concluded that all birds were sparrows, even though all sparrows were not birds. Other varieties were pictured in books or on Christmas cards, but I didn't have much faith in them. Until I was given a 'Birds shown to the children' book. It was a Golden Oriole which I decided to attract to our yard. This magnificent bird, with its carol of a name, enjoyed spiders and insects, the book stated, with fruit and berries in the autumn. Well, we had plenty of spiders and insects and I could manage apples and the brown mush of bananas with luck and Mum's blind eye. The oriole didn't arrive: sparrows increased.

Varieties of birds were not a feature of the Common but there were flowers to pick, all but the most extravagant of all, the may blossoms which shook the twisted branches with suds of creamy and pink blooms. Mayflowers must not be brought into a house; I did so and with screams of horror the branches were pushed out on to the windowsill. Bad luck! For a week we awaited it.

With Daisy I picked flowers for our mothers. One hot day we had made our usual hop over the paired lovers. The lovers kept strictly to their place, it was the first bit of the Common at the top of Earlsfield Road where the brick walls of gardens gave a small protection, from one side at any rate. Not that they were threatened, not by us, not by the Common Keeper. That lonely man was interested only in people who moved, in children who were too quick for him. We were careful not to jump on lovers and they kept eyes closed and arms and legs tidily together. They were sacrosanct.

Close by the lovers we found grasses, graceful with polished stems of tan and ruby and green. One by one we chose them, but as we walked home down Earlsfield Road the grasses were just bundles. Daisy began her old game of Tinker Tailor. She cheated, as she did in every skipping game, because she wanted to marry a sailor. For myself I took pot luck, preferring variety, and in any case I didn't want a husband, rich or poor, honest or scandalous.

'Sailor!' cried Daisy in triumph and the lady in front of us turned round, thus revealing the full glory of the flowers she held in her arms. Orange blossoms, roses, ferns, gladioli! Gosh!

She smiled but went on walking and talking to the man beside her. We walked on too, but without a word, walked sedately and as close as we could to the flowers which now waved over her shoulder.

Suddenly she stopped again, so suddenly that we almost fell into her. 'Would you like one of these flowers?'

It was like God or Miss Jones speaking to us out of school.

'Here you are.' She pulled out two roses and gave one into each trembling hand.

We let her go on down the road. Daisy and I looked at our bundles of grass, hesitated and then put them in an alleyway between the houses. Treading gracefully, we continued home with the roses nodding over our shoulders as lightly as in the lady's arms.

Chapter Seventeen

Elsie wrote once a month instead of once a week. She was at the end of a long tunnel and we were at the other; behind her shone a white Canadian sun, our end of the tunnel was lit by gas lamps and candles; she had the everlasting forests and I had Wandsworth Common and Earlsfield cemetery. I had Inman. Elsie would not come back and I didn't care. I would show her. I would show all of them.

But it was summer and summer didn't alter from one year to another. For Mum it began with the laburnum: 'The laburnum's out!'

For most of the year the laburnum, which hung black-twigged and sparse of leaves over our privet hedge, was ignored. But the shock of its burst of yellow always drove Mum to an explosion of spring-cleaning. Her sisters' spring-cleaning was already finished, in March or April as befitted the title, but only in this respect did Mum rebel. 'What's the use, I ask you, to clean before the streets are done? Tar all over the shop, and grit. I ask you.'

So, first the laburnum. Second, the house. Third – me. For until the house had been turned inside out, and whatever the weather, I wore winter clothes: gym slips, black stockings, thick shoes and a felt hat. As soon as the cleaning was finished, and whatever the temperature, I was stripped of winter, liberty bodice and all, and let loose into summer chill to 'go and play and keep out of my way, and – keep out of the tar, there's still puddles of it about but I can't wait no longer.' Air on my legs, nimble sandals on my feet, it was time to run and chase my friends, to whirl and be whirled until one or the other fell away, as unsteady as a drunk, but gasping and soon begging for more. 'Give us a twister! Go on! Give us a twister!'

It was no dancing goddess who opened up the summer for the street but the steamroller and the tar machine and the lorry which carried the gravel. The gravel arrived first. There was no warning, for Inman was the first of the roads to be tarred. The day before the operation men tipped piles of gravel along the gutters . . . and . . . went away. It was then our chance to scavenge the piles for the magic milk stones which possessed unspecified but undoubted powers. Next morning the tar, the black, oozing, voluptuous scented tar, and the swish and scrape of flung gravel and, last, the crunch, the elephant progress of the steamroller. It was a wonder to see the street change from patched grey to a golden beach. It was fascinating to tread the soft tarry stuff. Above all the smell. It filled lungs and homes, it hung above Inman for a week and by then we were into summer before the other streets like Wilna and Dingwall. For a while the sounds of scattered stones, the shouts of the road men, the impressive and unstoppable stroll of the steamroller and the overhanging haze of tar smell became so much a part of the environment that we took this to be permanent. We still walked pads of tar and stones indoors, we still acquired by mysterious processes tar on fingers and socks and inside pockets. And then one morning the men and the steamroller were gone, the road surface was smooth, its lava of black no longer oozed to be popped by our poking toes – not until the sun shone very hot, which it would do quite soon, for it was summer now.

Summer people were different, inhabited a country which was quite opposite where behaviour was informed by obscure rules, or by no rules at all. Beer, which had made the drinking women brisk and rowdy all winter, now transformed them into wandering and languid observers of our play.

Mum said, 'There they are, hanging about outside when they ought to be indoors, cooking their husbands' dinners. Poor fellas. Poor kiddies.' She had said, my mother who was steady against the persuasions of the seasons, 'Annie, I wouldn't stand for it the way those men knock the women about. Chronic. That's what I call it. Chronic.'

The women leant against front doors, or sat on steps or copings, minding how we played but not really watching us at all, and not saying much either, in spite of Mum's accusations. Like the cats they blinked in the sunlight and held up their heads to it. My mum could have done that, although I admitted our front door would have seemed odd with her sitting outside it. If the women were knocked about they must have forgotten; they were happy in the summer sun.

'Dun'arf take it out of yer, dunnit? Nice bit of sun though. Yer bones – yer feels it in yer bones.'

The school summer holiday was for ever, it made a hole in the year which was not to be repaired. Inside the hole we made a summer place. There were rules, of course there had to be rules, but we made them, that was the difference in our summer place. We gave concerts in back yards which were not like the concerts given in our winter kitchen to a durable audience. The back-yard concerts were prepared in advance, admission was by invitation, careful invitation, and there was a charge which was usually waived.

The summer also brought mad Jeannie back to the house where the Jacksons lived, and when we got used to her again we invited her to one of our concerts; this time it was in our yard.

'Mrs Jeannie isn't – you know – touched all the time,' Mum said. 'Now you be nice to her, poor soul, she won't hurt you.' As she spoke, her face was gentle. 'She's just a child,' she said to my dad. 'You seen her eyes, real deep blue? It's a bad time she has, locked up in the asylum.'

He said that there was more to Jeannie than blue eyes and in his opinion she shouldn't be allowed to hang around kids, and where was her husband and what was he doing about her? My dad's opinion was rarely given to Mum, he kept it for Sundays and for the subject of politics, so we had to take it seriously. I thought of the times when my dad clumped up the top to talk to the barber. Jeannie listened for the clap of his clogs, if just once he had turned his head in her direction he would have seen her blue eyes all right. She fixed them on him, every time he strode up the street; I think she believed in my dad more than anyone did, except me.

Jeannie too was a part of summer. When she came out to sit on the step we did our best to entertain her. We skipped – 'All in together, girls, this fine weather, girls – ' Or, the solitary skipper, 'Early in the morning, at eight o'clock, sure to hear the postman knock. How many letters? One and two and three and . . .' Sometimes Jeannie opened her lips in astonishment, sometimes she was serious, but she watched us always. We tried hard for her responses. 'Jelly on a plate. Jelly on a plate. Wibble, wobble, wibble, wobble, jelly on a plate.' No? Well. How about the bumps? Rene bumped as high as a mountain. Boys couldn't skip. It was the girls in the street who were dapper with the snap and slap of feet and rope, unsmiling girls and neat.

When we tried to speak to Jeannie we used loud voices, like the women used to her in the house where she lived, like – 'There you are then.' Or – 'Nice to be home eh? Jeannie?'

There was no answer; we didn't expect one. She inclined her head as if she were a queen. We stepped back when she stood up from the step, a bit afraid. Not that she was so tall, it wasn't that. But . . . she seemed so long . . . long and loose inside her frock, it was the same one all the time I think, it draped itself around her. She was as thin as grass. Sometimes she put on a veil, right over her face. 'It's a curtain,' Mum said, but I thought her beautiful.

At first when Jeannie came out of the loony bin we were careful of her; the Jacksons who lived in the same house as her even began by holding their breaths when they met her, as we all did when we passed the work-house or Wandsworth Prison or when an ambulance or funeral carriage passed us. But we soon got used to her. She was our summer visitor. It was nice to have her with us, she sat on the step or on the coping between the houses, stroking her bent head, rocking slowly to the songs she sang only to herself. Other people seemed to be caught up with one another, but Jeannie was quite absent from everyone. When she did look up she smiled as thoughtfully as though she smiled at her own reflection in a looking-glass, and her neck displayed a scar, a piece of cobbled sewing across her long throat. I remembered how Auntie Florrie had warned me to be grateful for my tidy scar. Jeannie's husband had cut her throat. That was Rene's story. The Jacksons said Jeannie had done it herself. Either way, no one had bothered to stitch it together properly.

It was time for us to give a concert in my back yard. I gave Jeannie a ticket, no charge, and she seemed pleased and granted me her small queenly nod. We handed her lemonade made from sherbet, and she took the best chair. However, we soon realized we shouldn't have invited her for she paid no attention, sat with her hands linked around her knees, her skirts right up high – too high – and started to rock backwards and forwards, singing to her Lord Jesus. All this put Maurice Jackson off his words. He had to be jogged into his words at the best of times.

'Mummy, Mummy, can I go out to play?' piped Evie Jackson in approved posh accents.

'Now you, Maurice. You say – yes – you're Mummy – yes – you are! It doesn't matter it you're a boy. We can't help it. You've got curly hair – you say: "No". Then you, Evie – you have to cry. You're fed up, see?'

'Now I come in,' said Rene. 'I'm a burglar.'

And Rene, who could make the best deep voice, stamped to the front of the stage. She was getting a bit too old for concerts, but she didn't mind because she called them a bit of a lark.

What happened next was a kind of success – well, it certainly made a buzz which brought my mum downstairs to see. Jeannie jumped up – when I say jumped I mean jumped high, too high, she knocked all the little children around her to the ground. In the middle of the tumble of legs and arms she was swearing. It was tremendous, her swearing: clots of swear words rolled out of her, too loud and muffled to remember. She pushed past my mother and ran through our house and out into the street.

The next day she was sent back to the loony bin and Mrs Jackson, who never came to our door, felt obliged to let Mum know the details, seeing that she, Mrs Jackson, lived in the same house as poor Jeannie.

'You should've heard them at it,' whispered Mrs Jackson, 'all night. Swearing? I'll tell you, Mrs Chamberlain, they were swearing chronic. My children, I put cotton wool in their ear 'oles.' Her voice had dropped so low that it hurt to catch the words. 'The bread knife again – yes – yes – shocking. Mind, old Beat was up to Jeannie's tricks.'

Old Beat, who lived in one room next to Jeannie and her husband, was enormous, and as leathery-skinned as a rhinoceros. Her hair, which was kept tight in permanent iron curlers like metal grubs, added to her superhuman appearance. No one had seen her hair emerge from those curlers, and this added to her mystery.

'She might show her curls to the King and Queen,' suggested Auntie Annie. And she was one of the jug-and-bottle women, the only one at our end of Inman. They said she was never short of the spondulicks for a glass of stout.

When the men came to collect Jeannie, Rene and I gave her some of Granny Warren's marigolds. She trembled when I put them into her hands and dropped them. Lord Jesus hadn't helped her much, for all her singing and gazing up to the sky. Mum said not to keep asking about the loony bin, it was just the ticket for some, very clean anyway. Apart from this I had no clue to the nature of the loony bin, so I made a picture of it as a great locked bird cage hung curiously in the sky. Mad Jeannie was taken and this time she didn't return.

Summer or winter, Saturday afternoons the laundry was empty, all the women had gone home, the packers in the packing room got rid of their last customers and Uncle George and my dad were out in the van doing last deliveries. The laundry was ours, my friends' and mine. The Archway, where the van was kept, had high wooden doors with a small door inset. We closed both against enemies and played first there in the Archway where balls might be thrown high and hard, the only hazard being the vats of starch. The starch forced some degree of skill-learning on us because of the disgusting business of retrieving balls which plopped into the vats.

Rene and Frankie gloated in the search in the slimy depths, they plunged hands, arms, shoulders deep into them, clenching fists and screwing up their faces, calling out 'Yuk! Tapioca!' Some balls were lost for ever.

Ball games didn't last long, there was a laundry to play

in. We accepted the warning of my mother and father: 'Don'ts'. The don'ts of everyday living were the fences and alleyways of our child country, marking routes to avoid, pointing out directions to interesting forbidden things. 'Don't . . . touch the mangles . . . go near the colanders . . . leave the irons alone.' Tempting and indifferent Mum was all of a piece with the parents in *Struwelpeter*; she expected·disaster with the same kind of tolerance as the Mama of Harriet who played with matches or the mother of the silly boy who sucked his thumb.

'Ah!' said Mama, 'I knew he'd come to naughty little Suck-a-thumb.'

No one as fearful as a long-legged Scissor Man awaited us in the empty laundry, but we lived in hopes. We hid in the vast drums of colanders, turned the wheels of mangles, ironed one another with cold irons, and faced the real challenge of the drying room. The drying room had no window, one door at the back of the furnace and day and night, weekday and weekend it was hung with lines of washing. This was, naturally, the place above all others in which to hide, it was a test, we knew that for a fact. It wasn't so awful if two people were hidden there, although if time went on and no 'It' came to find you the breathing of that other friend became the breathing of an enemy, the stir of the hanging shirts betrayed the passage of a stealthy and hostile approach. We practised being brave though, even if it curled toes in fear, and held tight to bravery even if the clothes began to move close. Once the person hiding there with me was found and I was not. Footsteps died away and I was alone, deserted, hunched among the embracing shirt sleeves and too frightened to unfold from them.

Altogether there were far too many things to be afraid of. Especially was I afraid of heights. If I felt the rush of air, saw the ground lifting to meet me, heard the crack of bones, mine, touched the hot explosion of blood, mine – why then should I not be afraid? Frankie Finbow wasn't afraid of heights, but even he was scared of the drying room.

For a long time I told them that the loft above the ironing room was locked up and anyway there were only a lot of old . . . things in it. One afternoon, however, the Jacksons pushed hard at the door, and as it opened in a creaky way, and slowly, they all went up the stairs before I could stop them. They came down pretty quickly.

'There's nothing up there,' Frankie said, pulling his lips down in the comic way he had.

'I told you.'

It was my loft. During the week it was fine to lie up there on the floorboards, to look down below through the gaps in the boards where the pipes were channelled to supply gas for light and for irons. The women were too lively with chat and work to look up at my eyes peering down, or to care if they saw them. I could see them in a curious overhead perspective, the way birds saw us, perhaps the way God saw us. It was an unnerving suggestion. I listened and heard everything – heard, that is, as you listen to music, not following each note but going along with the sounds, not fussy about them at all. Sometimes the women did provide music, sang the songs of Sunday evenings, and up in the loft I sang with them but they didn't hear. Sometimes they quarrelled, sometimes they had a good fight, enough to make one of them run down to the laundry machine room to fetch Mr Joe, quick. Then my dad's hairy and bald head appeared beneath me and the women gathered close about him. They spoke, didn't shout to him; they turned their faces up to him, the flush of colour was that of pleasure, not anger; very soon they smiled. I saw them. It was all made plain to me, the blessing he gave them. After he had gone downstairs they sighed and got on with the work and the clothes on the ironing tables smoothed the women's minds until they were quite flat and quite blank.

Only once did I go up into the loft by myself on a Saturday afternoon. As before, I stared down through the gaps. The silence and emptiness of that ironing room rose up to meet me. Tables and tables of resting irons, still tethered by the gas pipes; they were grey irons which I had previously seen as dull red weapons for the women to attack with bash and spit. Up there in a silence I was dangerously close to dreams; at any moment the room below might stir, the irons begin to slide of their own volition across the borders of day reality. When a floorboard snapped I jumped out of my skin. We practised at being afraid, or was it at being brave, but whatever it was I was up in the loft only once when no women worked below.

That episode marked a silent test of strength from which I had retreated but there were other challenges, and public ones. One was the water-tank ledge, a temptation to those who relished balancing high, a torture for me. The ultimate provocation was watching my dad up there on top of the wall, and my mother saying to our open mouths, 'Don't let me catch any of you getting ideas.'

The tank covered the flat roof of an outbuilding of the laundry; this formed one wall of our back yard, on this wall Grandma Thornley had grown her vines. Inside the building was the furnace which got my dad up at five o'clock every morning and next door to the furnace was the drying room. Up the wall was an iron ladder. The dare was to climb the ladder, to walk round the ledge, right round and back again. Frankie could do it, skipped up aloft, balanced the length of the ledge, started to play silly devils until one of us shouted, 'Stop mucking about, swankpot!' Rene did it, so did the Jacksons, though carefully. It was my turn. It wasn't my turn. They had all been picked by the game. OK. 'Eenie, meanie, mynie, mo – and *out* you go with a jolly good push – Eenie, meanie, mynie, mo – a-and – *out* you go with a – and it is you – it's *you*!'

Yes . . . Of course it was me.

'Last time I did go up.'

'You only went to the top of the ladder, you didn't even stand up on the wall!'

At any moment Frankie was to call out, 'Cowardy-custard, cowardy-cowardy-custard, stole her mother's mustard!' and no matter that we were all loving friends, pretty soon the others would join in. Frankie had a lot to learn about pride, swaggering as he did about his fearlessness on the heights. I wasn't admitting to pride myself.

'It won't be so bad this time,' comforted Rene, with her arms around me.

Before I reached the top of the ladder my hands were slipping, my feet were huge as they stood on the narrow ledge, there was nothing but air to hold on to. Like bird noises from below came cries of, 'Go on.' 'You'll be OK.' From Frankie, 'Gor! D'yer get that? She almost fell then!' I was halfway round! I was all the way round, hands in front of me like a sleep-walker.

A scrambling of feet on the coke piles in the laundry yard and I was aware of them watching me, and now aware that we were joined in this ordeal.

'Stick yer arms out, they helps you to balance!' croaked Frankie.

I stopped, put my arms out to the side, wobbled. Nothing to grab! Nothing! Below me was our back yard. Suddenly every detail of the landscape was made terribly clear. Each blade of grass, each leaf of the golden privet, cries from the street behind the houses, where people lived remote and comfortable and indifferent lives.

Then, the window of our kitchen opened and Mum shook a duster.

'Don't!' I moaned. 'Don't shake it! Don't! You'll shake the air! You'll knock me off this ledge! I'll fall! I'll fall!'

And I was falling and falling and – down . . . and down . . .

Mum held the cloth out like a flag, she held her hand out like a policeman, she didn't believe what she saw. Then – she did. She opened her mouth to scream . . . then – she didn't. She vanished from the window, leaving me to fall.

So – that was that. There was nothing I could do now, for I was only sensation, and one sensation: fear. Instead of blood, fear scalded me right down to toes which tried to dig into the bricks of the wall, right along to outspread arms to fingertips which tried to clutch thin air. And finally to eyes which fear made blind. I wanted one thing, and that was to give in to the tug of the black dirt of our yard.

Piercing the blindness, my dad's voice said, 'Steady now. Hold my hand, I'm touching you. Put your hand behind you, slowly. Just hold my hand. Stead-y, stead-y.'

It said, the voice, 'Gently. Gently. That's a good girl. Let me turn you round, that's right . . . yes . . . yes . . . that's right, don't look down. Careful. Hold on to me. Put your feet where mine have been. That's my girl.' And I was. I was his girl. I did what he said. His girl. Yes.

Afterwards bed wasn't a punishment, but a blessing granted. They whispered in the room. 'I thought I should've – when I saw her up there like a ghost – Joe – if she'd fallen, Joe . . .'

Mum was crying, leaning against the strong man and weeping, and my dad said, 'There,' he said. 'There, there,' in a humble way that was new to me and to him.

He used another voice later when he visited the bedroom: 'Don't you ever climb up there again. Worrying your poor Mum. Promise?'

Just to see, I went once more to the bottom of the ladder and placed one foot on the rung, and . . . sweat, as instant as rain . . . I wiped my hands and promised – this time to myself.

Saturday afternoon in the laundry wasn't all fright and testing. For example, there was the packing room to play in. The packers, Miss Biggs and Miss Spinks, were the last to leave; consequently the packing room was the final playroom on a Saturday.

Miss Biggs made sure that she was the last to leave, we watched through the window as she perked her head from side to side checking the place for odd cottons or scraps of tissue paper. Really she hated to go home – she would have liked to stay in Number 31 Inman all the time, to manage the packing room and all the customers and Uncle George and even my dad by herself; she sometimes said as much to him: 'I feel at home here you know, Mr Joe.'

He called her Ethel though everyone else called her by her proper name, Miss Biggs. She had worked for Grandma Thornley in the great days when the Earlsfield Laundry washed the shirts of Winston Churchill. He wasn't good at paying up but what an honour, and that was the toffs for you. Mum shook her head indulgently and forgave Mr Churchill. Miss Biggs was awe-inspiring herself, it had to be admitted in spite of the fact that she and I met eye to eye. Brought down to my level by her legs, which were as bowed as Auntie Lizzie's best chair (but of course without the claws), given by those legs a sway which was hard not to imitate, Miss Biggs was not to be taken lightly Mum said – we were not on any account to stare at those legs. Nor to look at cripples or drunks or children with Chinese eyes or blind people (they didn't see you looking?) or the man with a ball of skin bulging over his collar tight and orange and about to burst, or ladies with a coat of powder on their faces, white powder and red lips. This was all right for actresses and for Queen Mary.

Mum had seen Queen Mary in Clapham Junction. 'Like enamel it was, the stuff on Queen Mary's face.'

It was daring of her to tell tales on Queen Mary, especially as I thought of her as a statue.

Earlsfield was filled with forbidden people and as a consequence I must consider once more my own luck in having straight eyes, straight legs and no orange bulges of skin about me. That is, I should thank Mum for arranging things and not nag her for legs that were as elegant as Rene's.

'You've got good sturdy legs. They'll carry you through life.'

A turned-up nose? That too would see me through. If I blamed her too often she remembered the dear little girl I had been until I called that child an idiot and wished Mum could get rid of her. She clung like a shadow and always would, I supposed.

Miss Spinks, tall, humble, wary of Miss Biggs, and bossy when Miss Biggs was asked to work at one of the other depots in Clapham or Battersea, went home to put her feet up. Miss Biggs went home to put her feet in a bowl of hot water. Heaven, she called it. When she had rocked out of sight up Wilna we took over the packing room.

The shelves round the walls were detachable and could be slotted into a variety of positions. We pushed one plank into its slit, sat on it and slotted another across our laps. We perched in rows like portraits in the cinema. 'Like flies,' Frankie said. 'Like pigeons in a loft,' Daisy said, but she had an uncle who kept racing pigeons. There was no question of panic so high against the wall because the shelf enclosed us. We didn't concern ourselves with our bizarre appearance unless my dad came into the room. Then we saw ourselves.

Once in position, what did we do? Mostly we just were. Rather perky, pleased with what it felt like, sometimes we went up and down the walls for ages, trying out fresh positions and heights, pinned to those walls and grinning. We got pencils and bits of shiny packing paper and made ourselves into a club. The point of this turned out to be more keeping people out than writing them in. It was important to have unchosen folk; with a bit of effort we could make them into enemies.

Chapter Eighteen

'WELL, anyway, I don't want to go up the Common,' Daisy said.

'The lovers'll be there, it's Saturday.'

'I never want to be a lover,' I said. 'Do you?'

'Nor me. No fear,' Rene agreed, but in the thinking manner which she had developed since we returned from Haslemere.

'Neither shall I be one.' Daisy hurried to the pact. 'I'm going to have six children and they shall all have long yellow hair.'

'Boys too, I s'pose.' Teddy Jackson made faces. 'Blimey, what sissies!' Teddy was getting too big to go about with us and if he didn't realize it we did and were preparing to get rid of him.

Someone said, 'Let's go up the cemetery.'

The cemetery lay between the railway line and Magdalen Road. It had begun at the top of the hill, where there was a grey chapel and a house, but it was working its way downhill towards the library. Already the graves had swallowed up the tennis courts and some of the allotments, and I hoped the dead would leave the library alone as I should be old enough at ten to join it.

The cemetery walk was inspired not by season or weather but by the sudden and mutual conclusion that the cemetery was above all others the one place to visit, and together, though once inside the iron gates we wandered in different directions. I made for the recent graves, of which there was a steady supply. I envied the dead their flowers – no simple bunches for them, but mounds of blossom, flowers twisted into wreaths, into crosses, into hearts, one in the shape of a beer mug, one as round as a football. But the petals soon turned limp and brown.

Rene walked higher up the broad lane to examine the sculptures. We drifted together eventually to watch her imitating the attitudes of stony angels and to admire, with discretion, the way Teddy could calculate ages of the people inscribed on the tombstones. Smiler should see him; in a flash he told how old the person buried beneath our feet had been when he was called, how much older he or she was than the partner who shared the space, which had arrived first . . . how long ago . . . there was no end to his tricks. We gave him credit – had to, as we couldn't argue with his arithmetic – and some of his ability rubbed off on us as we were, after all, a gang. Daisy, who intended to become an actress before she married a sailor and had six plaited children, read out in her actress voice the verses on the headstones. By her recitations we came to know innumerable methods of dying. Few in fact died. Many were gone to rest; others were taken (an alarming notion), some had gone to sleep or had passed away or were departed (jolly – like boarding a train). Daisy was given little scope by the older inscriptions which were mere lists of names, the relatives went deep down into the earth, as packed tight as the houses in Inman and all asleep in Jesus, all sadly missed, and one testimonial did for all.

We were surrounded by these tired angels in Earlsfield cemetery yet we weren't unnerved, only at times confused. We had lined up in the usual manner to observe the progress of one man's coffin from Inman. We had often witnessed this man as a rolling drunk, we had heard the rows booming from his home; people said his wife had turned on him and knocked him down and he had died from his fall. She had been, they said, a good sport and had given him a good funeral. As of course she should. We could vouch for the funeral, even by Inman standards it rated high and went on for several days and nights. ('Where does the money come from?' was my mother's inevitable comment.) Now we read the flowers on the man's grave. 'Love from all at number three'; 'Cheerio, old pal'; 'Sadly missed at The Feathers'. And one: 'Dad's gone to be a sunbeam shining in the sky. We'll look up and – ' The rest was a smudge of rain and ink. We looked at one another, hesitated, but took the jump of faith. The old drunkard was an angel now, like the rest of them.

One or two graves made proclamations of their import-ance simply by the grand length and breadth of their plots. These were as wide as double beds, with a spread of granite chippings to hold the important people down. There was something splendid about their indifference regarding messages of solace or assurance, there was no need in any case to warn God that they were coming His way. He would know, would take it for granted, as we should who stood by the graves. No conduct or attend-ance report was necessary, all that was required was a register of birth and death and a rather imposing and elevated cross for the humbler, the flowery graves to look up to. Sometimes the chippings grew stonecrop, that was all.

The climax of our cemetery walk was where my sister Winnie and Grandma and Mr Thornley were buried in a sandwich with Grandma's sister. At the end of their row was the statue of a girl who had died young – at sixteen, Teddy worked it out. The statue and the kerb of her grave were as white as wedding cake and the jars beneath her statue were always filled with fresh flowers. We didn't doubt that the statue was a portrait of the girl, in spite of its wings. Rene copied the statue – well, we all did when we played the game of 'Statues', but Rene was best at it. One white hand pointed to heaven, the other lay on her breast (breast was OK for statues). She kept herself to herself, for no other name was recorded on her headstone, and we approved, for there were too many family sandwiches in the cemetery.

Beyond the horror, a boulder of granite strung around by iron chains, was my sister's grave. It was ordinary, neat and boring though I was thankful that my friends gave no opinion. Grandma Thornley's place was predictably more adventurous. The inscription on the stone made it quite clear that she and her final husband and a sister were to remain there for ever, until the Last Trump anyway, but – Oh crikey! What an uproar there was underground! Talk about a shemozzle – as Uncle Will would have said. The headstone was tipped sideways, the kerb was cracked in two places, and out from this stone pillow fight burst the trunk of a rose bush whose branches bristled with blood-red thorns. Only once a year was the grave made quiet, and that was in June when rose petals filled the grave.

Sometimes Mum met me from school in the summertime. For a while she would sit on the bench near our family's part of the cemetery. 'At the weekend,' she said, 'there's such a racket up here, all those people running about with watering cans, the taps running, and all that chat. It puts me off. I like it, though, up here in the week. Some of those people at weekends . . . the graves aren't . . . there as gardens. And then, you keep meeting – well, you don't have much choice. No, I like it quiet. A bit of fresh air.'

At the end of the summer day Mum and I sat and listened to the quiet. She looked tired always but peaceful, and I wondered if it was because she was near her first child, who would have grown to be the best of all. Wimbledon Common was where she looked, across the roofs and chimneypots of Earlsfield, and staring so she forgot me. I slipped my hand into hers and claimed her and she nodded and smiled herself back together again.

'We'll take a gander at Grandma's grave, shall us?'

'Can I?' I asked her one June evening, reached out to a fat rosebud.

'Well . . . well, I – ' She glanced over her shoulder, then, with a flash of her glasses – 'Oh! Crumbs! Why ever not! Just one though, eh?'

I tugged at the rose and tore my hand and my frock, the thorns clawed before I could skip back. Blood dripped on the broken kerb. 'I'll have a good go at those stains,' Mum said. She seemed to be on my side for once.

The oldest part of the cemetery was where the willows grew; they draped their branches over humps of grassy graves where lost folk were buried. The humps were without stone monuments, there were no vases of flowers, no empty jam jars, no visitors busied themselves or shared bright mourning chats there. In the spring snowdrops appeared, or crocuses which slid downhill from the cosseted graves. It wasn't the place to go with more than one other, and not the place to go at all by myself. Death was serious in the old part.

Once I was there alone. Once I saw a ghost. Afterwards I told Rene and she said, 'You're making it up. Come on, it's late.' So we ran away from the ghost through the twilight of November and told one another as we ran that – wasn't it awful nearly being locked in the cemetery? And –

'You never ought've gone off like that. I'm older than you. You never ought've gone in among those old graves.' And as we got near home, Rene said, 'Fancy you thinking . . . you saw the trees moving, daft 'aporth.'

I was still pricking with what I had seen, but after I had told Rene I told no one.

The cemetery walk stopped when I was ten, we were

all old, Rene and Daisy had not passed the exam for the Grammar School and they were glad. They could remain at Swaffield and make tea for the teachers. A better life there than at the swankpot Grammar. Homework too – at the Grammar. Who wanted homework? Elsie had written letters to me as sharp as needles telling me to work hard and not to waste myself and to tell her what I was learning at school in my scholarship year.

Dear Elsie,

At school I'm learning to swim but they won't let me swim in Wandsworth Baths because of my scar. Instead I'm learning to knit but I do not want to. I have written a book about explorers who find gold in South America. Edie is sewing the pages together and if you say you want to read it she will hurry up and finish it. Have you read *Westward Ho!*? Have you read the Dimsy books? I have joined the library. It is a bit difficult to work it out but I go with a friend you don't know and we manage to get the books we want sometimes. Can you tell Mum that it is all right for me to swim wet as well as dry? I sent away for the free book about the Children's Encyclopaedia and a man came one night and asked to speak to Miss Chamberlain. Guess what! He meant me! He wanted me to buy the whole set. Mum was cross. Do you think they would be useful? If so will you let Mum know? I've given up hope of having a dog.

With much affection,
Yours truly,
Ena.

P.S. I am top in most lessons but not in arithmetic which is awful, but don't worry about arithmetic.

Mum says that she has written about our great fire. My dad was really brave. His hands were burnt to shreds but he doesn't complain or boast. I missed it all, being asleep in the next room. Just my luck.

P.S.S. Sometimes my friend is top.

Although I had faced the truth that I would never become a games captain I thought that to swim, in itself affording intense and voluptuous delight, might also bring the kind of social prestige which skill in games apparently carried. I thought of Elsie, who swam in Canadian lakes, I held my head underwater in the sink and counted to ten. Like the rest I brought a piece of brown paper to the lesson; with the rest I lay down on the paper in the hall, face down, legs and arms stretched, arms out to push, legs, frog legs to kick, and – one and – two – and *three*! Brown paper crackled and was pushed aside by the sweep of limbs; we scrabbled and panted and inhaled the smells of dirt and polish from the floorboards. We swam. Dry.

A promise had been made: 'Next week bring a bathing costume and a towel.'

I did. And was told to join a class of younger children and knit. 'While we are off to the Baths you can practise. Knitting isn't your forte.'

Sulking was. I sulked in the corner of the room and knitted bad temper into a dishcloth for my mother, who would not be as grateful as the teacher supposed. Finally I threw it into the wastepaper basket. Sulks and bad temper paid off. I was left alone to read.

When the swimmers returned, full of boast, sleek-headed and fragrant with bleach, they told of a man who had ordered them to grab the end of a long pole. Then, one by one, he flung them into the water. Astonished by the picture they painted, I asked, 'What happened next?'

'We swam,' they said. As simple as that.

At first I blamed my mother for preventing me from swimming, but it was really the legend of my scar, which had followed me throughout the school, which now returned to bring me down. Week after week the swimmers came back from a morning in the fabulous water world, everlastingly hearty, all of them. They were rewarded with linen buttons and tapes to sew on their costumes. (A button signified that three strokes had been swum – with both feet off the bottom; a tape represented the width of the Baths swum successfully, and – the final accolade – the red tape: the length of the pool.) They were threatened by the teacher saying, 'Now then, Miss, if you don't behave you won't go swimming next time. You'll have to stay behind.'

Like me.

However, sulking and obvious gloom weren't helping. So, by devious means and with good works paid for, I saved enough money to take Rene and me to the Wandsworth Baths in the holidays. Then I had to save more for blackmail money, as Rita had said she would tell. We chose our moment, got out of the house with towels and costumes and ran to Wandsworth along Garratt Lane. Rene had taken swimming in her stride; in fact she had scarcely mentioned it. She was like that about school; for her it was just a place to go, wasn't much to do with Rene Collins.

'I can swim a width,' she said. There was no button on her costume.

'Really? I can swim a length.' Rita was in one of her bored moods.

The Baths were what Mum would call an eye-opener. No one had given an idea of the unearthly howling which came to the changing rooms from the pool itself, neither did I anticipate the blue clarity of the water or the tiles under it which slid up and down in my eyes. Voices wailed and clashed against one another and there was no sand. I had expected sand.

Rita jumped in from the side. I shivered in the shame of a dry costume that was inevitably too big, allowing for growth, and was absolutely bereft of a tape or a button.

'Come on, babies!' shouted Rita, jumping like everyone else as high as dolphins did in pictures. Rene crept down the steps, I followed and Rita waited ready to pull us under. It was me who had got her to the Baths, my generosity. Rene and I glued ourselves tight and bobbed carefully, teeth chattering.

Rene opened her eyes wide in candour. 'I – can't swim. I can't swim. I never had no button.'

Oh, but we were friends! We hopped in circles, gasping, began to shriek like the others, and Rita splashed a width to show us and with her eyes on us, she struck out sideways for the deep end. I forgot the brown-paper swimming and held grimly to the bar, found the bliss of jumping terribly high, found that it was fun until our lips turned blue. Swimming was easy and I would soon do it. Elsie hadn't bothered to help and I should write and tell her so.

Mum's reaction was unforeseen, but on second thoughts was in character.

'Well, you've not caught a cold. Perhaps you can go again – if you behave. By the way, where did you get the money?'

Chapter Nineteen

I T would soon be time to unpick my dresses and for the hems to come tumbling down my legs, for in the wardrobe mirror I was growing higher and surely Mum and Auntie Annie would notice. I kept the other changes in me private, though Mum called me a Dreamy Daniel with a more cutting anxiety. 'Buck up!' she said. 'Look lively.' I was forever staring into the sky, so she confided to Auntie Annie, 'with that vacant look on her face'.

'It's only her growing up,' she said.

Auntie Annie agreed and so did I until the next time when the familiar became extraordinary. And then it would happen again, anything might start the changing inside, a voice, or a silence, or a colour, but it was the sky which absorbed me, the spreading, moving sky above the street.

At the same time, though without connection, my friends and I were preoccupied with heaven and hell. We inclined to hell to be truthful, as it assumed a more enticing appearance, but saved thought of heaven up as a dessert. Both heaven and hell had featured in the dramatic episode of our fire.

Mum's candle had started the fire; she had been reading while she waited for my dad to come home from the Club, and had fallen asleep. The breeze had stirred the curtains across the candle flame and in seconds the room was ablaze. Dad had run up the stairs to the bedroom and beaten out the flames with the first equipment he could find – his own hands. 'Bare hands,' Mum told people. She was so much a mixture of pride at such a husband and horror at the loss of her curtains and

196

dressing-table that it was comical to see her struggling to make out which was the most important thing. At any rate the night voices stopped their quarrelling, so she must have made up her mind. The waste of it was that she hadn't woken me. I had to work out the whole scene in my mind and I guessed that I managed not too badly considering all I had to go on was Mum's description ('Your dad charged like a bull at the flames') and the sight of the charred flakes of the furniture and the sick smell of the curtain rags. And my dad's orange and glistening hands, of course.

Edie and I worked the whole story over. She had begun to take me out on the bus or the tram to new places: to Streatham Common or to Tooting Bec, where a man had been found hanging on a tree, or as far as Clapham Common, where there were two ponds, one as neat as a nursery rhyme with a round island in the middle of it. You could trace a child's story on to that pond, perfectly a circle, stone-edged, and – lots of ands – in the middle a round island, and on the island a small and tall tree, and on the tree a branch and on the branch a bird and . . .

Also there were paddle boats drawn up in a circle around the island to be hired out at weekends. She paid for me to work one on a Saturday when she had been given an unexpected half-day; Edie didn't care for water so I sat and pushed the boat around on my own. It was odd how far off the shore was when seen from the surface of the pond. Edie sat on the green iron seat and watched everything. Beside her sat a woman with a baby in a pram, she waved now and again to a boy in one of the paddle boats. Then Edie waved at me. She looked like a mother too from my distance. She looked carefree and happy.

Because she and I went over the story of the fire, inventing some better episodes and giving me a chance to take part in the adventure, I learnt how clever Edie was at story-telling.

'One day I'll take you to Wimbledon Common,' she said, 'and what if one day . . . we two hop on a bus to London. On the top of the bus. You see all kinds of things from the top of a bus.' She glanced at me as we walked across the mown grass of Clapham, excited but cautious.

'Don't tell, but I did that once, went on top of a bus all round the West End and changed buses and off again to Aldgate and Whitechapel.'

'Whitechapel!'

Pleased with the effect of her news, she spoilt herself. 'Messy place, Whitechapel, smelt of greens. And the women. What get-ups! Talk about loud! You've not set eyes on loud clothes till you've been down Whitechapel.'

The stories she told me made me almost willing to be her friend, almost got rid of the good reliable steady daughter whom Mum had presented for all my life. But when we got home the tales she told were lies, silly embarrassing lies.

'This man, Mum, he came out of the trees and winked at me. I know – cheeky cat! Said he liked the look of me and how about the pictures Saturday.'

'What did you say?'

Did she really believe Edie? When I stood there scowling?

'Well . . . I didn't speak to him, of course. Just gave him a look. You know.'

Elsie was the one to give a look, she was famous for it. Not Edie. Our friendship wasn't reliable or steady but it never quite went out.

But real life was spent out in the street with friends, loved friends, though they and I would have collapsed in scornful giggles at the mention of love. What brought the fear of hell and the Devil and heaven and God so

198

close to all of us when I was ten years old? Sunday School for years had vague connections with a vague goodness; school Assembly was straining hymns through the throat and the smells of wooden floors and the backs of taller girls who blocked the compulsory view of Miss Jones on her perch. But I at any rate had no illusions about Black Devil and White God, books had instructed me and as I was frequently at home being poorly the one benefit from Mum's care was that I had had more time than most to read – indeed, reading at these times was an occasion for praise. 'She's no trouble,' Mum said. 'Give her a book and she's lost for hours.'

Because the Chamberlains were Conservatives I was to go to the Church of England Sunday School and because we did things together my friends went there too, just to try it. It was boring. As we were there simply because families wanted their little bit of peace and weren't fussy about how they got it we decided to try out other places which might point the road to ultimate goodness. Indeed, we did have a strong leaning towards salvation and the place which advertised it most urgently was the Anchor Mission in Garratt Lane.

The Mission's posters faced two pubs, they welcomed anyone to come inside – especially, we found, did they welcome the men and women who sprawled on the pavement outside the pubs, heads lolling against the green wall tiles which were trailed with spit and dog wet. But children were allowed too, the man at the door said that we might as well, and to hurry up, it was chilly with the door open and they were just about to begin, which was like the pictures, except for the bright cold light of the afternoon. As soon as we understood what tune the gusty harmonium was aiming at we sang 'Onward Christian Soldiers' with much assurance, our voices rising above the mumbles of the older folk, and the minister shook his head at us. The routine was easy, no one knelt down, but the smell of beer and clothes was awful and Mum would have been furious if she had known. One old man in front of us turned round in the middle of a prayer and gave us each a piece of toffee out of a damp newspaper. He had no teeth, but smiled with his gums and, teeth or not, managed to suck his piece of toffee, making juices run from his lips while the minister made his announcements.

Without another hymn the man raced off on his sermon, which he introduced as an address. He made a great fuss about washing, about keeping ourselves clean as snow, and if it was directed at the people who steamed together in the growing warmth of the place it wasn't the kind of thing we had expected. We ducked our heads, whispering a plan for getting outside . . .

The minister's voice had stopped its nagging tone; he spoke softly about the Lamb, told us to wash in the blood of the Lamb. (Just let my dad hear that!) I began to feel sick, butcher's shops turned my insides and besides, this wasn't a real church – God wouldn't object if we . . . slid out.

But now the voice was loud, like a hand to hold us still. 'We have among us, my friends, a marvellous surprise. A new friend has come to speak to you.' (We looked at one another in alarm – was it one of us?)

But the friend stood and was beckoned to the front of the hall. He was a sort of carved man, bulky, without a neck, all in one piece with a blue and red face. He didn't hover like the minister but marched to the first row of chairs, stood like a wall, and glared at us. At *us*. We stopped whispering, sat up straight. Something was about to happen. We held our breath.

It didn't happen for a few minutes. The man chewed stuff around in his mouth, looked up at the roof, looked down at us again. *At us*. The old man in the next row slopped his toffee about and wiped his coat sleeve across his bristled chin. Our toffee was quite gone. I felt sick.

Then, at full tilt, the man began to speak from the front of the hall. He spoke very fast and in a growl and at first I couldn't make out a word of it. He stared straight at me and I stared back. I had to. Something of what he said made a kind of sense, but it was the way he spoke that made its mark. Afterwards the others said that the man was staring straight at them. I found that he was talking about himself, it was all about himself, it was amazing how interested he was in himself, but then he had lived an awful life, full of sin. Unfortunately he gave no details, only drunkenness and that he had treated his old mother badly and that now it was too late to do anything about her.

'She's passed over,' murmured Daisy.

He wiped his round nose and asked for water. He had given up the beer. The harmonium lady spilled the water in her pity for him. After that he rather went to pieces and didn't know how to stop his speech and he started all over again about his drunkenness and his shame. So the minister stepped forward to say, I supposed, a thank you. 'Shut yer gob. I ain't done yet!' the man snarled.

We had to sit still while he coughed and hawked but at last he got back on the track and said that since he had given up the booze and the old malarkey he was living a new life and was kind to old people and to little children and at that point his eyes moved away from mine, he faltered and seemed confused.

Taking advantage of the man's puzzled manner, the minister asked, 'What was it that made you give up the drink?'

Pause.

'Wasn't it . . . ? Wasn't it . . . ?'

'Yeh! Thssright!'

The joy on the man's face made us all light up. Exalted – that's how he was. The way the saved were meant to look. I had read about it.

"Im! S'right! Y'mean 'Im!' He thumped the minister in his joy, knocked him sideways.

'Jesus! Yeah! That's what done it! Bloody Jesus! Gor bless 'Im! Ta, mate!' The two men shook hands and put their arms round one another's shoulders as if they had run a race and both had come in first.

The harmonium panted and chairs scraped, but before we had finished gathering at the river some of the older people had shuffled to the back room behind the harmonium, from which came the clatter of tea cups. We followed. Rene said it wasn't worth having and where were the buns, as for me I didn't want to drink tea, there was altogether too much tea at our house. But – 'After all that jaw,' muttered Rene, 'I'm parched.' It was a chance, though, to get a closer look at the man who had been saved. He was hemmed in by a clutch of Mission ladies, but kept his end up by tipping back all the cups of tea they could pass him, biscuits also, two at a time he soaked them in his tea.

He didn't notice me, as I hung around trying to pluck up courage to ask him if it mattered that I didn't drink, that the fumes outside the pubs and inside our front room on Sunday mornings made me shiver. Also – and to make true confession – that I didn't sin; well, nothing to brag about. Could I then – working up to the question – could I, did he think – be saved in these circumstances? Could I – like him – go around in a cloud of light, could I be famous for my virtue? Or must I earn this? Come back later, when I was besmirched – as he had described his former state.

The women fed him, I could not get near, and it was a waste of time to ask him. I was incapable of the hatred which the man had directed at his wicked self, and with such gusto. Yes, it was hopeless for me to wait.

At the doors to the street the minister touched my head. 'And why is this young lady so downhearted? Didn't the service bring joy? Didn't a burden slip from your back?'

Far from relieving me, I thought, he and his friend had loaded me, as they loaded the sad old donkeys in Bible pictures. But as a last try I blurted, 'What do you do if – ?'

'To be saved? What do you do to be saved? Glory Hallelujah!' Waving the lady harmonium player over, he shouted, 'Gladys! D'you hear this? This little girl – this . . . little one – glory be – wants to be S-A-V-E-D!' As though it was a rude word.

Quite overcome by me, the minister hurriedly returned to the back room, which by now was almost as bare as the biscuit tin. The man who was saved was brushing crumbs from his scarf and scowling; the ladies turned from their washing-up and beamed. I was held fast and it was all getting beyond me. 'I only wanted – '

'Only? Only? I know what you only wanted, my dear child . . .' and he stuck his face into his chins, regarding me as did the ladies, with such amused affection that there could be no doubting their innocent joy, so why did I feel uneasy? Expressions on faces, words on lips, they struck the right note; in just this manner did the Good address the Young. I had read, I had seen the whole thing in book illustrations, except that the clothes we now wore were incorrect. So why did I try to pull myself free from the minister's too-possessive hand?

'No! I only wanted to ask the man with the red nose – not you. Not you! Can I – do I have to take up the drink . . . and the bad language and . . . ?' They stopped beaming at the sink. The minister let go. It was almost dark and my friends were gone from the street. The minister was in a state, he was puffing and cross and calling to the harmonium lady to sign this one up. The lady nodded to the minister, who nodded back. If this was a fearful story in a book, I had reached the page which I could not turn over.

I was marched along passages, back and back into a small room which was quite empty except for a fat spider and two wooden chairs; my chair wobbled when I sat on it. The lady closed her eyes at the minister, who nodded back. It was a code. Then the lady and I were alone.

She drew up her chair so that her glittering rayon knees touched my black woollen ones. 'I have to ask you questions. Your name?'

I told her my name.

'Address?'

I told her my address. There was nothing I wouldn't tell this person. She had me. The spider shifted and ran into a corner; the pen pitter-pattered across writing paper.

'Now, listen to me. You want to take the Lord Jesus into your heart?' Was that what I wanted? What I wanted . . . what I wanted . . . it came to me as suddenly as the salvation I had anticipated, and I was struck down. It was fame I was after, not goodness, not goodness at all unless it made me famous, splendid. I couldn't confess this to the pop-eyed interrogator in her den. She hadn't stayed behind to listen to this nonsense and she and Mum would have agreed on this one thing, if on no other. I was in this prison cell because of what Mum hated most. The Big Idea.

My eyes were open. They were also shining and the person opposite pressed her knees closer to grind against mine. 'The Lamb! The Lamb! You take Him into your heart?'

The capital letters were luminous between us.

'Yes. Yes. All right.'

Eye to eye we stuck it out. At last, satisfied, she sank back and released her knees.

'You've got to sign this little book. Can you read? This tells you that you are saved. And this is another book which tells you everything you must do from this day forward. Read it carefully and come back next week with the money. Oh yes – and when you get home you must tell your mother or someone that you are saved. That's important. Now, sign.'

It was black dark when I ran indoors but Mum wasn't prepared to be annoyed for long since all her sisters were downstairs having a chat with the men for a change. But – 'Why are you so late? Where have you been?'

On the way home I had made up my mind that salvation must wait a while; nevertheless my signature was in the book, and the person in the empty room had insisted . . .

'We – went to the Anchor Mission.'

There is a happy land. And that was far away, too far. I didn't need salvation, not yet anyway, not while I was happy here and pleased with myself.

Edie was buttering bread; she paused, her knife held aloft. Mum had turned from the stove.

'The Anchor – Why! That place! Oh Lor'!' The Mission was not much higher in her caste system than the pub.

'Did you sit near any of the – ugh! I'll have to go through you for – Well, I'm too busy just now. But . . . fleas . . . I've got all this – ' She dithered between the tea-time preparations and my potential fleas. 'Oh! What is it now?'

'Mum. Mum – I'm supposed to tell you.'

Edie had run out to the scullery to fill the kettle. In a panic before she could listen, I went close to Mum's ear: 'Mum, I've been saved.'

Desperately I whispered, willing her to understand,

205

or at least, not to laugh . . . or . . . tell. Like: 'Guess what young Een's been up to now? She's been saved. Would you ever – '

She said, 'Have you, ducks? Oh well, that's nice. Worth a penny in the plate, that is. Edie, cut the bread diagonal, Florrie likes it.'

I went to the bedroom, combed my hair, examined my reflection for signs of grace, found none, and wondered what my face would look like when I had really sinned.

Chapter Twenty

MISS Jones said, 'On our walk through life together –' and the phrase hooked itself into my mind. 'Our' and 'we' were nice round words but did not apply to Miss Jones and me. And – 'walk together' – immediately I was walking through a country, 'we' were walking through a country which was well known because I had invented it long ago. It was wide-open upland country, yet Inman Road ran alongside. 'We' included family and friends and the street, it was dear and nothing altered it. However, for me and only for me there was a way into another place, mine, where the clean skies were shadowed by trees, and where signs and silences of the very strangest kind took me into the depths of my domain. This was the second country. There was another but I had no right of entry, perhaps I never should have, and for most of the time I was quite content with our country, the one which belonged to me and everyone I loved.

Salvation had hovered but it didn't settle and soon the Anchor Mission became one more piece of Earlsfield to stay away from, like the Fever Hospital, like the Prison on the Common, like the Workhouse in Garratt Lane. Everyone avoided the Workhouse, no one went in, no one came out of the yellow-brick building; glancing slyly as we passed by on the opposite pavement we saw never a movement behind the dusty windows. Those windows were barred.

We knew, though, that in there were the people – hardly people of course – creatures as frail as skeleton leaves, who were wickedly poor, and peered out at us, and that within a certain radius their influence was exceedingly strong. Earlsfield was garrisoned with buildings like the Workhouse, ready to absorb the unmindful. The troops were in the streets, it was the enemy which was quartered indoors. You had to keep a sharp lookout, for example – The Central Hall in Southfields opened its smiling doors on Saturdays, hoping to entice us within on Sundays also. The Methodists of the Central Hall and the Missionaries of the Anchor Mission fought over the unwary speaking the same language, all sin and washing, whether in the River Jordan or in Blood, but I suppose the Methodists won. No one queued for the Mission's tea and biscuits, but the queues of children around the Central Hall on Saturday afternoons gathered that Hall into a python grip. It was named 'The Tuppenny Rush'. The grip came first and when the doors were finally opened and we raced inside to find the best seats – that was 'The Rush'. It was also one of the excitements of the afternoon. Into that bonfire of children the minister tried to pour a few words of peace. Fat chance. He led us into the Lord's Prayer. Led us? We were out in front of him, so far ahead that he was forced to gabble on the same note as the Amen – 'and if any boy has a firework will he hand it to me before the show begins'.

He waited, all alone on the platform, and we waited, began to stamp our impatience at him, for it was wonderful what we could do together, grinning and wild. The lonely man was patient, stood hands folded, head bowed, but no boy gave him what he asked for – a firework. So the film was begun, the piano played an accompaniment, for the films were silent in the Central Hall. Eventually the firework exploded. Approaching Guy Fawkes Day, fireworks outplayed the piano. We didn't try the Methodist Sunday School, although the minister never gave up but as we left the building said, 'We'll see you on Sunday then?'

The use of the Central Hall on Sundays somewhat tempered the atmosphere of sin which films inspired, although sin was always condemned and evil indicated at once: black stetsons for the bad cowboys, black horses for them to ride, and white for hero and heroine – who were invariably outnumbered, that was taken for granted; even in History lessons we learnt that fact of life. Only where Red Indians came into the film were goodness and badness confused and we had to await the development of character before we could judge.

I favoured the Red Indian. Thought him outmanoeuvred by the White Man and argued his case with friends. Actually it was the clothes, and especially the headdress, which I admired and which, when Rene was given a real Red Indian Headdress, feathers all down the back, I coveted.

The real place of temptation was the Premier Cinema in Garratt Lane. Its welcome was as warm as that of the Central Hall, if more expensive, but there were no prayers and no invitations to pray when you left.

Patrons occupied the back seats, which were covered in soft stuff with antimacassars to protect them. A lady came round in the interval to serve tea from a watering can. Rene's brother said that we should just get an eyeful of what went on in those posh seats in the evening performances. Once, when we were there in the front, in the afternoon, there was a commotion: the lady was pouring her hot tea into a patron's cup when, like a trumpet, a man's voice cried out, 'Christ! Right on me balls, you silly bitch!'

Bitch was rude. We raised our eyebrows and ate our monkey nuts with our friends in the front side rows. By the end of the film the floor would be crunchy and eyes would have adjusted to the distortion of elongated and slanting actors on the screen so that, blinking from the sweet disinfected darkness of the Premier, we came into a winter greyness and into a reality of short, straight, up-and-down men and women in the street. We had accompanied Betty Balfour, the lovable Squibs, through adventures and perils and we all wished we could have her for a friend. But there we were, we were all we had; we squinted at one another, rubbed our eyes and were reconciled to one another's friendship.

The pictures were black and white, the characters were black and white. Out in Garratt Lane it was a coloured world, and muddled. It had not always been so; I remembered a witch in our street. Now I saw that she had turned into an old and feeble woman. In the night there were angry, terrible voices and one or both might well be described as bad; but I knew that one voice belonged to my dad and one to my mother. How then could I name my parents as bad? And – Elsie? Was she a deserter or an adventurer? And still I couldn't quite let religion go.

'Mum, d'you say prayers?'

'What? Oh! Prayers. Sometimes, yes. I used to when I was your age.'

'What did you say? "Our Father"? Did you ask God for things?'

Careful, my mother. 'Yes. I suppose I've asked for things. Now and then.'

I closed in. 'Did He answer? Did He give you what you wanted?'

'Well, you can't have what you want in this world. Not the way things are you can't.'

I bet she asked for a new house in Morden.

'Then why do you make me go to Sunday School?'

'Oh! For heaven's sake!' No joke intended, none taken. I knew why, to get rid of me so that she and the aunts and Edie might heat up secrets over teacups and cards.

Sometimes I fancied myself as the missionary to my pagan family, saw them converted to religion of the strictest regime, church twice on Sunday and prayers before and after meals with lots of gratitude and supplication. Bent head, beseeching lips, I practised alone at the table until I was told to stop that mumbling and eat up the wholesome food and if I wanted so much to be good to look about me, there was plenty of tidying up to do.

I gave up God and the Devil for the time being, except occasionally to make a prayer, heartfelt, not to grow up like Edie (in spite of, well, loving her more) and perhaps, if possible, to grow a little bit like Elsie (in spite of the way she didn't answer letters). I was ten years old, a coming-of-age. Old enough to join the library. And to grow up.

The library wasn't for simple people, books were kept prisoner behind a metal fence and guarded by an old dragon who wore pince-nez. The craft of borrowing a book had to be acquired by observing other borrowers. Boards hung on the walls of the library with numbers on them, like the arrival and departure boards on Waterloo Station where Edie had taken me one half-day. The red numbers stood for books which were Out; the blue numbers were for books which were In. To decide which book you wanted to borrow you had to search in the drawers where numbers and book titles were linked. If by mistake you drew the wrong book (a school friend was taken by the title 'Sketches by Boz', thinking that it would be a kind of glorious comic) then you had to keep it until the next day. If you finished reading the book on the same day, the rule still applied. Some of us felt the injustice of this rule deeply. Starving us like that!

But once I had the hang of the library the world lit up, its air was more bracing, I breathed great gulps of the pure stuff. None of it affected the cynicism with which I regarded school work, however. Teachers, one after the other, had handed me on with the brief report, 'An imaginative child'. Mum wasn't too pleased with this account, neither did the teachers imply a compliment. I worked where necessary, and as little as possible, and even in compositions gave the teacher what she wanted; all this was easy because I was what they called quick – except in Arithmetic – and what in brief moments of honesty I knew was slick. The important thing was to be top or as near top as possible without overmuch exertion.

At home I wrote thrilling stories on the endless supplies of stuck-down envelopes but for school I played up to the teacher in the composition book. Subjects given were uninspiring; we had had them all before: 'A day in the life of a penny'; 'The spring', 'My sister'. Keeping Elsie remote from the nosy teacher, I described Edie; made her into a picture so that no one would recognize her, happy and light and pretty she was in my exercise book.

'I should like to meet your sister,' said my teacher.

Edie was pleased too when she saw her name in the book and read it through. She was so grateful that I was ashamed.

I was ten years old all through the library summer and in the autumn I was ready, more than ready, for Miss Howard.

Miss Howard was given the scholarship class – a misnomer, that title, as only a few girls could take the scholarship examination. The class was as large as any other in the school, over forty girls, and she taught all of us. We all took the exam named the preliminary scholarship exam; this eliminated the majority, and left the scholarship girls available for concentrated work. The failures – and there was no delicate avoidance of the word – would stay on in Swaffield School pleasantly mooching through the years until they achieved adult status at the age of fourteen. They weren't stupid, the failures, just accepted that whatever happened their parents wanted them to go to work as soon as possible and that the Grammar was not only expensive with its uniforms and such, but demanded evenings of homework. Better stay at Swaff. How this mild resignation affected Miss Howard we didn't stop to consider. She shared all her exhilaration of learning with them, she never stopped watching for signs in any of us of a kindled interest. She would have shaken us awake if it would have done any good. We didn't need shaking, my friends and I.

It was a delight to sit before her; quite apart from what she taught she was good to look at: she had grace. She was tall, slim, brown-skinned, her hair smoothly looped in a knot at the nape of her neck. New words were necessary to describe Miss Howard.

In place of the light and shade which made Elsie so captivating Miss Howard possessed a special faded beauty, suggestive of past suffering. Above all she indicated an existence which was different, which contradicted, which looked out to new landscapes and in to a new me. At once I wanted to impress her and tried to do so in the way I knew best. I wrote what I thought she would like to read. She gave my exercise book back with a brief comment: 'You can do better than this. Say what you really think.'

I was hurt, ashamed, but gradually all the slick patter of words was abandoned and I wrote with energy, made mistakes, forgot Miss Howard – while I was writing.

For a long time I did not speak her name at home, but she was always there, on the edge of vision, accompanied imagination, posed questions which had not been asked before. I suppose I was in love with her but I had nothing with which to measure love except book love, didn't take account of married love as demonstrated by the family, or affection exchanged between parent and child. And as for the lovers on the Common . . . Aside from family love, which was a duty or a nuisance, it seemed that love was limited to a relationship between men and women.

Of course her name had to be uttered at home at last, when I let slip the evidence of Miss Howard. 'She's telling us about the suffragettes, Mum. Were you one?'

She half turned from the sink, the cloth dripping on the floor. 'Suffragette indeed! Catch me making an exhibition of myself. A lot of so-called ladies who ought to have known better. They weren't working-class, ducks, ladies mostly, but not nice. They made themselves sick with tubes pushed down – ' and, seeing my expression, ' – but never you mind. We got the vote, I suppose, but I vote the same way as your dad, that goes without saying.'

She changed the conversation to more interesting things. 'That Miss Howard of yours,' (the name spoken at home, in familiar surroundings, made my cheeks red; I wondered that Mum could be so blunt with such a name) 'she never married, then?'

I caught her drift. If she wasn't married, what was wrong with Miss Howard? But before there was time to defend or resent . . .

'Course – it was the war. She'd be that age. Her young man got killed.' Thus investing Miss Howard with a devastating aura of sorrow.

'You've got a crush on your new teacher,' my brother teased, and I looked upon him with pity.

I tried to keep her untouched by my family after that: she was different, her difference required that critical comparison from me which was often painful, conflicting as it did with old loyalties. For once I understood Mum's obsession with the houses in Morden. A new home, a new personality. But Morden wasn't Epsom, where Miss Howard lived, where she walked on the Downs, where she picked green and bronze beech leaves for us to paint in school. When we were truly her children, in early summer, she brought a box filled with wild orchids and we peered at the intricate design. I had nothing to say but remembered Granny Warren's marigolds and the rose on Grandma's grave.

Just to partake a little of Miss Howard's journey to Epsom, two of us followed her from school down Swaffield Road to Earlsfield Station. We were discreet, kept our distance. Over her shoulder a fox fur was slung and its pinched foxy face glinted its glass eyes at us. She walked loosely with a swing that we tried to imitate. We skipped in and out of shoppers in Garratt Lane to the arches of the railway station, where we lost her in the sooty dark approaches.

Margaret MacDonald, who was older than the rest of us, had already passed the scholarship exam – more than that, she had been awarded a place in a boarding school, Christ's Hospital school for girls. She had to remain at Swaffield until the end of the summer term, she was a legend and was by this saved from making tea for the teachers. Miss Howard was up to the situation; she made a space for Margaret, she supplied atlases, a Baedeker, railway timetables, a dictionary, an encyclopaedia, books on art, on history; many of these she brought from her home. Margaret set out to plan a journey for herself across Europe by boat and train and on foot, from London to Budapest. It was an exploration of all the treasures of art and history and landscape and science and religion which might lie on her route, and the scope of her task took my breath away. As far as possible I listened to the conversation between her and Miss Howard, and was green with envy.

At the end of the afternoon we were one class again to

listen to the stories Miss Howard read. Other teachers had read stories, it was a way of folding up the school day, but listening to Miss Howard we were not folded up, we weren't docile or drowsy, we were alert, the atmosphere was tense. Blind Pew tapped along the moorland road, we saw cliffs above a sea that we had not seen before, we were on the brink – as upright as rabbits' ears. In the circumscribed unity of Miss Howard's class we sighed one sigh as the bell rang for the end of the day.

One cold springtime morning we sat the exam; as if in disgrace, we were set apart in the hall. Mum had given me a good breakfast to feed my brain, and a clean handkerchief and a kiss for luck. She had broken the rhythm of the week and washed my hair and given me a bath on the Monday before the exam on the Tuesday, which made me nervous. Like me my friends arrived at school in a similar clean and shaky condition. We closed in on Miss Howard, who alone could steady us; her hand placed on our shining heads and spotless dresses was enough. We were the scholarship girls, Miss Howard's own.

One cold summer morning the exam results were announced. Miss Jones was beside herself with the secret, she called on us to come to the front of the school, below her dais.

'Splendid news!' she shouted. 'All our girls have passed the Junior County examination!'

She laid into the clapping, teachers followed, finally the rest of the school clapped, enjoyed it and clapped furiously at last. Even those who hadn't got further than the prelim clapped and didn't appear to notice that Miss Jones's 'all' meant 'a few'. Neither did we, if we were honest. We were more than honest, we were relieved then quickly lifted up on the waves of applause, then – were dying to tell . . . tell parents . . . families . . . the milkman, the cat. After telling – what? We didn't think past the telling. We huddled together beneath Miss Jones fronting the clapping as if it was gunfire. Close friends we were, belonging, it was clear to us now. Rene's face I saw at the back of the hall. She wasn't clapping. Time was up and with the others I moved to back behind the lines but Miss Jones's fat hand dropped on my head.

'Not you.' She whispered violet cachou scents into my ear and lifted me on her dais.

'This girl' – she raised her voice. At once the picture of Mr Brocklehurst at Lowood School came to mind (and was I then to be placed like Jane Eyre upon a stool to remain there speechless all day?) – 'This girl has brought one more honour to Swaffield Road School. Last time Margaret MacDonald was given a place in Christ's Hospital. Now today another girl has been so appointed. Here she is!'

She gripped my scalp and twisted me to the tide of faces. People were silent, then they were clapping and this time I had to bear the brunt by myself, and with swallows and grimaces I tried not to cry. Also I had completely muddled myself by intruding Mr Brocklehurst into the occasion, also I was struck by the collusion of religion and medicine in the name – Christ's Hospital. I stumbled back to Miss Howard.

All morning I watched my friends. What did they think of me? Had I spoilt their glory? While we had felt no jealousy towards Margaret – for mine had been only for her journey across Europe – I was one of the group, or had been. What had I done?

At dinner time Rene ran home without me. She was turning somersaults over the railings when I got home, Evie Jackson was counting.

'Look out,' Evie muttered. 'Here comes clever-stick-make-me-sick.'

Mum wasn't sure how she felt about my news. 'It's a

boarding school, you say?' As though she hadn't heard of Christ's Hospital.

'Oh Lor'! There'll be the uniform and labels to sew on and fares to go and see you. Well, we'll just have to pull our straps tighter, that's about it. Run quick and tell your dad what you've done.'

'You're to be pleased and proud of me. They clapped at school. It was nice.'

It had been awful. And Miss Jones had tried to kiss me.

My dad didn't have to be told how to behave. 'That's great news.' He swung me round in the laundry and all the women smacked me on the bottom. 'Look at my little old woman, girls! Ain't she sweet? Wait till I tell them at the Club.'

Edie's reaction was much the same as Rene's. Bill said that the Christ's Hospital boys were a laugh because they wore frocks and yellow stockings. They weren't taken seriously at the Emmanuel, the school he had attended. I needed Elsie but she was beyond reach.

But apart from sour responses there were other considerations. The basic fact of a boarding school was leaving home, and I addressed myself to that. How would that be? An adventure? The path I had longed to take to a wider life? To meet jolly boarding-school girls with names like Paula and Betty? Midnight feasts with cream buns and sardines? I hadn't quite outgrown the bouts of sickness, and weren't the jolly girls all good at games? I wasn't. I had never played games like hockey and lacrosse. In drill lessons I was bored as well as unskilled, in country dancing I giggled like the others. I was to be the duffer, and I had read enough of the schoolgirl books to know the fate of the duffer. I could of course decide to be a bounder like Cora Grandways in the *Schoolgirl's Own*, she smoked and had cronies instead of friends, but the role did not appeal.

It was a miserable time. Success had seen off my old street companions. Right, so what if I had, during the last months, moved away from them into fresh company? Perhaps I should not have friends again, perhaps all the girls in Christ's Hospital were awful clever-sticks like me. I sobbed into the pillow, and when I woke my cheeks were stiff and salty. But I had to attend an interview with the headmistress of Christ's Hospital, and she required a medical examination of all prospective pupils.

After the interview and the medical I sobbed once more. The interview had been fun, the person who asked me questions seemed very interested when I said what I was to be – an author – although I was rather distracted by the way she kept playing with her large amber beads. She smiled a lot, not like Miss Howard but with the sort of smile that allowed her to examine me without my knowing. But I did, of course. In the doctor's room Mum went into the details of the years of suffering I had endured as a result of the TB operation.

'It still affects her,' Mum said. 'She's still delicate. Anaemic too.'

'Didn't the doctor and the nurse admire your scar?' Mum congratulated me on the way home in the tube train. 'You could tell they hadn't seen many as good as yours.'

I failed the medical. And was very miserable for an hour or so until Rene, who had heard the news by the mysterious Inman underground telegraph, forgave me for winning the scholarship and asked me round to play. The other scholarship girls welcomed me back, I was to be one of them after all, we should go to the same Grammar, we had a fairly wide choice but there was in fact no question but that we should go to Mayfield. It was the nearest, and they wore a navy uniform which was sensible and could be bought in many shops, shops which were not as expensive as Hardwick's in Wandsworth High Street, which was Mayfield's officially appointed supplier.

Public opinion was proving too much for my mother to resist pride in me, though even now this came to me at second hand. Elsie wrote a thanksgiving for my success – that was before she learnt of my failure in the medical. Eventually she declared herself still awfully pleased but wasn't it a shame and I should still set my sights high. The aunts and uncles felt that I had done right by the family, but must be watched in case of getting above myself.

'We've come from good stock,' Auntie Lizzie told Mum. 'We're on the up and up, sparrer. Can't say as I thought that young Ena, the runt of the litter, your little mistake so to speak,' (Mum was pressing her lips into a narrow pale pink bite and I was fascinated) 'and her always sickly and such a queer Dolly Daydream – there – never mind me – I have to say what I think before I forget it – but Em, I'll say this too, you've not done bad with the youngster in spite of everything.'

One by one the aunts and uncles put me in my proper place, which was marching along the family road behind the family banner. Nothing more was required of me, or of any of the new generation, but to follow the route marked out, and to march onward and upward with resolution but without too much show of ambition lest that take us out of sight of one another. The example of Elsie should be a lesson. It went without saying that we were not to slip back. No, we belonged – belonged, mind you – to the working class, and if we held to that belief we should know where we were in the scheme of things. It was quite a stir when they discussed what I had done, on Sunday after dinner.

'Climb the ladder, but only one rung at a time,' said

Uncle George. There were a few rules to successful living.

'You're no good without your health,' said Auntie Hepsie. The others nodded; they could point – and did – to those who had pots of money – or perhaps 'comfortable' was a word that was preferred – but in spite of that they suffered bad health, suffered chronic, they could go into the details but wouldn't, they'd turn you over and after Emma's fine blow-out – leave it there – but suffered all right . . . and, reassured, they returned to one more rule.

'Don't let them know your business. Keep yourself to yourself.'

Except for your relations, of course, your own flesh and blood. There was no one like your own kind so you told them everything, didn't you? And told them before they could tell you, if that was possible.

Warnings and advice were passed around the dinner table with the cruet, for I was one of them now; at the table and never beneath it. Along with the buzz of recommendation, disapproval was insinuated against my mother. A near thing, that, the kid failing her medical, and suppose she had passed it and was about to vanish into a posh school? And there was Elsie . . . off like that . . . Well, Edie was the steady one. And Bill. No nonsense about Bill. And Joe, he was ballast enough for Em's flighty children. Quite safe, now I wished like anything that I had passed the medical; once again I cursed my scar. I was back to the Big Ideas and to the Showing Them.

Auntie Annie made no comment, she hadn't noticed that anything remarkable had occurred, or almost occurred. What she did know was that when you passed an exam you had a little prize and in front of them all she gave me a florin. I gathered several florins for the last time, and without the sly handover. It was good to be done with the performance of the coin squeezed into the palm of my hand until it hurt, good to be finished with the dewy moustache kiss. Good not to be grateful. Though I did miss the money.

Chapter Twenty-one

Auntie May had given up hope of the Palais de Danse, but she still refused to go under and accept the disgrace of spinsterhood. 'Women are as good as men,' she said one Sunday afternoon. (She had realized how old I was and promised to tell my fortune if I sat quiet. None of the aunts minded my listening now, but their precious Sunday secrets weren't much after all.) 'Why should men have it all their own way?'

For some reason Auntie Lizzie sympathized. 'Of course – there is the child-bearing . . . Women have to cope with that . . .' She sighed, they all sighed – even Auntie Flo and Auntie May and Edie, who hadn't known the child-bearing, and so the sighs changed to talk of babies and I lost interest. So did Auntie May, for she continued her own argument.

'And why shouldn't a woman ask a man to marry her?'

They sat up. Her question was a drastic attack on what was proper; it was also sly. One Christmas, Uncle Jack, who was feeling merry and bright, had teased his wife by hinting that it was Lizzie who had proposed to him. This had not been forgotten. Edie's eyes moved from one face around the table to another, waiting for replies.

There were none unless a shrug was a reply, or a quick glance at Edie. She would be the next one, the next old maid. I had no care for Auntie May, who taught piano and told fortunes and was the life-and-soul, but Edie – my sister – couldn't they see? These old safe aunties, couldn't they see how she waited . . . on the alert . . . all ready-steady-go . . . not – not to be chosen, not to

223

belong, not to have a place for herself? And waiting with such terrible patience. Well, I didn't look forward to it but I would love her in her disgrace, and on my own terms.

Having got the reproaches for my necessary uniform out of the way, Mum threw caution out of the window and set out to enjoy a shopping expedition. In this she was quite shameless.

'Don't think I don't know what's what. You must have clothes to fit now. None of Annie's economy larks, making things too long so they last.' So I tried on the correct size in gym slips, the blazer with the badge pinned on to give the idea, the furry felt hat with its red and white check band – and became a stranger to myself in the shop's long mirror. Mum put her head on one side, assessing the stranger, and called her 'My little girl', and whispered that she was so proud.

Loaded with parcels, we walked alongside a file of men who shuffled in the gutter droning a chant which had no beginning and no end.

'Welsh miners,' Mum explained. 'They're unemployed. Fancy leaving their wives and children . . . here . . . slip them a sixpence but don't speak, mind.' One of the bent sorrowful grey men took my hand and shook it. I saw Mum's face, she would start polishing something when we got home.

After the excitement of shopping was over and the uniform had been exhibited, it was hung in her wardrobe to take up the smell of camphor. Then – nothing. An extraordinary period of nothing happened. And went on happening. It was the same for all of us in Number 29, I think. I avoided the friends nearby, saw no new friends who lived remotely at the top of the hill. I changed library books feverishly until the pince-nez of the librarian gleamed in an amiable manner every morning and Mum said that I should read the eyes out of my head.

She took me to the doctor to get an iron tonic, and asked for one herself. It was the heat, she said, on the way to the surgery, and 'Just look up in that tree.' Above my head, inches above, swung a column of hooked caterpillars, and when the doctor saw my pale face he immediately made up his medicine.

'A tricky time,' he said to Mum. 'Has she – ?' and Mum shook her head.

'Why don't you and Rene play any more?' she asked, forgetting that she had never quite approved of Rene.

'If only something would happen!' I moaned, but I didn't want it to, was absorbed by detail, nothing was to be whole and complete. I pushed at the oily puddle left by the laundry van to swirl it into a separation of purple and gold and green. I examined not the bloom but its petal, a fly wasn't a fly but a wing, a face not a face but a lip, or an eyebrow or a wrinkle; and . . . dust – dust was beguiling, its specks darted into the sunlight and out again, lost.

And it was hot. Even in the evening, especially in the evening. Coming indoors after watching the others play in the street, I found Mum with her elbows on the kitchen table, and Elsie's photograph in front of her. Edie sat by the window, she was embroidering another crinoline lady in a garden of hollyhocks. Neither looked up.

'I was just going to call you,' Mum said.

But she wasn't, for she was absent from home, from Edie and me and all. She would have let the night come down and left me in the street while she gazed at her lost girl. Edie bent her head and pushed her needle into the bonnet of the crinoline lady.

The walls of Inman Road throbbed with the heat, tar melted on the road, and on the Common the grass was as brown and as rough as coconut matting. Women in the street lived all day out of doors and my mother sat by the open window, hands lax, eyes half closed behind her glasses. When her hair drooped from its knot she was too lazy to pin it back. 'Why don't you read something to me?' she asked.

So I read a poem. I was alone and palely loitering and it brought a smile to her lips. 'Let's have a cup of tea,' she said.

At night, in the middle of the night, it was different, the heat was filled with noises, the machinery noises which pottered as ever through the walls into the bedroom, and other sounds which were dangerous. A drunken man blundered up the stairs to the kitchen, crashed the door open and laughed.

There was a shrill cry: 'I'll hit you!'

An idiot laugh. A slap. Another laugh. The sounds were growing faces and I lay straight as a post in my narrow bed.

And the next day and the next the sun shone and the air shimmered and the family were silent, as though we were in a painting, unable to move.

Clouds drifted high and a wind blew and a telegram arrived. Elsie was coming home.

'Elsie's coming home!' I told Rene, and Daisy and the Jacksons and Miss Biggs and Miss Spink and Big Ethel, who knew it already, and the library lady who seemed quite pleased.

'She hasn't been well, she has had a nervous breakdown,' I quoted Mum, 'and the sea trip will take about five days and it will do her good – ' I added, 'She won't stay long, she'll go back to Canada. I might go too.'

It was no surprise that Elsie at once resumed first place in our house; for Mum her return prompted a spring-cleaning and a cooking jamboree, and a dizzying of chatter as she ran up and downstairs. For me it meant a scatter of reminders to myself: I must tell her . . . I must show her . . . and I wondered if Elsie would still detest Inman Road. For Edie it meant the cancellation of our treat together, for the bus ride round London was due to take place on the day of Elsie's probable arrival in Southampton.

'We'll have a fine old time,' she had promised, 'we'll go all over the shop.'

And now? It didn't seem much of an old time . . . and . . . no question of it in any case, was there?

Procedure on the day went as before, but in reverse. Mum and Dad met Elsie on the quayside, I stayed behind with Edie. For hours I hung about in the hall, thought about putting on my uniform, decided against it; it was too hot, and there would be trouble. When a taxi drew up outside I hid in the front room.

'Where is she?'

I opened the front-room door. Every member of my family squashed together in the hallway. And Elsie was there. Taller, thinner, suntanned, and there were flat mauve shadows beneath her eyes. As she bent to kiss me I glimpsed a tooth filling of gold. Edie and Bill were shy and polite and Mum had red eyes, and Dad hurried off to his machines.

For the rest of the evening Elsie talked and we sat around her in a circle like the thieves in *Ali Baba*, blinking over the jewelled stories she was telling. We could all look at Elsie now that she was absorbed in her tales; her dress was narrow and decorated with rows and rows of small buttons, her hair was cut short and close to her head and was foreign-looking. Auntie Annie and the cousins came and Elsie went on telling until, right in the middle of the story about the Maid in the Mist at Niagara Falls which I had read about in the book she had sent us, she stopped.

'D'you mind? I'm fagged. Oh! The same bed?'

Edie and Mum and I looked at one another. We hadn't thought of that! The same bed? Same everything?

227

Then, with her hand on the door, Elsie turned to look back at our circle. She said, 'It's funny, it all seems so small, I'd forgotten about the dirt and . . . all those little chimneypots you see from the train as it goes into Waterloo. In Toronto even the sidewalks are wide – and stretch for miles . . . and . . . everywhere is so clean – clean.' She had the nerve to stare at Mum while she spoke. She came back to me where I sat (my bedtime forgotten), she pulled at my fringe. 'You've begun to grow at last. Mind you don't grow too tall.'

I dreamed that night in the room where two sisters were breathing, dreamed of myself, elongated, winding and sinuous and swaying over a tired and lovely face and over a mouth from which a gold tooth shone like a star.

Elsie's breakdown sufficed to make Mum into her mother once again. We were to rent a wooden house by the sea, in Shoreham. One part of the place was a railway carriage – what a joke! And because I was to go I would benefit, especially as I needed some good health before starting at the new school. And Edie would look after my dad and Bill, it was more useful practice. I scarcely said goodbye to Edie. We had gone a little way towards friendship, perhaps as far as we could. The only real words we used weren't spoken, they were underground. From Edie a question: 'Do you see me? Is this any better?' And from me, 'Sometimes I do – yes. But come out stronger – '

'How about this? Am I . . . oh, not lovely, of course not . . . but – ? It isn't too late for me, is it?'

Poor Edie, and for me, too much pity to bear. I should be Elsie's friend now.

On the whole it was as well that Elsie and Miss Howard didn't meet, though what a confrontation that would have been. In the limbo between schools I found that Swaffield was precious; the girls who stayed on were lucky; I liked everything about the place: the green-painted walls, the granite staircase, Miss Jones. And Miss Howard was left behind. 'I have something for you,' she said as we parted.

From her desk drawer she took a small box. 'Open it.'

The box contained a carved ivory flower, it was buried in cotton wool.

'It was made in Switzerland. The flower is an eidelweiss, a tiny flower which grows high up in the mountains. It is difficult to reach. Remember.' To all of us who were leaving she said, 'Come back to see us, won't you? At your first half term, perhaps?'

We would. We did. But she sat in front of her new class. 'These are my old girls,' she told them. She wasn't our Miss Howard any longer.

If Elsie was ill nothing showed unless it was that she was hardly Elsie now. On Shoreham beach she and I walked for miles along the wet sands until we reached the part where no other person walked. Higher up in the banks of pebbles yellow poppies grew but she wasn't interested; I found a dead sea bird twisted among seaweed and she couldn't stop shivering and told me not to keep finding things, or, if I must, to keep them to myself. Sometimes she chattered, a lot of frantic stuff, rubbish tumbled out. I didn't tell Mum about it, nor how sometimes Elsie shouted, 'I'd like to punch you! I'd like to knock you down!' It was better when she was silent, though after one long silent walk she whimpered, 'I can't type, you know, or play the piano. It hurts my fingertips so.' Worst of all was when she just sat, sat on the beach, her head bent to her knees, not seeing anything, alone but for me, and I had to leave her there because I must, just now and again, run and dive into the sea. 'The sea air is doing you both some good,' Mum said when we came back to the wooden house.

If Elsie was crying she could bear me to be close by,

but when she huddled into her head-on-knees position she ordered me to go away. Over and over again I leapt off the breakwaters into mattresses of drying seaweed, telling myself that I was fed up with this illness, that I had my own worries, a new school for heaven's sake.

'Buck yourself up!' I told Elsie in my head, using an aunt's voice. 'You should go away again,' using my own. 'You should send photographs, stay inside your photograph where you're happy.'

I saw how brave she had been and how she had lost her pluck which they had boasted about and condemned.

Thumping down into the orange and brown mess of weed for the last time – until next time – I ran back to Elsie in panic. She was gone, the camp of sandwich eaters were gone, a few moist jam crusts marked where they had been. Suddenly the beach was empty but for a heap of clothes and towel, the swimmer far out beyond the line of weed, who as I watched turned and swam in a fast crawl back to the shore. I ran then, the way one runs in a dream with long-legged bounding paces, very powerful, ran down near the trim little waves along the edge, ran up the banks of shingle to stop, panting to search the beach, hands shielding eyes from the level rays of the sun. It was getting late. I began to scream: 'El-sie! El-sie!' along with the floating sea gulls. A black dot in the water.

'El-sie!'

I wailed to strike her, I was blazing with temper. How dare she! I aimed myself into deep water, out of my depth at once with the tide coming in. I could swim, but my limit was the three strokes.

'Help me!'

She took her time but was there to hold me in the wash of the waves, she blinked the water from her eyes and smiled as peacefully as anything. 'Isn't it great, to go in the sea with your clothes on? I did it once in Canada.'

We waded on to the sand, our dresses clinging, flapping as the breeze caught them. We clung to one another, half crying, half laughing. I loved her now more truly than I had loved her when she was perfect, for she could never swim away from me again. Mum didn't say a word when she met us running up from the beach with our clothes sticking to us; she made certain, though, that Elsie and I didn't go to the beach alone again, except on our last day, when Mum waited to pay the milkman. She would join us later with a picnic. The last one. We had reached the point of last times. Mum was good at these, just as she was practised at goodbyes; saying polite goodbyes, waving goodbyes, all of that, and – goodbyes to things as much as to people. Goodbye sea. Goodbye beach. Goodbye house. Goodbye funny old stove . . . ice-cream kiosk . . . cat on the corner. She wasn't so good at hallos.

From the launching pad of the three strokes of swimming I had expected to go straight into a crawl and on this last day made a final attack on it. Elsie was to help me. She became lively in the water, rather too lively. She laughed as I swallowed salt water, as I sank and spluttered, she was doubled up with laughter and her laughing went on and on, loud it was – 'common' Mum would have said, if she hadn't known it was Elsie who laughed.

Afterwards, as had become customary after one of her outbursts of laughing – or crying – or anger – she became very quiet. If she had asked what I was thinking I should have replied, 'Nothing'. I was watching the freckles growing on my arm. If I looked sideways and close up at my skin the hairs were as long as fur.

'I believe in werewolves,' I said.

'So do I,' Elsie mumbled. She opened her eyes wide. 'Oh yes!' She lifted up her chin, opened her mouth and howled, a wolf howl, long and lonely. People were turning to see where the sound was coming from so I opened my mouth and howled with her; we howled for all the wolves in Canada. Then we stopped, for Mum was on the shingle with the bag of food, waving and smiling because it was our last day and our last picnic and we were all to be happy together.

Chapter Twenty-two

A<small>T</small> Mayfield a girl answered to my name when the register was called; she soon made the correct reply: 'Here', not 'Present'. She wasn't top, she said 'break' instead of 'playtime', she accepted that skill at games was the essence of success – of social success, at any rate, and that this was the only kind worth having. Gradually real people emerged from uniforms and some became friends. Swaffield girls lost one another and found one another and by the end of the autumn term they discovered that girls from Putney, girls from Southfields, and girls from Earlsfield were all much the same. The only ones who sustained a first impression of breezy superiority were those who had attended Mayfield in the Lower First because their parents paid for them. Scholarship girls were in the majority. I ran home on the final day of term a Mayfield girl through and through and ready for Christmas.

'Your Dad's been taken bad.'

A sequence of faces greeted me, neighbours lined the hall, the stairs, a zigzag of faces glistened with sentiment, for I was the latest to hear the news. At the top of the stairs Edie stood. 'Dad's had a stroke. No. No! you can't see him. Mum's making him tidy.' She added, 'I've seen him. I was fetched from work.'

My dad was not ill, he didn't know how to be. Also, he wasn't tidy except on a Sunday when his hands and face were washed pale. In his overalls he was a splendid and dirty giant who strolled like a buccaneer along the street to chat with the barber in the room at the back of

233

the shop. He could not be ill, not on a weekday, not to be tidy or to lie like a baby in bed.

'Your poor dad. Fancy Mr Joe having a stroke.'

A misunderstanding, but the people crowding the stairs would have it so. I threw my satchel into the corner and chewed the word – stroke. Stroke? To stroke was to be gentle, to be stroked was a consolation. They were too casual with words, those people, and my sister who chatted with them so importantly. Another word offered itself, so like, so opposite. It was – struck. A blow, savage, struck down. I saw a tree, struck by lightning, I saw Nebuchadnezzar gaping at his doom across the feasting table (we were up to Nebuchadnezzar in Scripture). Finally I understood that it wasn't an illness which my dad suffered, but a judgement.

At the same moment of enlightenment I was aware that right now it would be useless to explain my understanding. A chill stir of air crept through the house, whispers shuffled among the folk who waited on the stairs. What was Mum thinking about, allowing the street women and one or two of the laundry women to come into her house?

'The fire's almost out,' I called, but Edie was quite enjoying her chat. So I put more coals on, gingerly at first, then more and more until the top plate wobbled on the range. We should have a blaze. It really was cold. I sat down by the fender to guard the fire and to wait to stop shivering.

All the old books came back, as I knew they would, to help me. Think of the illnesses I had read through: Louisa May Alcott brought one after the other of her people to the sick bed; there was Helen Burns who died in *Jane Eyre*; there was the mother who died in *The Wide Wide World*, there was the tear-brown copy of *Jerry's Little Nell*. I drew myself up short, for these reminders were all of death. Again the idea of judgement came to relieve me. The people who had begun my reading adventures died because they were ill. I had been educated in the ways of illnesses: the books were as succulent with details of sickness as Auntie Annie's bread puddings were with sultanas and spices. Not one of these details applied to my dad, as far as I could gather from Edie's reports. As for accidental injury, my dad wasn't a child to fall as Katy did; as for epidemic, there was no scarlet fever to attack him; there was no war; there were no snakes or tigers or crocodiles to prowl or slide or yawn in our street. I was right then, my dad had been punished. Punishment was awful but came to an end at last, and repentance hurried things along. He must be sorry, throw off his bedcovers and the tidiness and get back to work.

That settled, I could not deny myself a small meditation on the manner with which I could have dealt with an illness, if he had had one. Again it was the old books which helped me; the new schoolgirl books from the library were too breezy and bracing to permit illness, unless it resulted from falling over a cliff in one of their adventures. Good old books had something relevant to say; moreover they were textbooks on behaviour during the long night of the crisis when all but the one girl who could truly help were excluded by the doctor: 'Call me if you need me. Otherwise – it's all up to your prayers now, my dear.'

Prayer couldn't fail on such occasions; either way it must be answered: One – 'The crisis is over, thank God! And thanks to you, my dear!' Two – 'He has joined the angels, and is at rest. You did all you could – more, much more!'

There was no sound now from the stairs, the neighbours had gone to feed their healthy families with news of Mr Joe and I came out of my night vigil in the sick room exhausted, very, but lifted up and respected ever after – when Mum stepped out of the bedroom carrying towels and a bowl of soapy water. Before I could explain what had happened to him she said not to worry, my dad would be better soon and not to sit hunched up like that, I would grow round shoulders.

I followed her about as she tipped water down the sink and hung up towels. 'Remember what Auntie May told my Dad? About his life line?'

She was too busy to listen. 'Life line? Oh, give me patience!'

'She told him he'd live for ever.'

She had said, though I couldn't repeat her words, 'Joe, what a life line you've got. Blimey, Joe, you'll outlive poor Emma!'

'I've not had time to think about tea,' Mum said, 'it happened this morning in the laundry. First thing I knew the women were barging up the stairs, bumping your dad upstairs to the kitchen. Fancy those women! Coming in like that! 'Course your dad couldn't help it, he was like a sack of coals. Helpless! And – Big Ethel fainted! Fancy! Big Ethel! Did you ever?' Her voice rose, astonished more by Big Ethel than by my dad.

'I want to see him.'

At last my anxiety was observed, misinterpreted, and rewarded. 'I don't see why not. I've made him quite respectable. You can speak to him but he won't answer, it's the stroke, see? Be a good little girl while I just . . .'

Little girl! She took the grown-up skin off me as neatly as she peeled an apple. I was pushed into the bedroom and the door closed behind me. Curtains were pulled but a fuzzed brownish glow shaped the room, and as I paused inside the door from out the heaped eiderdown a silence spread towards me. I must move, put one foot after another. I must see what lay on the pillow.

A head. My dad's head. No mistake about it, he wasn't burst open by lightning, not blinded; one bright small

236

eye rolled round to settle on me, the other was fast
asleep. And there was a mouth which chewed vaguely
then gave up the struggle to puff gentle puffs of air into
the silence. Nothing to be scared of, see? Except the
wide-awake eye which talked so furiously from its socket.
I stepped back a pace where it couldn't see me.

'Speak to him,' she had said, 'but he won't answer.'

His one eye would. So I kept quiet and kept clear of
the eye and hoped that someone would soon tell me to
run along. A step of light from the landing dwindled the
shadows of the corners of the room.

'That's enough,' Mum whispered as though she knew
what I knew, that it was a test of some kind which she
had put me through. 'Better go now,' she said, 'you can
come back later on and sit with your dad – later on then.
Dear Dad. He knows you're with him, ducks.'

Dear Dad? It was serious after all. The stroke had
made him my Dear Dad. I had said nothing in that
room, I had stepped out of reach, yet – 'He knows you're
with him.'

Out of the room and out of the house I ran three times
round the block on frosty pavements. There was something I could do, someone I could tell. I opened the
front door of Rene's house, shouted her name. She had
been my best friend. She must listen to me. Not that I
would tell of the eye. I shouted her name and when there
was no answer, no sound of voices or kettle steaming or
fire cracking, I still shouted, 'Rene! Rene!' Stood in the
hallway shouting her name to pieces.

Mum had forgotten Christmas was coming. Of course
the Christmas cake and the Christmas pudding were
already made and we had all helped by skinning almonds,
we had eaten the curious sugar out of the candied fruit,
we had all stirred the slobbery mess three times and

wished. Pudding and cake were in the cellar, the toad-stooled, frog-hopping root of the house, a hole where light entered only in moments by way of the coal hole or by candlelight, where things unidentified ran from one corner to another, where jellies were put to set, a place to which I was ordered to just run down to fetch them, because my legs were younger. If hell was kin to our cellar, then my dad must be saved from it. The Mission approach to salvation had not encouraged so I gathered together the bits and pieces of rescue which over the years had been gleaned. My opportunity came.

'I'm worn out,' said Mum. 'Be a duck and . . .'

I had kept clear of that bedroom, but now – 'I'll sit with my dad.'

Under the bed and behind the po and the tin box where special papers were kept was the Family Bible. I pulled it out; it was cold on my knees and I hoped that the eye wouldn't see how awkward I was at balancing the great book. I began at the beginning: 'In the beginning God created – ' The eyelid was closing so I dragged the pages over until the end was reached. Revelation.

'Blessed is he that readeth and they that hear . . .' It was a promising start. I glanced up at the pillow and detected a quiver of attention in the folded eyelid. But as I continued to read my voice became only one voice among the many who cried out in a tempest of words from the pages. I had not listened after the first sign of hope but suddenly was aware of what I was reading.

I read: 'And behold a pale horse: and his name that sat on him was Death, and Hell followed with him – ' The Holy Bible slid and thumped on to my feet.

'I'm sorry,' I said, but my dad didn't hear a voice that now was so butterfly-soft. I kicked the Bible under the bed where it belonged. 'Sorry,' I whispered.

I was ten years old and could not save my dad. It was

238

the first time I faced up to loving him. Loving him hurt, bad.

'I'm sorry,' I said, glaring at the eye. 'Sorry!' with my eyes stinging with tears that mustn't be seen. Mum was outside and held me into her apron before I could wriggle free.

'That child was really choked,' she was telling my sisters later. 'Crying her eyes out! Real tears! Well I never! Proper cut up she was!' Mum was proud of me; she didn't know of the pale horse who rode at my dad.

Ambulance men came like clowns to jog the loaded stretcher downstairs. A feathered hat fell off the hall stand on to my dad's face so I came from behind the front room door to remove it.

''Allo! 'Allo! What's this! Come to say goodbye to your daddy? Come on, give 'im a kiss then. Say ta-ta.'

My dad was shrunk small, he was laid beneath all the legs so very low. I felt ashamed. One eye tried with all its might to tell – the other was still asleep, his lips stuck at the words which his mouth pushed towards me; a dribble glued to his hairy chin.

First I was ashamed, then I was angry, angry with God and His punishments, angry with my dad for putting up with God. I had been – 'My little old woman', I had been – 'My youngest'. Always belonging to him, alive only because I belonged to him.

'Come on, girlie, give your daddy a kiss.'

Lips touched skin; the round eye pleaded. Closed. The eyelid squeezed moisture delicately.

'Quick. Here's Mum. She's goin' for a ride with us to see your daddy comfy. Can't take you, luv. Can't take little girls, not even pretty little girls.'

Stupid ambulance men, and I wasn't pretty. I stooped again a long way down to meet the forehead, broad and soft with sweat, and kissed it but I couldn't kiss the fumble of the lips. They had said, 'Don't pull faces, for

239

the wind might change and you'll be stuck like that and serve you right.' If the wind had changed for my dad he made no protest. But he should have done, he might have tried! His eye was silent, it hid behind an eyelid, its sign of life the veins which made the smallest possible quiver of existence.

On the pavement the street women lined up in appointed wedding and funeral regiments; my friends were there holding their breath against the infections of the ambulance. Evie Jackson crossed herself, we had told her not to but she could be stubborn.

'It's not as if you're a Roman,' we said. 'RCs can do it.' To be a Roman was to go too far, we understood this from conversations caught in our absent-minded way, a sort of trawling exercise for information which sometimes resulted in surprising hauls. A Roman Catholic school near the Common gave off a whiff of dangerous intrigue when we glimpsed the flapping nuns but we weren't tempted, it was simply that Evie Jackson continued to cross herself when the occasion suggested it. She said that you never knew.

So in the doorway of Number 29 I watched them take my dad away, and watched the women and my friends, and watched myself. Took my usual pace or two back for observation, but this time I didn't want to, wanted all of myself for my dad, was ashamed but couldn't help it. Took my picture and framed it – for reference.

Now I shut the door on the lot of them. Homework. Holiday work. What if I finished it at once? I rummaged in the corner among the pile of newspapers where my satchel had hidden itself and found the Atlas in the dresser drawer. Geography first.

Inside the Atlas my brother had written his name as the first owner: William Arthur Chamberlain, 29 Inman Road, Earlsfield, London, SW18. Because of Bill's long name I had been given a whisker of a name. 'By the time

I've finished writing my name on the exam paper the rest have started on the questions.' That was his complaint. Mine was the brevity of 'Ena'.

'The Queen of Spain is called Ena.' Stuck with Ena like a stamped letter I yearned for a string of long names: Veronica, Virginia, Victoria. The bliss of the initial 'V'! Daisy's father had presented me with a 'V' but only to poke fun: 'Ena-Dena-Valentine-Emily'. However, to face facts I had, when the Atlas was passed on to me, crossed out my brother's name and written my own inescapable title: Ena Chamberlain, 29 Inman Road, Earlsfield, London, SW18, England, Great Britain, Europe, The British Empire, The Northern Hemisphere, The Earth, The Milky Way, The Universe. With the addresses my eyes had stretched to vast wildernesses, I remembered the panic of wonder and how the line which I threw to such a universe was one day to reel in a shining fish.

On the evening when both my mother and father were gone there were no distances, instead there were walls, the walls of the kitchen where I sat, brick walls making a house into separate compartments, some lit, some filled to the brim with dark; in his bedroom downstairs back, Bill scratched over an insurance examination paper; in the bedroom upstairs my sisters blew their noses loudly and often. Listening I heard the other noises: the lavatory on the landing made an involuntary gurgle; a tap dripped, paused, dripped again; the walls and floors of the house made careful and creaking adjustments, and through the dividing walls the laundry groaned and squealed as it did when I was alone in bed.

I wasn't allowed to touch the gas lamp so I did, turned the tap to lower the light and turned it up again; fascinated by my skill I raised and lowered the thing and the mantle blossomed and folded, spreading illumination and alternately sucking in the shadows. The gas warbled to itself in a friendly way and I listened to it rather than to the other sounds of the house beyond the kitchen.

Well, Mum would come home to find my sisters' blotched cheeks and just to show her they would squeeze any tears that were left and just to show her I would not cry at all.

I pushed the Atlas aside, went over to the range, and sat staring at the coals behind the bars. Suppose I was wrong about my dad? Suppose Mum . . . ? Was she so safe – not drinking – not being anything but recognizably good . . . Both of them? Appalled, I drew closer to the fire but I was trembling, taken unawares by the question, a pale worm of a question which had wriggled out of some cellar of my mind. I made a prayer – with fists clenched – not like a girl in a book – as much a threat as a prayer: 'Please! Please!'

What happened next . . . a blank of staring . . . and then a voice telling me to be sensible, of course my dad could rouse himself and get strong again. Impatience made me happy, irritation brought confidence, confidence made me restless. I considered making toast for the others but it was too much bother. On the dresser was a glass dome containing a snowman and it wasn't for touching. I picked it up and shook the thing, and shook it and shook him until the demented creature was obliterated in snowflakes, all but his intermittent fat red grin. Inside my head the snowflakes whirled. Perhaps if I waited like the snowman, was as stubborn as he, perhaps I should land back in the place where I had started. I put him down and watched the slow settling of whiteness. He was safe inside his globe. I propped my head on my hands, my throat ached, there wasn't a sound in the house now. An empty house, then? It wasn't right to cry in an empty house.

For a long time I stayed quite still, waiting for the whirling inside to slow as it had for the snowman.

Sometimes there came glimpses of the girl who was waiting to become me, alluring suggestions of the person to whom I had promised myself with growing excitement. Now I turned my back on her, told her to run along, that I had made up my mind after all to stay as I was, a child with two parents in 29 Inman – always. Such a declaration must surely keep both feet on the ground, though about my head wild things rotated; disguised as family and friends they were revealed without warning as phantoms, as devils and not angels. For there were no angels, they had wings and had flown away. To tread down the vapours of nightmare I muttered names: Inman, Earlsfield, London. The floor of the kitchen spun faster and faster: Great Britain, The Empire . . . a widening elliptical radiance of names, and still the girl beckoned and still she wouldn't go away. There was a screech of pain which brought my sisters running.

'What's the matter? What are you shouting about? What's up?'

They didn't know and neither did I.

Mum came home. And my dad was quite comfy.

Chapter Twenty-three

I WAS sent from home to stay with a cousin I hardly knew who lived with her husband in the country outside Croydon. She took me out on freezing walks and once we had tea in a Fullers' tea shop. Her meals were different, and were called lunch and dinner, and we had napkins at every meal. I sat up straight at the table and was told to eat a little more dear and that I was a real help to her and I came to agree, seeing myself through her eyes.

Halfway through the week my cousin's husband, who was a teacher and meticulous in routine and in style of dress, put on a black overcoat and left the house much later then usual. When he returned at his regular time he was rosy with the cold air and formidably playful.

'When shall I go home? We haven't had Christmas yet.' I spoke to cover the awful dread of spending Christmas with these nice cousins. My dad wasn't mentioned.

I was at the top of the stairs when the doorbell rang. Elsie stood in the porch. She was dressed in black, her black umbrella dripped on the mat. Cousin and sister looked up at me, so deep down they seemed at the bottom of a pit; I had seen a workman digging in a trench in the road, they appeared like him, only pale-faced while the man had been as brown as the strange earth beneath the layers of the road.

There was plenty of time to attend to such ideas, all the time in the world. Elsie must have thought so too, for though she smiled in her new dreamy way, she said nothing. Of course I could have helped her, of course I knew what black clothes meant. I found that I was watching myself again but I was a girl watching a child and the child had decided – 'I should cry. I should be crying by now.' And the girl said, 'Go on! Cry then! You're a crybaby. Cry!'

Neither as child nor as girl could I squeeze out a tear in spite of a keen sense of what was expected of me, and of what (I saw this myself) was fitting the occasion.

At home it was the same. Edie was in black; Mum's black dress was covered by her new-for-Christmas crimson-and-orange-patterned overall which added a theatrical touch; Bill wore a black armband.

'Where's my black dress?'

'You? Oh, you're too young for black. Besides – we can't throw money about. We've got to draw our horns in now.'

It wasn't the usual to-and-fro of Mum's budgeting. We were poor, then. Really poor at last.

'I'll make myself an armband.'

I bit my lips trying not to tell how angry I was with her, angry and sore – worse than that – I hated her. Hated all of them. Inside I treasured a diamond of a heart.

Aunts and uncles came and went and we took their kind thoughts. The holidays went on and on and then we came to Christmas Day and we took that also.

'When are the aunts and uncles coming?'

Elsie roused herself to look shocked. 'They aren't coming this year.'

Christmas pudding made in the past, ages and ages ago, sat on the table with its obligatory spray of holly. Inside would be a sixpence for me. The child. Five chairs completed the table nicely and no sixth space was permitted – not even in case . . .

I went back to school and was glad. A friend asked me to stay one weekend and I was too pushy, asking 'When?

Next weekend?' Talk had been easy in Number 29 but now there was a sort of trailing silence unless someone made an effort to speak. Sentences assembled themselves in the mind but you had to think out where they might lead and it wasn't worth the bother. I was eager for homework.

True, there was business talk: the selling of the laundry, the sharing of the proceeds between Mum and Uncle George, and foreboding that there wouldn't be much over at the end of the sale. Lloyd George's name cropped up, for my dad had joined his insurance scheme from its start but had dropped it when money troubles came and because he, my dad, was so strong. There would be no widow's pension for my mother.

One day she said, 'We're buying a new house in Worcester Park.' She might have prepared me. I muttered, all the words stuck together like acid drops in my mouth, 'You've got your own way then.'

She took no notice. 'You'll still go to Mayfield. You can have a grant for travelling and a little bit for uniform. Three pounds a term.'

'We're poor, then?'

'Hard up, yes.'

Sometimes I caught her and Auntie Annie whispering about me. 'Ena? No, not a tear. Hard as nails. And I thought she was so fond of her dad.'

I went to see the new house and it *was* new – brand new, ghastly new. Uncurtained windows faced a concrete road, and other empty windows. 'We'll be the first in,' Mum said. 'You'll soon get to know people.' In the distance elm trees were gathering into green, so it was springtime. 'It doesn't matter to me about people. I've friends at school. I'm not a child.'

There wasn't much time left. A man swung his long legs in front of me as I walked home up the Earlsfield Road. Breathless, I chased after him, prepared to make

the rascal pay, to punish him before . . . before . . .
Then – the horror of a stranger's face, the wrongness of
it . . . 'I'm sorry. I thought you – '

'So you ought to be – jumping at me like that – and in
school uniform – I've a good mind to – '

'Please, I thought you were . . . someone I knew.'

Hunting a father took all my patience. I sauntered by
the barber's shop up and down outside while the muzzles
of soapsuds were wiped from the faces of men who lay
back close to the windows. One by one they were made
as clean and as pink as babies. The barber caught sight
of me and grinned and shook his head. He bent across
his customers and they glanced in my direction and
looked stern.

My mother couldn't help me. She had been wife for
longer than she had been mother and now she was
widow, but it was on the title of wife that she had built
her home; everything had changed, and must she change
also? The aunts came to pick about the ruins, uncles
steered clear or came on weekdays to rumble on about
business matters. Because Mum was shut up behind her
glasses, and so monosyllabic in her welcome, they took
Bill aside and told him that he was the man of the house
now. Elsie was planning a dreary marriage; Edie crept
about my mother as if she were an invalid, making her
cups of tea which she left to grow cold, making her toast
of a perfect even brown. There were no more airy cakes
made in the range, no roast dinners. Like Rene I ate
random meals or none at all. There were no more
Sundays. 'We mustn't impose,' the aunts said. 'You
come to us, Emma.' But we stayed at home in Number
29. It was all we had.

All this time Mum and I were growing closer and
closer and although, like shadows on the perimeter of
our arena, others moved, they were unconscious of our

bitter communion. For that is how it was; we were wrestlers, preparing to close on one another.

'Answer me,' I threatened, 'or else . . .'

She bit her lips and withheld grief, as she had withheld the words of love from my dad. It was no excuse for her to offer the old endless housework or the past marvels of her cooking.

The night before we moved from Inman Road I was woken from deep sleep; it was a physical sensation, as if hands had shaken me awake and pulled me upright. But no hand was on me, no voice spoke. Except from inside my head.

'Your dad is dead.'

I threw myself on the pillow, tugged it round my ears. I was innocent of death, I knew nothing of it.

But – 'Your dad is dead.'

The room was silent, there was no sound of sisters' breathing.

Then came the tears. Then they came.

Rivers, floods, oceans of tears I gave to my father, helpless and wondering I loved him for the first time without reservation and at last, lifted out of the rocking tide, I lay drained and stranded under the moist bed-sheets. 'Tears can clean you right out,' Mum had said more than once. They did. I was as clean and as empty as our new house.

The machinery was abandoned and creaked and squeaked into a grim silence. The women went home and some came to say goodbye. Big Ethel had fainted for love of my dad and she put on her best shawl and cap to say goodbye.

'Good luck, kid,' she whispered in her husky voice. Then, screwing her face into vast hands, she shuffled to the corner of Inman, blew her nose on her shawl and yelled, 'Keep yer pecker up, lovey!'

It wasn't often that an entire family left Inman, one

by one to the cemetery was the custom, so at least we gave the street a show, but when the van had disappeared with the furniture, all of it on display to them at last, they went back to their own doorsteps. Pink-eyed Rene was hiding and Daisy's mother wanted me to stay with them one day. Mum nipped round to say goodbye to Auntie Annie, whom we should see on Sunday.

The experience of solitude had been known to me, I remembered it for it was rare and in retrospect desirable, but in this house at this time it was more than I had bargained for. There was an extraordinary evacuation, a kind of sucking out of air room by room from the toadstooled cellar to the laburnum-tapped windows of the front bedroom, a sly and steady draining, breath by breath and then sound by sound. A floorboard creaked for the last time, the lavatory on the landing swallowed; gurgled – once – and stifled the sound. On the windowsill a fly fizzed, circled on its back like crazy and stopped dead, not a quiver of its surrendered legs. I pressed tight up against the wall. Yet even as the house moved into utter silence and as I watched and listened to it do so (the dust settling and settled on the silk steel of the range, the soft descent of dust and its repose on the floorboards) I watched myself. I was, it seemed, not quite convinced, not quite delivered from the hope of – what? Notes from the piano in the front room? The chatter of sparrows? The tread of the man on the stairs? Voices raised of sisters, one beautiful, the other good? And then I thought of the dumbness of Grandma Thornley, who now was laid face down in the removal van.

She had seen to it. She had stopped time. I saw the spider arrested motionless. Only seconds before it had spun a thread, passing back and forth, to hold me still. No! As if the silk were an iron chain I flung away from it, and raced downstairs to the scullery and to the door which led into the laundry. Where I must be. The door was padlocked. I screamed, kicked the door and screamed the house full of screams and my mother was holding me, she was alive. Alive and kicking, her. 'What d'you want in that old laundry? Don't you get yourself in a state, ducks.'

'I'm almost as tall as you,'. I said.

She sniffed and wiped her nose. Looked down. 'Blimey! look at me! No, down at my feet! You know what? I've sent my bloody shoes off in the van! I've got to walk out of here in slippers!' Purple slippers stuck out beneath her coat. And – bloody? The end of the world, then.

But the O of her mouth was too much for me and as she looked up and saw me exploding into laughter she caught it too, resented the laughing at first, then let it go and blow it and what the . . . and Oh! Oh! Oh! Oh stop! No! It hurts, it hurts!

Red-nosed and damp-eyed we padded along the road to the railway station, and still aching and warm-blooded with laughter we boarded the train. We had a carriage to ourselves and Mum put her slippered feet as if to bed, cosily side by side, on the seat opposite. She didn't care, not a bit, for other people who might want to sit there later. I couldn't take my eyes off her reckless face, for she was changing every minute.

As we approached Wimbledon Station she remembered what to do, she sat up as straight as Queen Mary and smoothed the dry tears from her cheeks.

'D'you know what?'

She turned her new brave face to me.

'D'you know what you never did? You never said goodbye to Inman Road!'

'No, Mum,' I said. 'I never did.'